# The Ancient Secret
## of
# THE FLOWER OF LIFE
## Volume 1

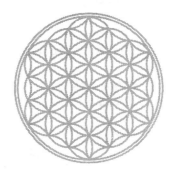

An edited transcript of
the Flower of Life Workshop
presented live to Mother Earth
from 1985 to 1994

Written and Updated by
Drunvalo Melchizedek

Transcribed, first edit by
Livea Cherish

Book editor, Margaret Pinyan

Computer graphics originated by
Tim Stouse and Michael Tyree

ISBN 1-891824-17-1


Published by
Light Technology Publishing
P.O. Box 3540
Flagstaff, AZ 86003
1-800-450-0985

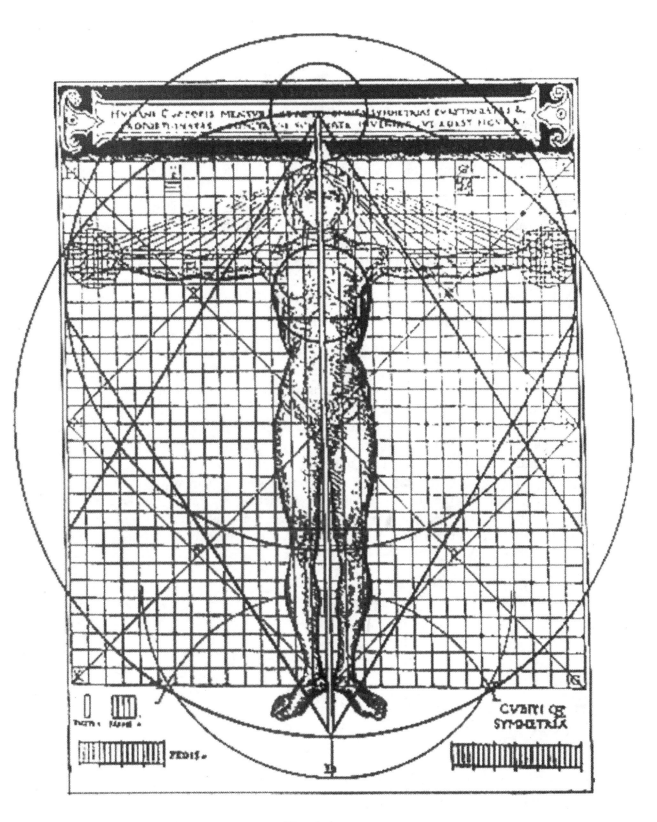

Vitruvius's canon
with Flower of Life sacred geometries.

## Acknowledgments

There are so many beings—in the hundreds—who have helped bring this work to completion. I can't name them all, but I feel a need to recognize a few.

First of all, the two angels who entered my life long ago and who have lovingly guided my life, you are most honored. Thoth, the ascended master from Atlantis, Egypt and Greece, has given me a great deal of the information in this book. My family, my wife Claudette and my children, who have been my greatest love and inspiration in life. The 200 facilitators teaching this work of the Flower of Life in 33 countries, who have given me invaluable feedback, support and love that has kept me strong. The thousands of students who have written loving letters telling how this work has changed their lives; this has given me strength to continue. Livea Cherish, who put this work into book form from the video format, and Margaret Pinyan, whose fine editing ability allows this book to read so smoothly. Tim Stouse, who created about half the computer graphics, and Michael Tyree, who created the other half; they have made it possible to understand what was being said. And O'Ryin Swanson, the owner of Light Technology Publishing, who had the faith in me to publish this work.

To the rest of you who are too numerous to name, I thank you all from my heart with the prayer that this work will actually help people understand who they really are so that together we can create a more loving world—and perhaps even a more loving universe. Thank you, dear ones.

# PREFACE

Only one Spirit.

Long before Sumeria existed, before Egypt had built Saqqara, before the Indus Valley flourished, Spirit lived in human bodies, dancing in high culture. The Sphinx knows the truth. We are much more than we know. We have forgotten.

The Flower of Life was and is known by all life. All life, not only here but everywhere, knew it was the creation pattern — the way in, the way out. Spirit created us in this image. You know this is true; it is written in your body, in all your bodies.

Long ago we fell from a very high state of consciousness, and the memories are just now beginning to emerge. The birth of our new/old consciousness here on Earth will change us forever and return us to the awareness that there is truly only one Spirit.

What you're about to read is a journey of my life through this reality, how I learned about Great Spirit and about the relationships that each of us have with all life everywhere. I see Great Spirit in the eyes of everyone, and I know that He/She is within you. You already hold within your deepest being all the information I will be sharing with you. When you first read it, it may seem like something you've never heard before, but it isn't. This is ancient information. You can remember things that are deep inside you, and it's my hope that this book will trigger these things so you can remember who you are, why you came here, and what your purpose is for being here on Earth.

It is my prayer that this book will become a blessing in your life and give you a new awakening about yourself and something about you that is very, very old. Thank you for sharing this journey with me. I love you deeply, for in truth we are old friends. We are One.

Drunvalo

# CONTENTS

## Note to the Reader

The Flower of Life Workshop was presented internationally by Drunvalo from 1985 until 1994. This book is based on a transcript of the third official videotaped version of the Flower of Life Workshop, which was presented in Fairfield, Iowa, in October 1993. Each chapter of this book corresponds more or less to the same-numbered videotape of that workshop. However, we have changed this written format where necessary to make the meaning as clear as possible. Hence, we've shuffled paragraphs and sentences and occasionally even whole sections to their ideal locations so that you, the reader, can glide through this with the greatest of ease.

Please note that we have added current **updates** throughout the book, which are in **boldface**. These updates will usually begin in a new paragraph directly below the old information. Since so much information was presented in the workshop, we have divided the subjects into two parts, each with its own table of contents. Volume 2 will follow later.

# INTRODUCTION

Part of my purpose in presenting this work is to assist people to be aware of certain events that have happened on this planet or are presently happening or are about to happen, events that are radically affecting our consciousness and the way we're living today. By understanding our present situation, we can open to the possibility of a new consciousness, a new humanity emerging on Earth. In addition, perhaps, my dearest purpose is to inspire you to remember who you really are and give you the courage to bring your gift to this world. For God has given each one of us a unique talent which, when *truly* lived, changes the physical world into a world of pure light.

I'll also be giving mathematical and scientific evidence to show how we got here, as spiritual beings in a physical world, in order to convince the left-brain analytical part of us that there is only one consciousness and one God, and that we are all part of that Oneness. This is important, for it brings both sides of the brain into balance. This balance opens the pineal gland and allows the prana, the life-force energy, to enter the innermost part of our physical being. Then and only then is the body of light called the Mer-Ka-Ba possible.

However, please understand that the evidence I originally learned this information from is in itself not important. The information could in most cases be completely changed to different information without affecting the outcome. In addition, I made many mistakes because I am now human. What is most interesting to me is that every time I made a mistake, it led into a deeper understanding of the Reality and a higher truth. So I say to you, if you find an error, look deeper. If you get hung up on the information by overestimating its value, you will totally miss the point of the work. What I have just said is paramount to understanding this work.

I'll also be giving my personal experiences, many of which are, I admit, outrageous by the ordinary world's standards. Perhaps they are not so outrageous by the old world's standards, but it is you who must decide if they are true or are just stories — or if it even matters. Listen deeply with your heart, for your heart always knows the truth. Then I intend to share with you, as much as I can in the second volume, a specific breathing technique that will help you return to the vastly higher state of consciousness from which we all came. It is the remembrance of the breath connected to the lightbody of the Mer-Ka-Ba. This is one of the primary purposes of this work.

At this point a short story of how this book came about is in order. You will read about the angels, so I will not begin there, but rather with the later events. In 1985 the angels asked me to begin teaching the meditation of the Mer-Ka-Ba. I first learned it in 1971 and had been practicing it ever since, but I did not want to become a teacher. My life was easy and fulfilled. Basically, I was comfortable and didn't want to work so hard. The angels said that when someone is given spiritual knowledge, they must share it. They said it was a law of creation.

Knowing they were right, I opened my first class to the public in the spring of 1985. By 1991 my workshops were filled and overflowing, with hundreds of people on the waiting list. I didn't know how to reach everyone who wanted this information. In fact, I could not. So in 1992 I made a decision to release a video of one of my workshops and let it go out to the world.

Within less than a year it was exploding in sales, but there was one big problem. Most of the people who were watching the videos could not really understand what was presented because it was outside the context and content of their spiritual understanding. I gave a lecture to ninety people in Washington State, all of whom had seen the video tapes but had never been to one of my live workshops. It was there that I realized that only about 15 percent of the people actually knew how to live the meditation by using only the instructions on the video tapes. It was not working. Eighty-five percent were confused and unclear about the instructions.

Immediately I took the video tapes off the market. This, however, did not stop the video from continuing to be sold. People wanted the information, so they began to copy the existing tapes and give, sell or lease them to people worldwide. By 1993, it has been estimated that there were approximately 100,000 sets of these tapes in the world.

A decision was made. It was determined that the only way we could be responsible with this information was to have a trained person in the room when someone watched the video tapes. Trained means that we had carefully instructed a person to know and live the Mer-Ka-Ba. That person could then orally teach another. This is how the Flower of Life facilitator program was born. There are now over 200 trained facilitators in at least 33 countries. And the system has worked very well.

Now things are changing again. People are beginning to understand higher consciousness and its value and concepts. It is now time to release this book to the general public, which is now ready, we feel. A book has the advantage that people can take more time to study the drawings and photos carefully at leisure. And it will also have current updated information such as follows:

**Update: The times they are a-changing for sure! According to Dow Jones Company, Inc. in their magazine *American Demographics*, February 1997, a ten-year scientific study has revealed that a brand-new culture is emerging in America and the Western world at this moment. Some have called this new culture the New Age, but it has had other names, depending on the country.**

From our experience, we believe it is a worldwide emerging culture. It is a culture that deeply believes in God, family, children, spirit, Mother Earth and a healthy environment, femininity, honesty, meditation, life on other planets and the unity of all life everywhere. The members of this new culture believe, according to the study, that they are few and scattered. The survey revealed, however, to everyone's complete surprise, that "they" are *one in every four adults in America — an amazing 44 million adults strong!* Something huge is happening here. Now that the money movers are aware of this enormous new market, you bet things will change. Everything from movie and TV content to the use of energy to the foods we eat and much more will be affected. Our very interpretation of the Reality may even eventually change. You are not alone, and it will not take long now for this fact to be apparent to everyone.

Ever since the angels first appeared in 1971, I have been following their guidance. This is still true today. It was the angels who gave me the meditation of the Mer-Ka-Ba, and it is the meditation that is important here, not the information that is presented. The information is used just to bring us to a point of clarity so we can enter into a particular state of consciousness.

Understand that as I received the scientific information in the early years from 1971 to about 1985, I thought it was for my own personal growth. When I would read a scientific paper or magazine, I would discard it, not realizing that in the future I would have to prove what I was saying. Most of the articles have been located, but not all. Yet this information needs to go out. You, the reader, have strongly requested it. Therefore, wherever I can I will document my statements, but some proofs are lost, at least for the moment.

Also, part of the information is from nonscientific sources such as angels or interdimensional communications. We understand that "straight science" needs to be separated from a source who is considered psychic. Scientists are concerned about their credibility. As a side note, I would like to comment that this is similar to a male saying to a female that her feelings are not valid and that only logic is true or valid, that logic *must* be followed. Naturally, she knows another way; it is the way of life itself. It flows. It has no "male logic," but it is equally true. I believe in both, in balance.

If you can conceive of a person using both science and psychic abilities together to explore the Reality, you have come to the right place. Whenever possible I will differentiate between the two types of sources so that you are clear. This means that you must go within yourself to see if this information is true within your world. If something does not feel right, then discard it and go on. If it feels right, then live it and see if it is really true. But it is my understanding that the mind will never really know the Reality until it has joined with the heart. Male and female complete each other.

When you read this work you have two choices: You can come from your left brain, your male side, and take notes and carefully see the logic in each step, *or* you can come from your right brain, your female side, just let go and don't think — feel, watch it like a movie, expanded, not contracted. Either way will work. It is your choice.

Finally, as I prepared this book, I had to make another decision. Should the final stages of the meditation, the Mer-Ka-Ba itself, be released? I still feel that an oral teacher is best. Would you jump to the final stages of Tibetan Buddhism after reading one book? What has been decided is that everything will be given here up to the time of the 1993 video, with the precaution that you carefully enter the Mer-Ka-Ba and still seek out a Flower of Life facilitator. That information will be given at the end of the second volume. Much has been learned after and beyond these writings that can only be given orally and experientially.

The reason I am giving out the full information is that there are now at least seven other authors who have reprinted this work in one form or another. Some have taken it word for word, some have paraphrased me, and some have used my artwork and sacred geometry drawings. Some have asked and some have not. But the end result is that the information is out. Much of it has been distorted and sometimes it is just plain not true. Please know that it is not to protect myself, but to be responsible for the integrity of the work. This information belongs to the universe, not me. It is only the purity of the information that I am concerned with, and your clear understanding of it.

The exact instructions for the meditation are on the Internet [www.floweroflife.com], but of course not the hidden knowledge. That is experiential. You must live it. There is other information on the Net that states it is coming from me when it is not. There is also information out about the Flower of Life that is simply wrong or out of date. Hopefully, this work will make clear what has been veiled or distorted. I understand that these people were coming from their hearts, looking for the truth, but it is still my responsibility to you.

Therefore, in order to be clear and set the record straight, I am writing this book for all of you who wish to truly understand and know the truth.

In love and service,
Drunvalo Melchizedek

O N E

# Remembering Our Ancient Past

## How the Fall of Atlantis Changed Our Reality

A little less than 13,000 years ago, something very dramatic happened in the history of our planet that we're going to explore in great detail, because what happened in the past is now affecting every aspect of our life today. Everything we experience in our daily living, including the particular technologies we use, the wars that erupt, the foods we eat and even the way we perceive our lives, is the direct result of a certain sequence of events that happened during the end of Atlantean times. The consequences of these ancient events have entirely changed the way we live and interpret reality.

Everything is connected! There is only one Reality and one God, but there are many, many ways that the one Reality can be interpreted. In fact, the number of ways to interpret the Reality are just about infinite. There are certain realities that many people have agreed on, and these realities are called levels of consciousness. For reasons we'll get into, there are specific realities that extremely large numbers of beings are focusing on, which include the one you and I are experiencing right now.

At one time we existed on Earth in a very high level of awareness that was far beyond anything we can even imagine right now. We hardly have even the capability to imagine where we once were, because who we were then is so out of context with who we are now. Because of the particular events that happened between 16,000 and 13,000 years ago, humanity fell from that very high place through many dimensions and overtones, ever increasing in density, until we reached this particular place, which we call the third dimension on planet Earth, the modern world.

When we fell—and it was like a fall—we were in an uncontrolled spiral of consciousness moving down through the dimensions of consciousness. We were out of control, and it was very much like falling through space. When we arrived here in the third dimension, certain specific changes took place, both physiologically and in the way we functioned in the Reality. The most important change was in the way we breathed prana, a Hindu

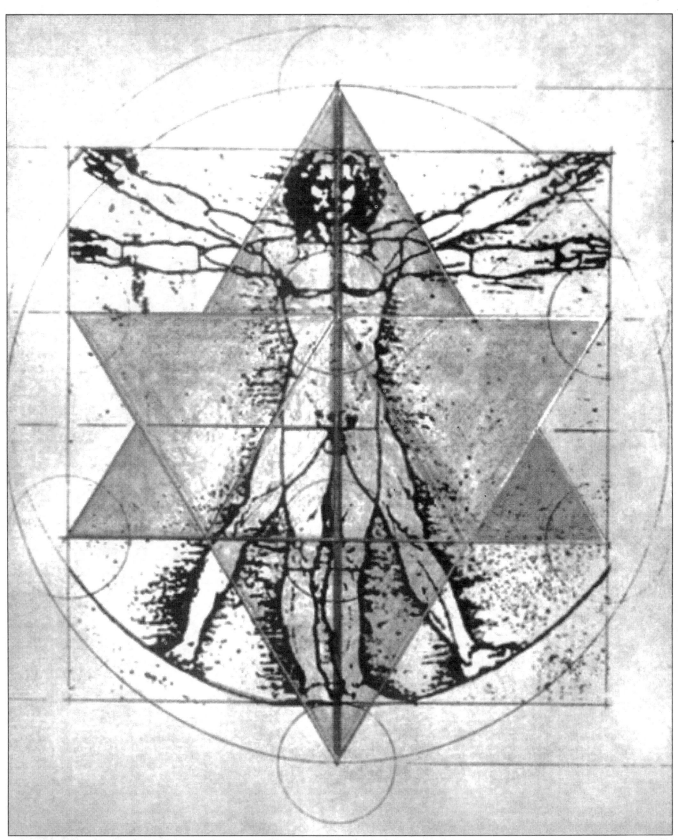

Fig. 1-1. The star tetrahedral field that surrounds each of us.

word for the life-force energy of this universe. Prana is more critical to our survival than air, water, food or any other substance, and the manner in which we take this energy into our bodies *radically* affects how we perceive the Reality.

In Atlantean times and earlier, the way we breathed prana was directly related to the electromagnetic energy fields that surround our bodies. All the energy forms in our fields are geometric, and the one we will be working with is a star tetrahedron, which consists of two interlocked tetrahedrons [Fig. 1-1]. Another way of thinking of it is as a three-dimensional Star of David.

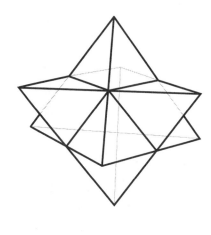

The apex of the upward-pointing tetrahedron terminates one hand's length above the head, and the apex of the downward-pointing tetrahedron terminates one hand's length below the feet. A connecting tube runs from the upper apex to the lower point through the body's main energy centers, or chakras. This tube, for *your* body, has the diameter of the circle you make when you touch your longest finger to your thumb. It looks like a glass fluorescent tube, except it has a crystalline structure at the ends that fit into the two apexes of the star tetrahedron.

Before the fall of Atlantis, we used to bring prana simultaneously up and down this tube, and the two prana flows would meet inside one of our chakras. Specifically how and where the prana meets has always been an important aspect of this ancient science, which today is still being studied throughout the universe.

Another major point in the human body is the pineal gland, located almost in the center of the head, which is a huge factor in consciousness. This gland has degenerated from its original size, comparable to a ping-pong ball, to its present size, that of a dried pea, because we forgot how to use it a long time ago—and if you don't use it, you lose it.

Pranic energy used to flow through the center of the pineal gland. This gland, according to Jacob Liberman, author of *Light, the Medicine of the Future*, looks like an eye, and in some respects it *is* literally an eyeball. It's round and has an opening on one portion; in that opening is a lens for focusing light. It's hollow and has color receptors inside. Its primary field of view—though this has not been determined scientifically—is upward, toward the heavens. Just as our eyes can look up to 90 degrees to the side from the direction they face, the pineal gland can also "look" as much as 90 degrees away from its set direction. Just as we cannot look out the back of our heads, the pineal gland cannot look down toward the Earth.

Held inside the pineal gland—even in its shrunken size—are all the sacred geometries and understandings of exactly how the Reality was created. It's all there, in every single person. But these understandings are not accessible to us now because we lost our memories during the Fall, and without our memories we started to breathe differently. Instead of taking in prana through the pineal gland and circulating it up and down our central tube, we started breathing it in through the nose and mouth. This caused the prana to bypass the pineal gland, which resulted in our seeing things in a totally different way, through a different interpretation (called good and evil or polarity consciousness) of the One Reality. The result of this polarity consciousness has us thinking that we're inside a body looking out, somehow separated from what's "out there." *This is pure illusion.* It feels real, but there is no truth at all to this perception. It's merely the view of reality we have from this fallen state.

For example, there is nothing wrong with anything that happens, for God is in control of the creation. But from one point of view, a polarity view, looking at the planet and how it evolves, we should not have fallen down here. In a normal curve of evolution, we should not be here. Something happened to us that was not supposed to happen. We went through a mutation—we had a chromosome breakage, you might say. So the Earth has been on red alert for almost 13,000 years, and many beings and levels of consciousness have been working together to figure out how to get us back onto the path (DNA) where we were before.

The effect of this "mistaken" fall in consciousness and the ensuing efforts to get us back on track is that something *really good*—something unexpected, something amazing—has resulted. Beings from all over the universe who have been trying to help us with our problem have initiated various experiments on us in an effort to assist, some legally and some without license. One particular experiment is resulting in a scenario that no one anywhere had ever dreamed would become a reality, except one person in a single culture from a long-distant past.

### The Mer-Ka-Ba

There's another major factor that we're going to focus on in this story. Thirteen thousand years ago we were aware of something about ourselves that we've since completely forgotten: The geometric energy fields around our bodies can be turned on in a particular way, which is also connected to our breath. These fields used to spin at close to the speed of light around our bodies, but they slowed down and stopped spinning after the Fall. When this field is turned back on and spins, it's called a Mer-Ka-Ba, and its usefulness in this Reality is unparalleled. It gives us an expanded awareness of who we are, connects us with higher levels of consciousness and restores the memory of the infinite possibilities of our being.

A healthy spinning Mer-Ka-Ba is fifty to sixty feet in diameter, proportionate to one's height. The rotation of a spinning Mer-Ka-Ba can be displayed on a computer monitor using the appropriate instruments, and its appearance is identical with the infrared heat envelope of the galaxy [Fig. 1-2]—the same basic shape as the traditional flying saucer.

The word Mer-Ka-Ba is made up of three smaller words, Mer, Ka and Ba, which, as we are using them, came from ancient Egyptian. It is seen in other cultures as *merkabah, merkaba* and *merkavah*. There are several pronunciations, but generally you pronounce it as if the three syllables are sep-

Fig. 1-2. Infrared photo of a galaxy, called the Sombrero galaxy, showing its heat envelope.

arate, with equal accents on each. *Mer* refers to a specific kind of light that was understood in Egypt only during the Eighteenth Dynasty. It was seen as two counterrotating fields of light spinning in the same space, which are generated by certain breathing patterns. *Ka* refers to the individual spirit and *Ba* refers to the spirit's interpretation of its particular reality. In *our* particular reality, *Ba* is usually defined as the body or physical reality. In other realities where spirits don't have bodies, it refers to their concepts or interpretation of the reality they bring with them.

So the Mer-Ka-Ba is a counterrotating field of light that affects spirit and body simultaneously. It is a vehicle that can take spirit *and body* (or one's interpretation of reality) from one world or dimension into another. In fact, the Mer-Ka-Ba is much more than this, because it can *create* reality as well as move through realities. For our purposes here, however, we will focus mainly on its aspect as an interdimensional vehicle (Mer-Ka-Vah means *chariot* in Hebrew) that will help us return to our original higher state of consciousness.

### Returning to Our Original State

To be clear, returning to our original state is a natural process that can be easy or difficult according to our belief patterns. However, simply becoming involved with the technical relationships of the Mer-Ka-Ba, such as correcting our breathing patterns or mentally realizing the infinite connections to all patterns of life, for example, is not enough. At least one other factor is even more important than the Mer-Ka-Ba itself, and that is the understanding, realization and living of divine love. For it is divine love, sometimes referred to as unconditional love, that is the primary factor that allows the Mer-Ka-Ba to become a living field of light. Without divine love, the Mer-Ka-Ba is just a machine, and this machine will have limitations that will never allow the spirit that created it to return home and reach the highest levels of consciousness—the place where there are no levels.

We must be experiencing and expressing unconditional love in order to move beyond a certain dimension, and the world is fast heading toward that higher place. We are heading away from the place of separatism where we see ourselves inside the body looking out. That view will be gone soon, to be replaced with a different view of reality where we'll have the sense and knowledge of absolute unity with all life; and that sense will grow more and more as we continue to move upward through each level on our journey home.

Later we will explore special ways of opening the heart—to kindle compassionate, unconditional love so that you can have a direct experience. If you can just let this happen, you may discover things about yourself that you didn't know before.

> *Dear reader: There are procedures in the workshops that cannot be reproduced on the tapes or in this book because they are totally experiential. They are just as important as the knowledge, for without them the knowledge is worthless. The only way we can give these experiences now is through oral tradition through a living workshop. But that may change in the future.*

## A Higher, Inclusive Reality

Another component we're going to focus on has many names, but in present-day terms it's usually referred to as the higher self. In the higher-self reality, we literally exist in other worlds besides this one. There are so many dimensions and worlds that it almost surpasses human capability to conceive of it. These levels are very specific and mathematical, and the spacing and the wavelengths in and between these levels are identical to the relationships within musical octaves and other aspects of life. But right now your third-dimensional consciousness has probably been severed from your higher aspect, so you're aware only of what's going on here on Earth. This is not the norm for beings existing in a natural unfallen state. The norm is that beings first become aware of several levels at once, like chords in music, until finally, as they grow, they become aware of everything everywhere at once. The following example is unusual, but it demonstrates what is being talked about.

I'm in communication with someone right now who is aware of many levels at once. The scientists who are studying her are speechless; they cannot understand how she does what she's doing. She might be sitting in a room, yet she claims to be watching from outer space. NASA checked her out by asking her to "see" a specific satellite and give specific information that could be known only if someone were actually there. She gave them readings off their instruments, which I'm sure seemed impossible to the scientists. She said she was flying alongside the satellite and simply read them. Her name is Mary Ann Schinfield. She is legally blind, yet she can walk around a room and no one would know that she cannot see. How does she do it?

Recently she called me, and while we were talking she asked if I would like to see through her eyes. Of course I said yes. Within a few breaths, my field of vision opened up, and I was looking at or through what looked like a huge television screen that filled my field of vision. What I saw was astounding. It seemed that I was moving very fast through space without a body. I could see the stars, and at that moment Mary Ann and I, seeing through her eyes, were moving alongside a string of comets. She was very close to one of them.

It was one of the most real out-of-body experiences I have ever had. Around the perimeter of this "TV screen" there were about twelve or fourteen smaller TV screens, each one giving extremely fast images. One of them up in the upper right-hand corner was flashing rapidly moving images such as triangles, light bulbs, circles, wavy lines, trees, squares etc. It was this screen that told her what was in the immediate space where her body was located. She could "see" through these seemingly unrelated images. There was another screen in the bottom left-hand corner where she communicated with other extraterrestrial life that was within this solar system.

Here is a person who is in a three-dimensional body on Earth, but has full memory and experience of living in other dimensions. This manner of interrupting the Reality is unusual. People do not normally see inner TV screens, but we do exist in many other worlds even though most of us are not aware of it.

You presently exist on probably five or more levels. Though there is a break between this dimension and others, when you connect with your higher self you mend that break, after which you start becoming aware of the higher levels and the higher levels start paying more attention to you—communication begins! This connection to the higher self is probably the most important thing that could happen in your life—more important than understanding any of the information I'll be giving. Connecting with the higher self is more important than learning to activate the Mer-Ka-Ba, because if you connect yourself to your Self, you will get absolutely clear information on how to proceed step by step through *any* reality and how to lead yourself back home into the full consciousness of God. When you connect with your higher self, the rest will happen automatically. You will still have to live your life, but everything you do will have great power and wisdom within your actions, thoughts and emotions.

Exactly *how* to connect with one's higher self is what many people, including myself, have been trying to understand. Many people who have somehow made this connection often don't know how it happened. In this course I'll attempt to explain exactly how to connect with your higher self. I'll do my best.

## Left- and Right-Brain Realities

There's one more component to this picture. I'll be spending perhaps half of our time on left-brain information like geometries and facts and all kinds of information that to many spiritual people would seem totally unimportant. I'm doing this because when we fell, we divided ourselves into two—really three, but primarily into two—main components, which we call male and female. The right brain, which controls the left side of our body, is our feminine component, though it's truly neither male nor female. This is where our psychic and emotional aspect lives. This component *knows* that there's only one God and that oneness is all there is. Though it can't really explain it, it just knows the truth. So there are not a lot of problems with the female component.

The problem is on the left side of the brain—the male component. Because of the nature of how the male brain is oriented—a mirror image of the female—it has its logical component forward (more dominant), while the female has its logical component toward the back (less dominant). The left brain does not experience oneness when it looks out into the Reality; all it sees is division and separation. For that reason, the male aspect of us is having a difficult time down here on Earth. Even our major sacred books such as the Koran, the Hebrew Bible and the Christian Bible have divided everything into opposites. The left brain experiences that there is God, but then there's also the devil—perhaps not quite as strong as God, but a huge influence. So even God is seen in terms of duality, as one pole of the opposing forces of dark and light. (This is not true in all sects of these religions. A few of them see that there is only God.)

Until the left brain is able to see the unity running through everything, to know that there is truly one spirit, one force, one consciousness moving through absolutely everything in existence—until it knows that unity beyond any doubt—then the mind is going to stay separated from itself, from its wholeness and from the fullness of its potential. Even if there's the *slightest* doubt at all about unity, the left-brain aspect will hold us back, and we can no longer walk on water. Remember, even Thomas walked on water for a short moment when Jesus asked him to, but one little cell in his big toe said, "Wait a minute, I can't do this," and Thomas sank into the cold water of polarity reality.

## Where We're Going with This Information

I'm dedicating a lot of our time to showing you beyond any shadow of a doubt that there is only *one image* in everything. There is one and only one image that created all that exists, and that image is the same image that has formed the electromagnetic field around your body. The same geometries that are in your field can be found around everything—planets and galaxies and atoms and everything else. We will examine this image in great detail.

We're also going to go into the history of the Earth, because it is very important to our present situation. We cannot really understand how we got here if we don't know the process that led us to this point. So we'll spend a

considerable length of time talking about what happened a long time ago; then slowly we'll come forward until we get to what's going on today. It's all tied together. The same old thing has been going on all along, and it's still going on—in fact, it has never stopped.

Those of you who are predominantly right-brained may feel inclined to skip this left-brained material, yet it is *most* important for you to hang in there. It is through balance that spiritual health returns.

When the left brain sees absolute unity, it begins to relax and the corpus callosum (the band of fibers joining the two hemispheres) opens in a new way, allowing an integration between the two sides. The link between the left and right brain widens, a flow starts, information is passed back and forth, and the opposing sides of the brain begin to integrate and synchronize with each other. If you're hooked up for biofeedback, you can actually see this happening. This action turns on the pineal gland in a different manner and makes it possible for your meditation to activate the lightbody of the Mer-Ka-Ba. Then the whole process of regeneration and recovery of our previous higher levels of consciousness can proceed. It is a growth process.

If you are studying any other spiritual practice, you do not need to stop in order to begin the work with the Mer-Ka-Ba—unless, of course, your teacher does not want to mix traditions. Other meditations that are based on truth can be extremely useful once the Mer-Ka-Ba is spinning, because then noticeable results can evolve very, very quickly. I will repeat myself just so you know for sure: The lightbody of the Mer-Ka-Ba does not contradict or inhibit any other meditation or religion that upholds the belief that there is only one God.

So far we've talked only about the ABCs of spirituality. These are just the beginning steps. But these first steps are the most important ones I know.

Your left brain may love all this information and file it away in neatly labeled pigeonholes; this is fine. Or you can just relax and read this like an adventure story, a mind-stretcher, a fantasy. However you read it, the fact that you *are* reading this book is what matters, and you will receive whatever you're meant to receive.

In the spirit of oneness, then, let us embark upon this journey of exploration together.

### Challenging the Belief Patterns of Our Parents

Many ideas we believe today and "facts" we've been taught in school are just not true, and people are now beginning to realize this worldwide. Of course, usually these patterns were believed to be true at the time they were taught, but then concepts and ideas changed, and the next generation was taught different truths.

For example, the concept of the atom has changed dramatically so many times over the last ninety years that at this point they don't really adhere to a concept. They use one, but with the understanding that it may be wrong.

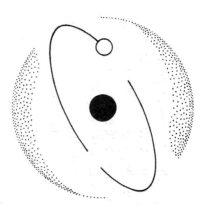

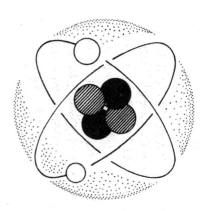

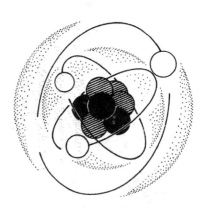

At one time the atom was thought to be like a watermelon and the electrons were like seeds inside the watermelon. We really know very little about the Reality that exists around us. Quantum physics has now shown us that the person performing the experiment influences the outcome. In other words, consciousness can change the outcome of an experiment, depending on its belief patterns.

There are other aspects of ourselves we hold true that may not be true at all. One idea that has been held for a long time is that we're the only planet in existence with life on it. In our heart of hearts we know this is not true, but this planet will not admit this truth in modern times even though there is powerful evidence of UFO sightings that have been coming from all over the world nonstop for over fifty years. Any subject other than UFOs would have been believed and accepted by the world had this subject not been so threatening. Therefore, we're going to look at evidence that suggests there is a higher consciousness in the universe, not only in the stars, but perhaps right here on the Earth.

*As a side note, I suggest that you see two videos aired on NBC Television as a special, hosted by Charlton Heston: "The Mysterious Origins of Man" and "The Mystery of the Sphinx." Both are distributed by BC Video at 1-800-508-0558.*

## Gathering the Anomalies

### The Dogon Tribe, Sirius B and Dolphin Beings

This drawing [Fig. 1-3] is truly remarkable. The information in it came from a book about Sirius, *The Sirius Mystery* by Robert Temple. He had, I was told, between ten and twelve different subjects to choose from, each one of which would lead to the same conclusion but from a totally different point of view. I'm glad he chose the one he did, because it happens to relate to another aspect of what we will be talking about.

Robert Temple was one of the first people to reveal certain facts—though scientists have known for a long time—about an African tribe near Timbuktu called the Dogons. This tribe holds information that is simply impossible for them to have by any standards in our view of the world today. Their information destroys everything we think we know about ourselves in regard to being alone.

You see, the Dogons have a cave on their land that stretches way back into a mountain, and in this cave are wall drawings over 700 years old. One particular man, the holy man of their tribe, sits at the front of this cave to protect it. This is his lifetime job. They feed him and take care of him, but no one can touch him or get close to him. When he dies, another holy man takes his place. In this cave are amazing drawings and bits of information.

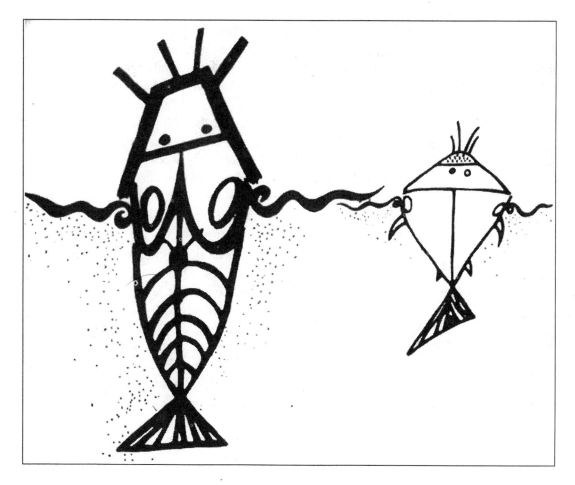

Fig. 1-3. Dogon drawing of Nommo, the great culture hero who brought civilization to Earth. Because both eyes are shown in the drawings, they are presumed to be plan views, which means the tail is opposed (like a dolphin) rather than lateral, as it is with a fish. The waterline is clearly indicated, implying that the Nommo is air-breathing. This drawing came out of the Australian magazine *Simply Living*.

I'm going to tell you about two of these bits—and these are only two of many.

First of all, we're referring to the brightest star in the sky (with an apparent magnitude of -1.4)—Sirius, now called Sirius A. If you look at Orion's Belt, those three stars in a row, and follow the line downward to your left, you see a very bright star, which is Sirius A. If you follow them upward about twice the distance, you see the Pleiades. The information in the Dogon cave specifically showed another star rotating around Sirius. The Dogons are very specific about this star. They say it's very, very old and very small, and that it's made out of what they called the "heaviest matter in the universe" (which is close, but not actually correct). And they say that it takes "close to fifty years" for this small star to rotate around Sirius. This is detailed stuff. Astronomers were able to validate the existence of Sirius B, a white dwarf, in 1862, and only about fifteen or twenty years ago could they validate the other information.

Now, stars are very much like people, as you will begin to see. They're alive, and they have personalities and many qualities like we have. On a scientific level, they have growth stages. They start out as hydrogen suns, like ours, where two hydrogen atoms come together in a fusion reaction to form helium. This process creates all the life and light that's on this planet.

**Update:** A magnetar (magnet + star) has been discovered only recently; it is a neutron star that rotates about 200 times per second, generating an enormous magnetic field. Scientists detected on August 27, 1998, what they described as a starquake. Their instruments picked up radio waves from SGR 1900+14. The radiation overwhelmed gamma-ray detectors on seven spacecraft, causing two to shut down, including the Near Earth Asteroid Rendezvous (NEAR) spacecraft.

As a star further matures, another fusion process begins—the helium process—where three helium atoms come together to form carbon. This growth process continues through various stages until it gets all the way up through a particular level of the atomic table, at which point the star has reached the length of its life span. At the end of its life, as far as we know, there are two primary things a star can do. New data on pulsars and magnetars give other options. One, it can explode and become a supernova, a huge hydrogen cloud that becomes the womb for hundreds of new baby stars. Two, it can rapidly expand into what's called a red giant, a huge explosion that engulfs all its planets—burns them up and destroys the whole system, then stays expanded for a long time. Then slowly it will collapse into a tiny old star called a white dwarf.

What the scientists found rotating around Sirius was a white dwarf, which corresponded exactly to what the Dogons say. Then science checked to see how much it weighed, to see if it really was the "heaviest matter in the universe." The original computations—made about twenty years ago—determined that it weighed about 2000 pounds per cubic inch. That would certainly qualify for heavy matter, but science now knows that this was an extremely conservative estimate. The newest estimate is approximately 1.5 million tons per cubic inch! Black holes aside, that would surely seem to be the heaviest matter in the universe. This means that if you had a cubic inch of this white dwarf, which is now called Sirius B, it would weigh about one and a half million tons, which would go right through anything you set it on. It would head toward the center of the Earth and actually oscillate back and forth across the core for a long time until friction finally stopped it in the very center.

In addition, when they checked the rotational pattern of Sirius B around the larger Sirius A, they found it to be 50.1 years. Now, that absolutely could *not* be a coincidence! It's just too close, too factual. Yet how did an ancient primitive tribe know such detailed information about a star that could be measured only in this century?

But that is only part of their information. They also knew about all the other planets in our solar system, including Neptune, Pluto and Uranus, which we have discovered more recently. They knew exactly what these planets look like when you approach them *from space*, which we have also only recently learned. They also knew about red and white blood cells, and had all kinds of physiological information about the human body that we've recently learned. All this from a "primitive" tribe!

Naturally, a scientific team was sent over to ask the Dogons how they knew all this. Well, that was probably a big mistake for these researchers, because if they accepted that the Dogons really have this information, then by default they must accept how they got it. When they asked, "How did you learn this?" the Dogons replied that the drawings on the walls of their cave showed them. These drawings show a flying saucer—it looks just like that very familiar shape—coming out of the sky and landing on three legs;

then it shows the beings in the ship making a big hole in the ground, filling it with water, jumping out of the ship into the water, and coming up to the edge of the water. These beings look very much like dolphins; in fact, maybe they *were* dolphins, but we don't know for certain. Then they started communicating to the Dogons. They described where they came from and gave the Dogon tribe all this information.

That's what the Dogons said. The scientists just sat there. Eventually they said, "Nooo, we didn't hear that." Because it didn't fit into anything they thought they knew, they just kind of hid the information somewhere under a carpet in their minds. Most people, scientists included, just do not know what to do with these kinds of facts. There has been a lot of information like this that we just don't know what to do with. Since we can't find a way to integrate this unusual information with what we already think we know, we just stick it away somewhere—because the theories don't work, you know, if we keep it.

Here's another thing the Dogons knew. This little drawing was on the walls [Fig. 1-4], but the scientists didn't know what the heck it was . . . until

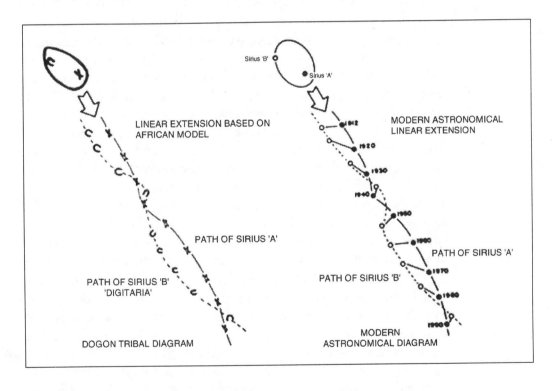

Fig. 1-4. Two linear extensions, representing the revolution of Sirius B around Sirius A. The diagram on the left is based on Dogon drawings; the projection of the right was calculated by Robert Temple.

computers calculated the orbits of Sirius A and Sirius B. As seen from Earth, this pattern shown in the Dogon cave is identical to the pattern made by Sirius B moving around Sirius A—in a specific time frame, which happens to be from the year 1912 to the year 1990. The dolphins, or whoever those beings were, gave this present-day diagram/time pattern to the Dogons at least 700 years ago!

Now, as this has unfolded in my life, I've discovered that both 1912 and

1990 were very important years. In fact, the period between these two years was probably one of the most important periods ever in the history of the Earth. I'll explain more about this as we go on, but briefly, in 1912 time-travel experiments began, as did experiments between the extraterrestrial Grays and humans. (We will explain later.) And 1990 was the first year that the ascension grid for our planet was completed. And many other events happened during this period. The fact that the Dogon wall drawings pinpointed this period could be considered clearly prophetic.

## A Trip to Peru and More Dogon Evidence

I first came upon this Dogon information in 1982 or '83. I found myself around a group of people who were working with the Dogon tribe, who were actually going there and communicating with them. Then in 1985 I took a group of people to Peru, including one of these Dogon researchers. We checked into a plush hotel in Cuzco called the Hotel San Agustin, intending to go walking the following day on the Inca Trail, about forty miles over the mountaintops. You walk up to about 14,000 feet, then drop down to Machu Picchu about 5000 feet below. It's beautiful.

Our hotel was a Spanish adobe palace hidden behind high walls in the center of town. We were paired off so we could get cheaper rates. I was with the Dogon researcher, and he was constantly telling me about what they were learning, including a lot more than we're discussing here. We got a room, and the room number was 23. He got all excited and exclaimed, "Room 23!—a very auspicious number!" From Africa, where the Dogons live, the star Sirius disappears below the horizon and is out of sight for a couple of months; then it appears again on the morning of July 23, when it rises about one minute before the Sun. It appears, bright ruby-red, just above the horizon, almost exactly due east. Sixty seconds later the Sun emerges. So you can see Sirius for just a moment, then it's gone. This is called the heliacal rising of Sirius, which was a very important moment for most of the ancient world, not just for the Dogons and Egypt.

This is the moment when Sirius and the Sun and the Earth are in a straight line across space. In Egypt, almost all the temples were aligned with this line, including the gaze of the Sphinx. Many of the temples had a tiny hole in the wall somewhere; then there would be another tiny hole through another wall, then through another wall and another, going into some dim inner chamber. In that chamber there would be something like a cube or Golden Mean rectangle of granite sitting in the middle of the room with a little mark on it. At the moment of the heliacal rising of Sirius, a ruby-red light would strike the altar for a few seconds, which would begin their new year and the first day of the ancient Sothic calendar of Egypt.

Anyway, here we were in Peru, getting the room and remarking about the number 23. We walked into the room and set our things down; then we both looked at the bed, and on the bedspread we saw this image [Fig. 1-5].

We just stood there in amazement, looking at it for about five minutes before we could even speak, because the wheels in our heads were going around so fast, trying to figure out how this could be.

If you look again at the image of the beings who got out of the flying saucer, they looked very similar. They were half in and half out of water—air-breathing mammals—and their tail fins were horizontal, not vertical like fish. The only sea creatures with such fins are cetaceans such as dolphins and whales.

But the Dogon image is from Africa . . . and here we were in Peru, staring at a very similar-looking mammal. This just didn't compute. So we asked the hotel personnel, "What do you know about this emblem?" They didn't know much. They were mostly of Spanish descent and weren't tied much into Indian legends. They didn't know the old stories of creation, so they had no idea what it meant. Here's a picture of the whole insignia [Fig. 1-6]:

In order to find out more, we rented a little car and drove around the area asking other people. We finally ended up at Lake Titicaca, talking to some Uros Indians. At one point I asked, "What do you know about this?" They said, "Oh, yeah," and proceeded to tell me a story that sounded very much like what the Dogons had told! This is their creation story: A flying saucer came out of the sky and landed in Lake Titicaca on the Island of the Sun. These dolphinlike creatures jumped into the water, came up to the people, told them where they came from, and in the beginning, began an intimate relationship with the pre-Inca peoples. It was this connection with the Sky People, according to the story, that launched the Incan empire.

Fig. 1-5. Logo on bedspread in Cuzco hotel.

I just sat there with my mouth open. Afterward, *Simply Living* magazine out of Australia published a whole series of articles on this subject. When people started investigating, they found that cultures all over the world have similar stories. There are *twelve different cultures* in the Mediterranean alone that tell a similar story.

We'll come back to the dolphins a lot in this work because it seems they played a huge role in the unfoldment of consciousness on this planet.

Fig. 1-6. Logo of Hotel San Agustin, Cuzco.

## Deciphering the Hebrew Bible Code

**Update:** There is a book called the *The Bible Code* by Michael Drosnin. This book, once it is known by the public, will have a tremendous effect on consciousness and will greatly break down the sense of separation from God.

Dr. Eli Rips, an Israeli mathematician, has discovered that there is a sophisticated computer code in the Hebrew Bible. It has been checked by Yale and Harvard and even the Pentagon, all of whom have further proved it is true. This is a scientific discovery, not just someone's fantasy. What they have found is that (probably) all persons and events that occur in time and space have been written in the Bible thousands of years ago, which clearly shows that the future is known. Detailed information such as the date and place *you* were born and the date and place that *you* will die (in the future) as well as the primary achievements of your life are already written in the Bible. This may sound outrageous, but it is true. The odds have been calculated to be at least one in a million. Read the book for yourself. Is this the "secret book" that the Bible says is hidden and will not be opened until the "end of time"? According to the Mayan calendar, we are entering "the end of time."

## A Sanskrit Poem and Pi

Let's look at something totally different now to suggest that the ancient beings of this world were perhaps more evolved than we give them credit for. Figure 1-7 is a phonetic translation of a Sanskrit poem. It was shown in an article published in *Clarion Call* magazine, in the early eighties, I believe. The English translation is shown below the Sanskrit.

> gopi bhagya madhuvrata
> sṛngiśo dadhi ṣandhiga
> khala jīvita khatāva
> gala hālā raṣandhara
>
> "O Lord [Krishna], anointed with the yogurt of the milkmaids' worship, O savior of the fallen, O master of Shiva, please protect me."

Fig. 1-7. From *Clarion Call* magazine: "Mathematics and the Spiritual Dimension" by David Osborn.

Over many years researchers have discovered that each one of these Sanskrit sounds corresponds to a numerical value. It took them a long time to figure this out. Figure 1-8 shows all the various sounds that are possible in Sanskrit. Each sound has a numerical value from zero to nine, and some syllables have two number values. For instance, *ka*, a primary sound, translates as *spirit* and corresponds to either zero or one, depending on its usage, I assume.

When researchers took these different sound values and applied them to this particular poem, a mathematical figure came up that is extremely significant: 0.3141592653589 . . . continuing out to thirty-two digits. This is the exact number of *pi* divided by ten carried to thirty-two digits! No one has ever figured out how to calculate for the decimal point, which is why this is pi over ten. If you move the decimal point one digit to the right, then it would be 3.1415 etc., the diameter of a circle divided into its circumference. Well, they might have known about the diameter of a circle divided into its circumference, but in our culture's understanding of who these ancients were, there is no possibility that they could have calculated it with that kind of accuracy. Yet here is undeniable evidence.

| | | | | = | |
|---|---|---|---|---|---|
| ka | | | | = | 0 |
| ka | ṭa | pa | ya | = | 1 |
| kha | ṭha | pha | ra | = | 2 |
| ga | ḍa | ba | la | = | 3 |
| gha | ḍha | bha | va | = | 4 |
| gna | ṇa | ma | sa | = | 5 |
| ca | ta | śa | | = | 6 |
| cha | tha | ṣa | | = | 7 |
| ja | da | ha | | = | 8 |
| jha | dha | | | = | 9 |

pi/10 = 0.31415926535897932384626643383279

Fig. 1-8. All Sanskrit sounds, with their numerical values.

There are many, many of these poems and many, many other writings in Sanskrit. I don't know how far they've come in deciphering all of it, but I think that when all is said and done, it's going to be pretty remarkable.

How did they do that? Who were these people, really? Is it possible that our understanding of them is not exactly correct? Were they maybe a little more advanced than we thought? This poem definitely suggests this.

### How Old Is the Sphinx?

The following is also probably one of the most important discoveries on the planet ever. It's happening right now at this moment. However, it began about forty years ago with R.A. Schwaller de Lubicz. He's a famous self-educated Egyptian archaeologist who has written many books. He and his stepdaughter, Lucie Lamy, have demonstrated a profound understanding of sacred geometry and the Egyptian culture.

While observing the Sphinx, Schwaller de Lubicz became especially interested in the tremendous wear on its surface. Toward the back of the Sphinx there are wear patterns that cut twelve feet deep into its surface, and this type of wear pattern is totally different from the patterns on other buildings in Egypt [Fig. 1-9]. The wear patterns on other buildings, supposedly

Fig. 1-9. Sphinx with scaffolding.

built at the same time, are textured by sand and wind, which is consistent if the buildings are, as believed, around 4000 years old. But the wear patterns on the Sphinx look like they've been smoothed with water. According to mainstream thought, the Sphinx, the Great Pyramid and other associated buildings were built about 4500 years ago in the Fourth Dynasty under Cheops.

When this discrepancy was brought up to Egyptian archaeologists, they refused to listen. This went on for about forty years. Other people noticed it, but the Egyptians simply would not admit the obvious. Then a man named John Anthony West became interested. He has written many books on Egypt, including *Serpent in the Sky* and a fine Egyptian guidebook. When he heard about the Sphinx dispute, he went to look for himself. He could see that the wear was incredibly excessive and that it did look like water had caused the wear. He also found, like Schwaller de Lubicz, that he could not get the accredited archaeologists to listen to his beliefs about the Sphinx.

There's a reason for this denial, I believe. Please understand, I am not trying to discredit a major religion. I am merely reporting. You see, there are around 5000 Egyptian archaeologists in the world, and they all pretty much agree with each other in most ways. This agreement has become a tradition. They make little changes, but not too many (and not too fast, either), and most agree on the age of the pyramids. All of these archaeologists are Muslim, with a few exceptions, and their holy book is the Koran. The Koran, in its traditional interpretation, says that creation began about 6000 years ago. So if a Muslim were to say that a building is 8000 years old, he would be disputing their bible. They cannot do that, they simply cannot, so they won't even talk about it, won't even discuss it.

If you say that anything is more than 6000 years old, they will not agree. They will do anything to protect their belief, making sure that no one knows about any man-made objects that might be more than 6000 years old. For instance, they've enclosed the pyramids of the First Dynasty, which are older than Saqqara, and built military fortifications around and within the walls so nobody can get to them. Why? Because they are older than or close to 6000 years. So John Anthony West stepped outside the Egyptian archaeology world and brought in an American geologist named Robert Schoch, who did a computer analysis that gave a totally different, scientific point of view. Lo and behold, beyond any doubt at all, the Sphinx *does* have water wear patterns—and in a desert that's at least 7000 years old, it puts it well over the age of 6000 years.

On top of that, computers have calculated that it would take a minimum of 1000 years of continuous, torrential rains dumped on the Sphinx—nonstop for twenty-four hours a day—to cause that kind wear. This means the Sphinx has to be at least 8000 years old minimum. Because it's not likely that it bucketed rain nonstop for 1000 years, they figured that it's got to be at least 10- to 15,000 years old, maybe a lot older. When this evidence gets out to the world, it will be one of the most powerful revelations on this planet in a very, very long time. It's going to have a bigger effect on the world's view of itself than probably any other discovery. This evidence has not entered the schools or general knowledge yet, though it has gone all around the planet. It has been looked at and checked out and thought about and argued over, and in the end most scientists have agreed that it cannot be doubted.

So the age of the Sphinx has now been put back to at least 10,000 years, maybe 15,000 or a lot more, and it's already changing the entire worldview of the people on the cutting edge of archaeology. You see, judging by everything we presently think we know, the oldest civilized people in the world were the Sumerians, and they go back to approximately 3800 B.C. Before that, conventional knowledge says there was nothing but hairy barbarians—no civilization at all anywhere on the whole planet. But now we have something man-made and civilized that's 10,000 to 15,000 years old. That changes everything!

In the past, when something new like this is discovered that has a major influence on the viewpoint of the world, it takes about a hundred years for it to get to the people, for the average person to say, "Oh, yes, that is true!" But this time it'll happen a lot quicker because of television, computers, the Internet and the way things are today. Now scientific circles, for the first time ever, are actually beginning to look at the words of Plato in a new light when he talked about another culture, another continent, from a dim past called Atlantis.

The Sphinx is the largest sculpture on the planet. It was *not* done by hairy barbarians, but by a very sophisticated culture. And it was *not* done by anybody we now know here on Earth. From a scientific point of view, this is the first solid evidence to be accepted about the true age of civilization. There has been lots of other evidence, but people just kept putting it under the table. This information on the Sphinx has made a crack in our worldview. This took place about 1990, and the crack is now widening. We now have the accepted evidence that there absolutely *had* to have been someone on Earth who was highly civilized as early as 10,000 years ago. You can see how that's going to completely change our view of who we think we are.

### Edgar Cayce, the Sphinx and the Hall of Records

I find it extremely interesting that the Sphinx is causing this change, especially in view of what the A.R.E. [Association for Research and Enlightenment] has been saying. The A.R.E., a foundation based on teachings of "the sleeping prophet," Edgar Cayce, says that the Sphinx contains the opening to the Hall of Records. The Hall of Records is an alleged underground chamber containing physical proof of superior ancient civilizations on Earth.

Cayce is a very interesting prophet. He made about 14,000 predictions in his lifetime, and by 1970, 12,000 of those predictions had come true and 2,000 were still in the future. And in all those predictions, he made only one tiny mistake. Out of 12,000 predictions, that's incredible. You can almost forgive him for that one mistake: He received a letter from a man in France asking for a health reading, but Cayce mistakenly gave a reading on the inquirer's twin brother. That was his only mistake. Every other thing came true exactly as Cayce had predicted—up until 1972. However, after 1972 mistakes began to happen, and I'll explain why at the right time. (For those who think Cayce's prediction that Atlantis would rise to the surface before 1970 did *not* come true, check out the January 1970 issue of *Life* magazine. Islands *did* come to the surface in the area where Cayce said Atlantis was located; some sank again and some are still above water today.)

According to Cayce, the right paw of the Sphinx is the opening to the Hall of Records. Both Thoth and Cayce have said that there are physical objects hidden in a room underground near the Sphinx that absolutely prove that there were advanced cultures on this planet long before us. Thoth says that these objects will prove the existence of these advanced cultures as far back as five and a half million years. In comparison, our level of culture is but a child to these ancient cultures.

In fact, according to Thoth, civilization on this planet actually extends back *500 million years*, and our very first culture originally came from the stars. But something colossal happened five and a half million years ago that affected the akashic records. I cannot understand how that could even take place, because of what I understand the akashic records to be. According to what I know, anything that occurs, occurs forever in vibrational form. So I don't understand how the akashic records can be destroyed; yet I'm told this is true.

### Introducing Thoth

Who is Thoth? What you're seeing in this illustration [Fig. 1-10] is Egyptian hieroglyphics. Everything in the picture is hieroglyph, not just the images at the top. "Hieroglyph" means *holy writings*. These hieroglyphs are drawn on papyrus, which was supposedly the first paper in the world. The person depicted here is a man named Thoth, pronounced with a long *o*. (Some

Fig. 1-10. Hieroglyphs for Thoth.

people say Thawth, but he pronounces it Thōth.) The hieroglyph shows his head as an ibis, a bird. So whenever you see this man with wide shoulders and a strange-looking bird head, it's a hieroglyph depicting this particular being, Thoth. He's holding papyrus reeds because he was the person who introduced writing to the world. The introduction of writing was a profoundly important event, probably the most influential act that has ever occurred on this planet in this cycle. It made more changes in our evolution and consciousness than any other single act in our known history.

Thoth is also holding in his left hand something called the ankh, which is the symbol for eternal life. The ankh is an extremely significant symbol in this work, just as it was one of the primary symbols in Egyptian times. There is an electromagnetic energy field surrounding our bodies shaped like the ankh. The remembrance of it, according to the Egyptian point of view, is the beginning of our returning home to eternal life and true freedom, so the ankh is a primary key.

All these things are an introduction. I'll be skipping all over the place, talking about many different subjects that won't seemingly be tied together; then slowly, as we proceed, I'll bring them all together in one coherent picture.

On my second trip to Egypt, I went everywhere looking for this little bird called an ibis. They supposedly lived in the reeds, so I looked through the reeds with my camera. I kept looking for one the whole time I was there. I looked from one end of Egypt to the other but never saw a single ibis. I had to wait until I got back to the Albuquerque Zoo to take this picture [Fig. 1-11]. They look kind of like short-legged storks with bright pink feathers.

Here is Thoth writing [Fig. 1-12]. This is a copy off a wall, and this next photo [Fig. 1-13] is an actual wall sculpture. He's kneeling here, holding the pen and writing. This was a revolutionary act that had never been attempted before in this cycle. According to the

Fig. 1-11. Ibises in the Albuquerque Zoo.

Fig. 1-12. As Thoth is said to have invented writing, he is often depicted with a papyrus roll and stylus. Copy of a wall sculpture.

Fig. 1-13. Thoth writing (figure on right), an original wall carving.

conventional version of history, this act took place in Egypt during the time of Saqqara, but I have my doubts. I personally believe that it took place about 500 years earlier. Saqqara was built during the First Dynasty, approximately 3300 B.C. When we talk about the pyramids older than Saqqara, you will understand why I believe this.

# My Story

## Berkeley Beginnings

Some of you may not accept the possibility of communication with beings on other dimensional levels, but this is what took place in my life. I didn't ask for it, it just happened. As it turned out, I had almost daily communication on interdimensional levels for a number of years with this man Thoth. Now that I understand it more, my personal relationship with Thoth really began when I was in college at Berkeley.

I majored in physics and minored in mathematics until I was just about to receive my diploma. I needed only one more quarter to graduate. I decided I didn't want the degree, because I had discovered something about physicists that turned me off to the idea of becoming involved in a science that I believed was no science at all. This is all changing now. This in itself could be a book, but the why of it is related to the same thing I said about archaeologists. Physicists, just like archaeologists, will turn their heads away from the truth if it means too much of a change too fast. Perhaps the real truth is that this is human nature. So I switched to the other side of my brain and started majoring in fine arts. My counselors thought I was nuts. "You're going to give up a physics degree?" they asked. But I didn't need it, didn't want it. Then to graduate I had to go for two more years majoring in fine arts and art history.

Changing majors makes sense now, because when you study the ancient writings, you find out that the ancients perceived art, science and religion as interwoven, interconnected. So the programming I was putting myself through was appropriate for what I'm doing now.

## Dropping Out to Canada

I got my degree in 1970. After going through Vietnam and looking at what was happening in our country at that time, I finally said, "I've had it! This is it! I don't know how long I'm going to live or what's going to happen, but I'm just going to be happy and do what I've always wanted to do." I decided to get away from everything and go live in the mountains like I had always wanted. So I left the United States and went to Canada, not knowing there would be thousands of Vietnam War protesters following me a year later. I married a woman named Renee, and the two of us went into the middle of nowhere and found a little house on Kootenay Lake. We were a long way away from anything. You had to walk four miles from the nearest road to get to my house, so we were really isolated.

I began to live my life exactly like I had always wanted to live. I had always wanted to see if I could live on nothing, so I gave it a try. It was a little scary at first, but it got easier as time went on, and pretty soon I became adept at natural living. I lived a wonderful and full life on basically no money. After a while I realized, Hey, this is a lot easier than holding a job in a city! I had to work hard for only about three hours a day, then I had the rest of the day off. It was great. I could play music and run around and have a good old time. And that's exactly what I did. I had fun. I played music about ten hours a day, with lots of friends who came from miles around. Our place had gained quite a reputation by then. We just had fun. In doing this, which is very important to my understanding now, I discovered something about myself. It was from this—"returning to my inner child" is how I phrase it these days—that my inner child was released, and in that releasing, something happened to me that was the catalyst that led into my life as it is today.

## The Two Angels and Where They Led Me

While in Vancouver, Canada, we decided that we wanted to know about meditation, so we started studying with a Hindu teacher who lived in the area. My wife and I were very serious about wanting to understand what meditation was about. We had made hooded white silk robes to show respect. Then one day, after practicing meditation for about four or five months, two tall angels about ten feet high appeared in our room! They were right there—one was green and one was purple. We could see through their transparent bodies, but they were definitely there. We did not expect this to take place, nor did we ask for it. We were just following the instructions that our Hindu teacher was giving us. I don't believe he fully understood either, as he kept asking us many questions. From that moment on my life was never the same. It wasn't even close.

The first words the angels said were, "We are you." I had no idea what they meant. I said, "You're me?" Then slowly they began to teach me various things about myself and the world and about the nature of consciousness. Finally my heart completely opened to them. I could feel tremendous love from them, which totally changed my life. Over a period of many years they led me to about seventy different teachers. They would actually tell me in meditation the address and the phone number of the teacher I was to go see. They would tell me either to call first or just show up at his or her house. So I would do this—and it would *always* be the right person! Then I would be instructed to stay with that person for a certain length of time. Sometimes, right in the middle of a particular teaching, the angels would say, "Okay, you're done. Leave."

I remember when they sent me to Ram Dass. I hung out in his house for about three days, wondering what the heck I was doing there; then one day I went to touch him on the shoulder to say something, and I got a zap that practically knocked me to the floor. The angels said, "That's it. You can leave now." And I said, "Okay." Ram Dass and I became friends, but whatever I was supposed to learn from him was over within that one second.

The teachings of Neem Karoli Baba, Ram Dass's teacher, are very important to me. It was his belief that "the best form to see God is in every form." I've also been exposed to Yogananda's work and cherish who he was. Later we'll be talking about Sri Yukteswar and some of his work. I've been intensely involved in almost all the major religions. I've resisted the Sikhs because I do not believe that military preparation is necessary, but I've studied and practiced almost all the rest of them—Muslim, Jewish, Christian, Taoist, Sufi, Hindu, Tibetan Buddhist. I've deeply studied Taoism and Sufism—I spent eleven years with Sufism. However, through all this study, the most powerful teachers for me have been the Native Americans. It was the Indians who opened the doorway for all my spiritual growth to take place. They've been a very powerful influence in my life. But that's another story, some of which I'll give in time.

All the world's religions are speaking of the same Reality. They have different words, different concepts and ideas, but there's really only one Reality, and there's only one Spirit moving through all life. There might be different techniques to get to different states of consciousness, but there's only what is real, and when you're there you know it. Whatever you want to call it—you can give it different names—it's all the same thing.

### Alchemy and the First Appearance of Thoth

At one point the angels led me to a Canadian man who was an alchemist and who, amongst other things, was actually turning mercury into gold (though it can also be done from lead, which is more difficult). I studied alchemy for two years with him and watched this process with my own eyes. He had a sphere of glass about 18" in diameter filled with a liquid, and little bubbles of mercury would rise into it. They would go through a series of fluorescent colors and changes, rise to the top, turn into little balls of solid gold, then sink down to the bottom. Then he would collect all these little balls of gold to use for his spiritual work. He owned an ordinary-looking little house in Burnaby, British Columbia, on an ordinary-looking street. If you drove down the street, his house would look like any of the others. But *under* his house was a hidden laboratory. He had taken the millions of dollars in gold and dug straight down, building a huge complex filled with everything from electron balances to you-name-it so that he could further his work. He didn't care about money at all. And of course the purpose in alchemy is not to make gold or money, but *to understand the process* of how mercury or lead changes into gold.

It's the process that's important. Because the process of going from mercury to gold is identical to the process that a human follows going from this level of consciousness into Christ consciousness; there is an exact correlation. As a matter of fact, if you were to study *all* of alchemy, you would have to study every single chemical reaction in existence, because every reaction has a corresponding *experiential* aspect to something in life. It's the old "as above, so below" saying. (By the way, Thoth is the man who originally spoke those words when he was known as Hermes in Greece.)

At one point I was sitting in front of this alchemist teacher, and we were doing a particular kind of open-eyed meditation where we were locking breaths and breathing a certain way. He was sitting about three feet away

Update: In light of the new findings around white-powder gold discovered by David Hudson, it may be that there is a physical correspondence with gold as well as a spiritual one.

from me, and we had been in this meditation for maybe an hour or two, a pretty fair length of time. Then something happened—something I had never seen before, ever! He kind of went fuzzy, then disappeared right before my eyes! He was just gone. I'll never forget it. I sat there for a moment and didn't know what to do. Then I hesitantly reached over and felt for him. There was nobody there. I thought, Wow! I was totally in astonishment. It blew my mind (as we would say in the '60s and '70s), it definitely did! I didn't know what to do, so I just continued to sit there. Then pretty soon a different person appeared in front of me, somebody completely and absolutely different! It wasn't even close. My alchemist teacher was about thirty-five years old and this guy was maybe sixty or seventy, and a lot shorter—maybe five feet three or four.

He was a little guy, and he looked Egyptian. He had dark skin and his hair was kind of long, but pulled back. He had a clean-shaven face except for a thick beard growing from his chin that was perhaps six inches long and tied in five places. He was dressed in simple tan-colored cotton clothing with long sleeves and pants and sat cross-legged facing me. After my shock wore off, I just looked into this person's eyes. There I saw something I hadn't seen before except in babies' eyes. When you look into a little baby's eyes, you know how easy it is because there's nothing going on, no judgment, no nothing. You can just fall into their eyes, and they'll fall into yours. Well, that's what it was like to look at this man. There were just these big baby eyes in this old body. He didn't have anything going on. I had an instant connection with this person, and there were no barriers. He touched my heart like no one had ever done before.

Then he asked me a question. He said there were three missing atoms in the universe, and did I know where they were? I had no idea what he meant, so I said, "Well, no." Then he gave me an experience, which I'm not going to describe, that sent me way back in time to the beginning of creation and brought me forward again. It was a very interesting out-of-body experience. When I came back, I understood what he meant about the three missing atoms—at least I thought I did. And I said, "Well, I think what you mean is this," and proceeded to tell him what I thought. When I finished, he just smiled, bowed and disappeared. A little later my alchemist teacher reappeared. My teacher didn't know the change had taken place. Everything that happened seemed to be only in my experience.

I went away from that totally preoccupied with the experience. At the time, the angels had me working with four other teachers, so I was going from one to the next to the next, and my life was really full. But I couldn't think about anything except this little man who had appeared to me. I never asked him who he was, and he didn't return. Time went on, and finally the experience started to fade away. But I always carried the question, who was that guy? Why did he have me go look for those three atoms, and what was this all about? I had a longing to see him again, because he was the purest person I had ever met—ever. Twelve years later I found out who he was. It was Thoth. On November 1, 1984, he reappeared in my life . . . and taught me so much. But again, that's another story for later.

## Thoth the Atlantean

This man, Thoth of Egypt, goes almost all the way back to the beginning of Atlantis. He figured out, 52,000 years ago, how to stay conscious in one body continuously without dying, and he has remained in his original body since then—until 1991, when he moved into a new way of being far beyond our understanding. He lived through most of the period of Atlantis and even became king of Atlantis for a period of 16,000 years. During those times he was called Chiquetet Arlich Vomalites. His name was actually Arlich Vomalites, and Chiquetet was a title that meant "the seeker of wisdom," because he really wanted to *be* what wisdom was. After Atlantis sank (we will discuss this subject in great detail soon), Arlich Vomalites and other advanced beings had to wait for about 6000 years before they could begin to reestablish civilization.

When Egypt began to come to life, he stepped forward and called himself Thoth, keeping that name all through the time of Egypt. When Egypt died, it was Thoth who started the next major culture, which was Greece. Our history books say that Pythagoras was the father of Greece and that it was from and through the Pythagorean school that Greece unfolded and from Greece that our present civilization emerged. Pythagoras says in his own writings that Thoth took him by the hand, led him under the Great Pyramid and taught him all the geometries and the nature of the Reality. Once Greece was born through Pythagoras, Thoth then stepped into that culture in the same body he had during the time of Atlantis and called himself Hermes. So it is written, Arlich Vomalites, Thoth and Hermes are the same person. True story? Read *The Emerald Tablets,* written 2000 years ago by Hermes.

Since that time he's had many other names, but I still call him Thoth. He came back into my life in 1984 and worked with me just about every day until 1991. He'd come in and spend maybe four to eight hours a day teaching me about so many things. This is where the largest body of the information I'll be sharing with you came from, though it correlates with other information and has been substantiated by many other teachers.

The history of the world, especially, came from him. You see, while in Egypt, where he was called the Scribe, he wrote down everything that took place. He was the perfect person for it, right? He was constantly alive, so as a scribe he would just sit there and watch life go by. He was a good impartial witness, as that was a major part of his understanding of wisdom. He seldom talked or acted except when he knew that it was in divine order. Eventually Thoth discovered how to leave Earth. He would go to another planet where there was life and just sit there and watch. He would never interfere, wouldn't say a single word. He'd be absolutely silent and just watch —just to see how they lived their lives, to get wisdom, to understand—for

Fig. 1-14. Shesat, Thoth's wife.

maybe a hundred years on each planet. Then he would go somewhere else and watch.

Altogether, Thoth was gone from Earth for about 2000 years studying other life forms. But he considers himself an Earth person. Of course, we have all come from somewhere else at one point or another in the game of life, because the Earth is not that old. It's only about five billion years old, and spirit is forever, always has been and always will be. *You* always have been and always will be. Spirit cannot die, and any other understanding is just an illusion. But Thoth considers himself from here because it was here that he made the first step that led him into immortality.

This is Thoth's wife, Shesat [Fig. 1-14]. She's a most extraordinary person—in some ways at least as extraordinary as Thoth, if not more so. She was the first person to bring me consciously to Earth, which was in, roughly, 1500 B.C. I was not physically here, but we had made a conscious link across the dimensions. She connected with me because of problems the Egyptians were having within their country that, from her point of view, would eventually affect the whole world and the outcome of humanity. We worked very closely together. I still have a very deep love for her and a really close connection, though she's no longer here. Neither is Thoth. In 1991, together they left this entire octave of universes and stepped over into a completely different kind of experience of life. Their actions are important to us, as you will see.

In 1984, Thoth came back into my life, twelve years after my first experience with him while meditating with my alchemy teacher. The first thing he did was to lead me through an initiation in Egypt. He had me travel all over Egypt and perform ceremonies and accept initiations at certain temples. I was asked to enter a particular space under the Great Pyramid, repeat long phrases in the original Atlantean language and enter a state of consciousness where my body was only light. I'll tell that story when it's time, I promise.

## Thoth, Geometries and the Flower of Life

After I had been back from Egypt for three or four months, Thoth came in and said, "I want to see the geometries that were given to you by the angels." The angels had given me the basic information/geometries of how reality is related to spirit, and the angels had taught me the meditation I'm going to give to you. This meditation was one of the first things Thoth wanted from me. That was the exchange: I received all of his memories and he received the meditation. He wanted the meditation because it was a lot easier than the method he was using. His way of staying alive for 52,000 years was very tenuous—it was like hanging on by a thread. It required him to to spend two hours every day in meditation or he would die. He had to spend one hour with his head to the north and his feet to the south, in a very specific meditation; then he had to spend another hour in the reverse position doing a different meditation. Then once every fifty years, in order to keep his body regenerated, he had to go into what's called the Halls of Amenti and sit for ten years or so before the Flower of Life. (This is a pure flame of consciousness that resides deep in the womb of the Earth and to which humanity's level of consciousness is completely dependent for its very existence. More later on this subject.)

Thoth was very interested in this new meditation because what took him two hours to accomplish takes only six breaths with the Mer-Ka-Ba meditation. It's quick, efficient and far more accurate; and its potential is much greater, as it leads into a permanent form of awareness. So Thoth began to give me vast amounts of what he knew. When he would appear in my room, we would not speak with words like we're doing now. We would speak using a combination of telepathy and holographic images. His thoughts to me were holographic, I guess you would say. But there was even more going on than that. If he wanted to describe something to me, I would taste, feel, smell, hear and see his thoughts.

He said he wanted to see what the angels had given me in terms of geometries, so I gave it to him telepathically, with a little ball of light, third eye to third eye. Then he looked at the whole thing, and about five seconds later said that I was missing many levels of interconnected information. So for many hours of every day I would sit there making drawings and figuring out what all this stuff was that we now call sacred geometry.

At that time I had no words for this way of seeing. I didn't know what it was, and in the beginning I had no idea what it really meant. And I didn't know anybody else who was aware of it except in the past. I thought I was the only one in the whole world. But the more I became involved, the more I realized that it's been going on forever and it's everywhere throughout the Earth's history and throughout the universe. He taught me in this way for a long time. Finally we came up with a single drawing [Fig. 1-15], which he said contains everything—all knowledge, both male and female, no exceptions. This is the one:

I know this is an outrageous statement to make this early in this writing, but this one drawing, according to Thoth, contains within its proportions every single aspect of life there is. It contains every single mathematical formula, every law of physics, every harmony in music, every biological life form right down to your specific body. It contains every atom, every dimensional level, absolutely everything that's within waveform universes. (I'll explain in just a moment about waveform universes.) After he taught me, I

Fig. 1-15. Flower of Life.

Fig. 1-16. Flower of Life on wall in Abydos, photo by Katrina Raphaell.

understood the above statement; but to just throw out that statement right now sounds incredible. God willing, I will prove what I'm saying. Obviously, I cannot prove that this drawing contains every single aspect of creation, because there are too many things that exist to do that in one book. But I can show you enough proofs so that you'll be able to see that you can carry it over to everything.

Thoth then told me that I would find this image of the Flower of Life in Egypt. There were two times that I doubted him in all the years I worked with him, and this was one of those times. My little mind went, "No way!" because I had by now read almost every book there was on Egypt, and I had never seen this anywhere. In my mind I scanned through everything I could think of. No, I thought, that symbol is not anywhere in Egypt. But he said I would find it, and then he left. I didn't even know where to begin to look for it.

About two weeks later, I saw my friend Katrina Raphaell, who has written, I believe, three books on crystals. She had just returned from Egypt and was in a grocery store in Taos, New Mexico, when I walked in. She was standing at the film counter and had just gotten back the photographs from her most recent trip to Egypt. She had a stack about ten inches high sitting on the counter and was taking them out, thirty-six at a time, and stacking them. We started talking, and at one point she said to me, "Oh, by the way, my guiding angel told me that I'm supposed to give you a photograph as soon as I see you." I said, "Okay, what is it?" She said, "I don't know." She turned away from the pile and went through it behind her back, pulled one out at random, handed it to me and said, "This is the one I'm supposed to give you."

Now, Katrina had no idea of the work I was doing, though we had been friends for a couple years, because I didn't talk to many people in those days about my work—and I definitely had not talked to her. The picture she pulled out was this one—the Flower of Life on a wall in Egypt [Fig. 1-16]!

That particular wall is probably one of the oldest walls in Egypt, in a temple that's almost 6000 years old, one of the oldest temples on the planet. When I saw the Flower of Life in that photo, I couldn't say anything but "wooooowww." Katrina asked, "What is that thing, anyway?" All I could say was, "You don't understand, but wooooowww!"

# The Secret of the Flower Unfolds

## The Three Osirian Temples in Abydos

This temple is in Abydos [Fig. 2-1]. It was built by Seti the First and dedicated to Osiris. Behind it is another very old temple called the Osirian Temple, where the wall carving of the Flower of Life was found by Katrina Raphaell. There is still a third temple, also dedicated to Osiris and also called the Osirian Temple. Figure 2-2 is what the plan looks like.

Evidently, when they were digging back into the mountain to build the Seti I temple, with full knowledge that the third Osirian temple was there, they found the older, second Osirian temple between the two. Seti I changed the plan for the newer temple into an L shape to avoid destroying the more ancient temple. It's the only L-shaped temple in all of Egypt, which strengthens this idea.

Some people say that Seti I built the older temple, too. However, the older one is a completely different construction design and has much larger stone blocks. Most Egyptian archaeologists agree that it is a much older temple. It is also lower in elevation than the Seti temple, which gives credence to its age. When Seti I began construction of his new temple, the second one looked like a hill. The third temple, the long, rectangular one in the back, is also dedicated to Osiris, and it is one of the oldest temples in Egypt. Seti I was building his temple on this site because the other (third) temple was very old and he wanted to dedicate a new temple to Osiris. We'll look at the Seti I temple, then the third one, then the second and oldest one.

Fig. 2-1. Temple of Seti the First. This view is of the small projection at far right of the L-shaped building in Fig. 2-2.

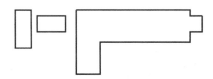

Fig. 2-2. Plan of the three adjacent Osirian temples at Abydos.

## Carved Bands of Time

In recent times archaeologists have discovered something very interesting about the wall carvings in Egyptian temples. Tourists usually notice that there appears to be a great deal of vandalism on the walls, where a lot of the hieroglyphs, especially ones of the immortals, had been chipped off and destroyed. What they might not notice is that the chipping is in a specific horizontal band, from about eye height up to about twelve to fifteen feet. There is no chipping above or below that. I didn't even notice that when I was there; it just didn't click. It didn't click for a lot of Egyptian archaeologists either for hundreds of years, until somebody finally said, "Hey, the destruction is always in this very specific region." From that realization, they began to understand that there was a difference between the region below the destruction and the one above.

They finally figured out that there are time bands on the walls. The band from about eye height down to floor level would represent the past; the band from eye height up to about fifteen feet or so would represent the present (the time the temple was built); and higher than that (these temples sometimes go up forty feet and more) would tell about what will occur in the future.

The archaeologists then realized that the only people who could have understood this relationship and actually chipped the hieroglyphs was the priesthood of the temple. The priests were the only ones who would have known that they were chipping out only the present. An ordinary vandal would not have been so precise in selecting only the band representing the present. Besides, the destroyers did not come in with a sledgehammer; they actually chipped certain things out very carefully. It has taken all these centuries to figure this out.

## The Seti I Temple

This is the front of the Seti I temple at Abydos [Fig. 2-3]. This is a small portion of a huge, huge temple.

I know now of at least two proofs that the Egyptians could see into the future. I have a picture of one of these: Way up high on one of the beams in this portion of the first temple at Abydos is something that, if you've never seen it before, is hard to believe, but it's there. I'm going to get a picture of the other one the next time I visit Egypt, because I know exactly where it is.

I think these two pictures are absolute proof, beyond any doubt at all, that they were able to see the future. *How* they did it I don't know; that's up to you to figure out. But the fact is, they did. At the very end I'll show the picture that proves this.

Fig. 2-3. Front of the Seti I temple at Abydos, looking down the length of the temple facade in Fig. 2-1.

### The "Third" Temple

This is the third temple of the three—a long, open temple [Fig. 2-4]. This temple was considered the most sacred spot in all of Egypt by the ancient kings and pharaohs, because they believed that this was where Osiris had experienced resurrection and become immortal. King Zoser, who built the beautiful funerary complex at Saqqara with its famous Step Pyramid, supposedly for his burial, did not bury himself there. Instead, he buried himself at this little unpretentious back temple.

They don't allow anyone into this third temple. But I couldn't stand to just look down into it. There was nobody around that I could see, so I dropped down over the wall into a courtyard. I managed to get about five minutes of space before the Egyptians began yelling at me to get out. I thought they were going to arrest me, but they didn't. The hieroglyphics in there are extraordinary—nothing like you would see anywhere else. The simplicity and perfection of the drawings is remarkable.

Fig. 2-4. The Osirian "third" temple at Abydos. Top of the wall is at ground level.

### The "Second" Temple's Sacred Geometry and Flower of Life

This is the second temple of the three [Fig. 2-5], which is lower than the other two. It was buried under the earth before they dug it out. (The ramp, seen at the right edge, was built to allow access from the higher ground level.) I took this picture from the third temple, looking toward the Seti I temple, whose back wall can be seen in the background. The second temple is where the Flower of Life drawings in Katrina's photo were found.

Fig. 2-5. Second (middle) temple at Abydos. Reeds are growing in the water covering its floor. The arrow at right indicates the wall where the Flower of Life is inscribed.

They allow you to go into only one place in the second temple, which happened to be the perfect place. The second temple is mostly filled with water now because the Nile has risen, but when it was first found, it was open and dry.

Here are two inside views [Fig. 2-6] of the center of the temple before it filled with water. There are three distinct areas: (1) the steps that come in from below to the center of the temple, where there is an altarlike stone; (2) the altarlike stone itself; and (3) the steps that go back down on the other side of the altar, which can't be seen here. You will see these three levels represented in the three phases of the Osiris religion. You can see the two sets of steps in the plan of the Osirian "second" temple on the next page [Fig. 2-7].

Fig. 2-6. Steps inside the second temple, before it became partly filled with water. [From Robert Lawlor's *Sacred Geometry*.]

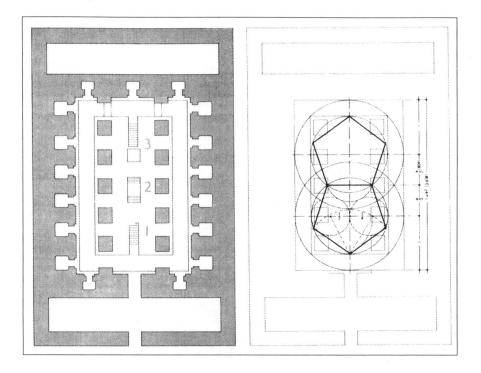

Fig. 2-7. Plan of the Osirian second temple (from *Sacred Geometry—Philosophy and Practice* by Robert Lawlor).

Lucie Lamy shows here what the original plan of the temple looked like. The two back-to-back pentagons show the sacred geometry that was hidden in its plan. Now I need to give you some background on this geometry.

The shape shown at A [Fig. 2-8] is an icosahedron. The surface of an icosahedron is made up of equilateral triangles arranged into five-sided pentagonal shapes, shown at B, which are called icosahedral caps in sacred geometry. Here the triangles are equilateral. If you were to take the icosahedral caps off the icosahedron and fit them onto each surface of a dodecahedron (twelve pentagons put together as at C), the resulting shape happens to be the stellated dodecahedron D, of the specific proportions of the Christ consciousness grid around the Earth. Without this grid there would not be a new consciousness emerging on this planet. You will understand before the end of this work.

Two of these icosahedral caps hinged together are like clamshells, indicated at E. These caps are the key, as they demonstrate the geometry used in the Christ-consciousness grid. And that's what, I feel, they're depicting in the geometry and plan of this ancient temple. I find it very appropriate that they used back-to-back pentagons in the plan for a temple dedicated to Osiris and resurrection. Resurrection and ascension lead into Christ consciousness.

Fig. 2-8. Shapes. D is the Christ consciousness grid.

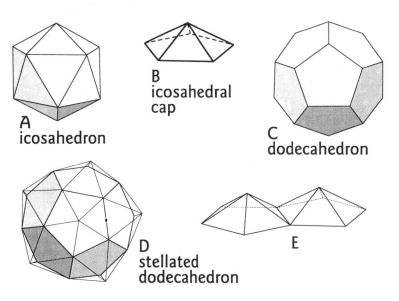

A icosahedron

B icosahedral cap

C dodecahedron

D stellated dodecahedron

E

Figure 2-9 is down in the second temple. The arrow indicates the place where Katrina unknowingly took a photograph of the Flower of Life. Here's the same picture taken with my camera [Fig. 2-10]. My photo came out better than hers, and you can see in the shade that there's another Flower of Life pattern on the same stone, side by side. To the left of these two Flower of Life patterns, on the same stone, are other related figures. The stones that

Fig. 2-9. Looking through the second temple. Arrow shows wall where Katrina took photo.

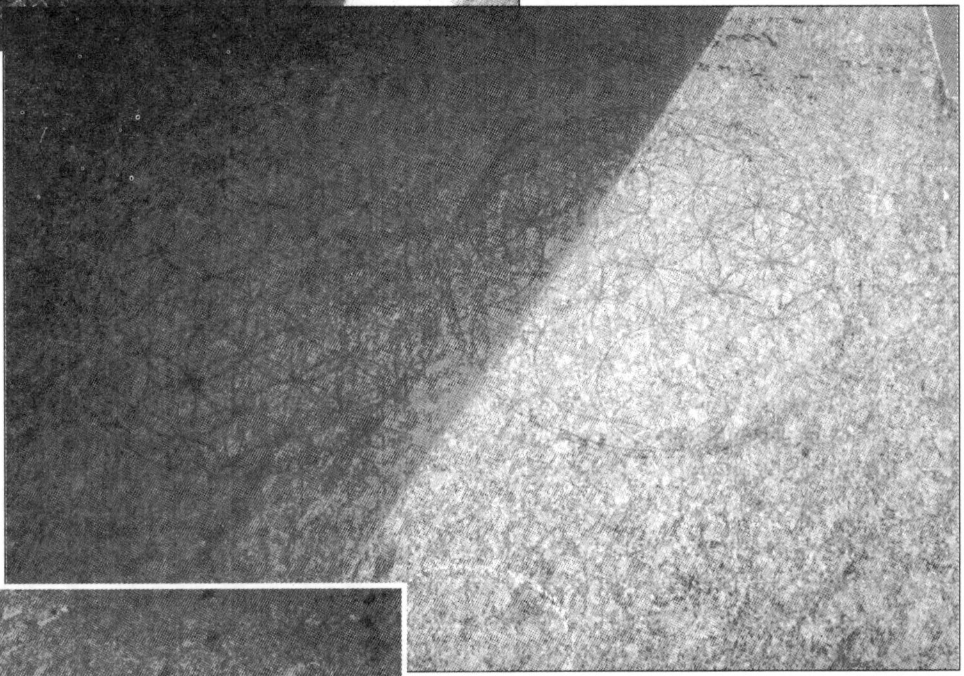

Fig. 2-10. The same Flower of Life that was in Katrina's photo [Fig. 1-16].

Fig. 2-11. Seed of Life on left. This is the same stone wall as above, but farther to the left.

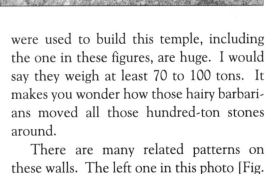

were used to build this temple, including the one in these figures, are huge. I would say they weigh at least 70 to 100 tons. It makes you wonder how those hairy barbarians moved all those hundred-ton stones around.

There are many related patterns on these walls. The left one in this photo [Fig. 2-11] is called the Seed of Life, which comes directly out of the Flower of Life pattern, as shown in Figure 2-12.

There was water at the bottom of this wall, so I couldn't get in there. But I was wondering what was on the other side of the stone, so I leaned around, put the camera on automatic and took a picture to see what would come out. This is what I got [Fig. 2-13]. You can barely see it in this photograph, but it shows many of the components that are aspects of what we're going to be studying in this course.

Fig. 2-12. Seed of Life in middle of Flower of Life.

Fig. 2-13. Flowers of Life, with other components at top.

Fig. 2-14. Coptic sign.

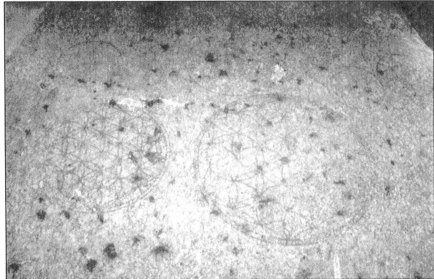

It was an amazing feeling to look at these drawings because they were so familiar to me, and I knew what they meant. And here they were, arranged on an Egyptian wall thousands of years old. The drawings were ancient, yet I knew exactly what they were.

## Carvings of the Copts

This next shot shows a wall in the second temple taken from a long way away using an 80mm lens. On this wall is a drawing, which you can barely see in this photo [Fig. 2-14], though we could see it clearly when we were there. It looks like Figure 2-15.

It's a symbol for Christianity, but it originated with a group of Egyptians called Copts, who lived at the time when the Egyptian empire was dying. They later became the very first Christians, if we include two other Egyptian groups who were connected with them—the Essenes and the Druids. You might not think that these two other groups had Egyptian roots, but we believe they did.

Fig. 2-15. Coptic symbol.

Fig. 2-16. Coptic design #1.

This is a Coptic symbol, and when I saw it, I realized it was probably the Copts who made these drawings related to the Flower of Life, not the original builders. The Copts came much later, but they probably knew this was a place for resurrection and used it for the same purpose. The building would have been several thousand years old when they made these drawings. In this case the drawings would have been no older than 500 B.C., which is when the Copts began.

This is the actual Coptic symbol, a cross and the circle [Fig. 2-16], sometimes found inside a triangle.

This is another one, in which you see the cross and the circle, though it's very worn [Fig. 2-17]. At the top you see the six loops of the center of the Flower of Life. In Egyptian drawings, whenever you see a sphere over a head, it means that the focus is whatever is inside the sphere. That's what they're thinking about or what the purpose is at that moment.

Fig. 2-17. Coptic design #2.

Fig. 2-18. Another Coptic design.

Figure 2-18 is another way this symbol is sometimes used—four intersecting arcs with an outer circle around them.

I find this photo very interesting [Fig. 2-19]. You see the fish breathing air. This was done *before* Christ. It's Coptic. It has thirteen little notches, or scales, if you want to call them that, and it's breathing air. We've seen a fish breathing air before, with the Dogons and in Peru. Now here it is in Egypt—and it is seen in other places around the world as well.

Fig. 2-19. Fish breathing air.

## The Early Church Changes Christian Symbolism

When you go back and really study some of the older writings, you find that there was a big change in the Christian religion about 200 years after Christ died. In fact, he wasn't very well known for about 200 years, at which time the Greek Orthodox Church, which was the most influential church of the day, made many changes in the Christian religion. They discarded many beliefs, added others, and changed things around to fit their needs. One thing they changed was an important symbol. All the way back to the time of Christ, from everything we've been able to read, Christ was not known as the fish, but as the dolphin. It was changed from the dolphin to the fish during the Greek Orthodox editing. Today Jesus is referred to as the fish, and even modern Christians use the fish to represent Christianity. What this means exactly, I don't know. I can only speculate when we talk about dolphins. In addition, the Greek Orthodox Church also removed from the Bible all references to reincarnation, which previously had been fully accepted as part of the Christian religion.

Fig. 2-20. Flower of Life.

**Update: In recent times we have found the Flower of Life image in eighteen more places, including Sweden, Lapland, Iceland and the Yucatan.**

## The Flower of Life: Sacred Geometry

This image of the Flower of Life [Fig. 2-20] is not only found in Egypt, but all over the world. I'll show you photographs of it worldwide in volume 2. It's found in Ireland, Turkey, England, Israel, Egypt, China, Tibet, Greece and Japan—it's found everywhere.

Almost everywhere around the world it has the same name, which is the Flower of Life, though elsewhere around the cosmos it has other names. Two of the main names would be translated as the Language of Silence and the Language of Light. It's the source of all language. It's the primal language of the universe, pure shape and proportion.

It's called a flower, not just because it looks like a flower, but because it represents the cycle of a fruit tree. The fruit tree makes a little flower, which goes through a metamorphosis and turns into a fruit— a cherry or an apple or something. The fruit contains within it the seed, which falls to the ground, then grows into another tree. So there's a cycle of tree to flower to fruit to seed and back to a tree again, in these five steps. This is an absolute miracle. But you know, it just goes right over our heads. It's so normal that we simply accept it and don't think much about it. The five simple, miraculous steps in this cycle of life actually parallel the geometries of life, which we'll continue to see all through this work.

### The Seed of Life

As I was showing earlier [Fig. 2-12], in the middle of the Flower of Life are seven interconnected circles which, if you take them out and draw a circle around them, would create the image called the Seed of Life [Fig. 2-21].

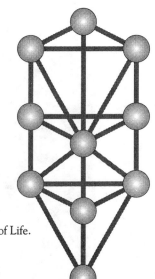

### The Tree of Life Connection

Another image in this pattern, which you're probably more familiar with, is called the Tree of Life [Fig. 2-22]. Many people have thought that the Tree of Life originated with the Jews or Hebrews, but it did not. The kabbalah did not originate the Tree of Life, and there is proof. The Tree of Life does not belong to any culture—not even the Egyptians, who carved the Tree of Life on two sets of three pillars in Egypt at both Karnak and Luxor around 5000 years ago. It's outside any race or religion. It is a pattern that is intimately part of

Fig. 2-21. Seed of Life, extracted from flower.

Fig. 2-22. Tree of Life.

nature. If you go to distant planets where there is consciousness, I'm sure you'll find the same image.

So if we have a tree, then a flower, then a seed, and if these geometries do in fact parallel the five cycles of a fruit tree that we see on Earth, then the source of the tree would have to be perfectly contained within the seed. If we take the images of the Seed of Life and the Tree of Life and superimpose them, we can see this relationship [Fig. 2-23].

See how perfectly they fit? They become like a key, one fitting directly over the other. In addition, if you look at the Tree of Life that was found on Egyptian pillars, you'll see one more circle above and one below [Fig. 2-24]. This means there were originally twelve components, and the twelve-component version also fits perfectly over the whole Flower of Life image. (There is a thirteenth circle to the Tree that can either be there or not.)

I'm approaching sacred geometry as though you never heard the words in your life. We're starting from the very bottom, and we'll slowly build on this until we get to the place where it makes sense. First you can see the synchronicity of the way sacred geometry forms move together and fit perfectly into each other. This is a right-brain way of understanding the special nature of this geometry. As we study more and more complex patterns, you'll keep seeing the same kind of amazing relationships moving through everything. The odds of some of these geometrical relationships happening at all is probably a zillion to one, yet you will consistently see these mind-boggling relationships unfold.

### The Vesica Piscis

In sacred geometry there's a pattern that looks like this [Fig. 2-25]. It's formed when the centers of two equal-radius circles are placed on each other's circumferences. The area where the two circles intersect forms what's called a *vesica piscis*. This configuration is one of the most predominant and important of all relationships in sacred geometry, as you'll begin to see.

There are two measurements in the vesica piscis—one that runs through the center across the narrow width, and one that connects one point to the opposite point through the center—that are keys to a great knowledge within this information. What many people don't know is that every line in the Tree of Life, whether it has 10 or 12 circles, measures out to either the length or the width of a vesica piscis in the Flower of Life. And they *all* have Golden Mean proportions. If you look carefully at the superimposed Tree of Life, you'll see that *every line* corresponds exactly to either the length or the width of a vesica piscis. This is the first relationship that became visible as we came out of the Great Void. (The Great Void is another key that will be discussed soon.)

Fig. 2-23. Superimposed Tree and Seed of Life.

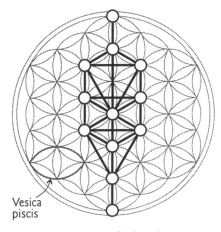

Vesica piscis

Fig. 2-24. Tree of Life with two extra circles.

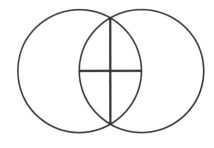

Fig. 2-25. Vesica piscis with key axes.

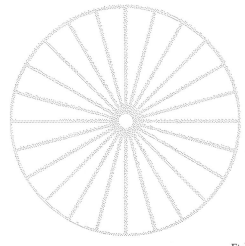

Fig. 2-26. Wheels on an Egyptian wall.

## Egyptian Wheels and Dimensional Travel

These wheels [Fig. 2-26] are some of the oldest symbols known. So far they've been found only on the ceilings of certain very old Egyptian tombs. They're always found in sets of four or eight, and nobody knows what they are. The world's most famous Egyptian archaeologists don't have the vaguest idea what they mean. But to me they're proof that the Egyptians knew that the Flower of Life was more than just a pretty design and that they knew most, perhaps even more, of the information that will be shared here. In order to understand where the wheels are in the Flower of Life, you have to study the tremendous levels of knowledge contained within it. You would never get there by just looking at designs. It's nothing that you could just happen on—you'd have to know the *ancient secret* of the Flower of Life.

This photo shows most of a set of eight of these wheels [Fig. 2-27]. The next picture [Fig. 2-28] is very dark and hard to see details. This is a ceil-

Fig. 2-27. Wheels; not all eight are visible here.

ing, and it was pitch black where I took the picture. Walking toward the right along the bottom of the drawing are seven people with animal heads. They're called *neters*, or gods, and each of them has an orangish red oval above its head, which Thoth called the *egg of meta-morphosis*. The neters are concentrated on the time when we go through a certain stage of resurrection, which is a rapid biological change into a different life form. They're holding an image of that transition as they're walking along the line, then suddenly the line comes to an end and there's a 90-

Fig. 2-28. Wheels, neters and 90-degree turn at right. The dark circles are above the heads of figures, the seven at the bottom having animal heads.

degree shift upward, and they're walking perpendicular to their first direction.

This 90 degrees is a very important part of this work. The 90-degree turn is crucial to understanding how to make resurrection or ascension real. The dimensional levels are separated by 90 degrees; musical notes are separated by 90 degrees; the chakras are separated by 90 degrees—90 degrees keeps coming up over and over again. In fact, in order for us to enter into the fourth dimension (or any dimension, for that matter), we must make a 90-degree turn.

Probably at this point I need to make sure we have a common understanding about what dimensions are—like third dimension, fourth dimension, fifth dimension and so forth. What are we talking about? I'm not talking about dimensions in a normal mathematical sense, as in the three axes or so-called dimensions of space: the x, y and z axes—front to back, left to right and up and down. Some people call these three axes the third dimension and say that time becomes the fourth dimension. This is *not* what I'm talking about.

## Dimensions, Harmonics and the Waveform Universe

What I'm seeing as the various dimensional levels has to do more with music and harmonics than anything else. There are probably different connotations of what I'm talking about too, though most people who study this pretty much agree. A piano has eight white keys from C to C, which is the familiar octave, and in between those are the five black keys. The eight white keys and the five black keys produce all the sharps and flats in what's called the chromatic scale, which is thirteen notes (actually twelve notes, with the thirteenth beginning the next octave). So from one C to the next

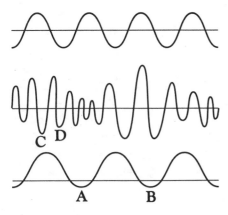

Fig. 2-29. Sample sine waves.

is really thirteen steps, not just eight.

Keeping that in mind, I want to show you the concept of a sine wave. Sine waves correspond to light (and the electromagnetic spectrum) and the vibration of sound. Figure 2-29 shows some samples. We're all probably familiar with this. In the entire Reality we're in, every single thing is based on sine waves. There are no exceptions I know of except the Void itself and perhaps spirit.

Everything in this Reality is sine wave, or cosine, if you want to look at it like that. What makes one thing different from another is wavelength and pattern. A wavelength extends from any point on the curve to the point where the entire curve starts over, as from A to B on the longer wavelength, or from C to D on the shorter wavelengths. If you get into a really long wavelength, they look almost like straight lines. For example, your brain waves are about ten to the tenth power centimeters, and they're almost like straight lines coming out of your head. Quantum physics or quantum mechanics looks at everything in the Reality in one of two ways. They don't know why they can't look at it in both ways at once, though the geometries tell why if you study them very carefully. You can consider any object, such as this book, as being made up of tiny particles like atoms; or you can forget that idea and just look at it as a vibration, a waveform, such as electromagnetic fields or even sound, if you like. If you look at it as atoms, the laws can be seen to fit that model; if you look at it as waveforms, the laws can be seen to fit *that* model.

Everything in our world is a waveform (sometimes called pattern, or sine-wave signature) or could even be seen as sound. All things—your bodies, planets, absolutely everything—are waveforms. If you choose this particular way of looking at Reality and superimpose that view over the reality of the harmonics of music (an aspect of sound), we can begin to talk about different dimensions.

## Wavelength Determines Dimension

The dimensional levels are nothing but differing base-rate wavelengths. The only difference between this dimension and any other is the length of its basic waveform. It's just like a television or radio set. When you turn the dial, you pick up a different wavelength. Then you get a different image on your TV screen or a different station on your radio. It's exactly the same for dimensional levels. If you were to change the wavelength of your consciousness, and in so doing change all your body patterns to a wavelength different from this universe, you would literally disappear out of this world and reappear in the one to which you were tuned.

This is exactly what the UFOs do when you see them shooting across the sky, if you've ever seen one. They shoot across at unbelievable speeds, then make a 90-degree turn and disappear. The people onboard those ships are not being carried through space like we are on airplanes. Spaceship passengers are consciously connected psychically to the vehicle itself, and when they get ready to go into another world, they go into meditation and link all aspects of themselves into oneness. Then they make either a 90-degree shift or two 45-degree shifts all at once in their minds, actually taking the whole ship, along with its passengers, into another dimension.

This universe—and by that I mean all the stars and atoms going infinitely out and infinitely in forever—has a base wavelength of about 7.23 centimeters. You can pick any spot in this room and go infinitely in or infinitely out forever within this particular universe. In a spiritual sense this 7.23-cm wavelength is Om, the Hindu sound of the universe. Every object in this universe produces a sound according to its construction. Each object makes a unique sound. If you average the sounds of all the objects in this universe, this third dimension, you would get this 7.23-cm wavelength, and it would be the true sound of Om for this dimension.

This wavelength is also the exact average distance between our eyes, from the center of one pupil to the other—that is, if you take a hundred people and average them. It's also the exact average distance from the tip of our chins to the tip of our noses, the distance across our palms and the distance between our chakras, to give a few more examples. This 7.23-cm length is located throughout our bodies in various ways because we are emerged within this particular universe, and it is embedded within us.

It was Bell Laboratories that discovered this wavelength, not some spiritual person sitting in a cave somewhere. When they first put up the microwave system that went around the United States and pulled the on switch, they found static in their system. You see, Bell Labs just happened to pick for the system's sending frequency one slightly longer than seven centimeters. Why they chose that wavelength, I don't know. They tried to find the static, looked through their equipment, tried everything they could. First they thought it was coming from inside the Earth. Eventually they looked into the heavens and found it, and said, "Oh, no, it's coming from *everywhere!*" In order to get rid of the static, they did something that we as a nation and a planet are *still* suffering from: They upped the power 50,000 times over what they would normally need, which created a very powerful field, so that the 7.23-cm wavelength coming from everywhere would not interfere.

### Dimensions and the Musical Scale

For reasons such as the above, I believe that 7.23 centimeters is the wavelength of our universe, this third dimension. As you go up into dimensional levels, the wavelength gets shorter and shorter, with higher and higher energy. As you go down in dimensional levels, the wavelength gets longer and longer, with lower and lower energy, more and more dense. Just as with a piano, there's a space between the notes, so that when you hit one note, there's a very definite place where the next note is. In this waveform universe we exist in, there is a very definite place where the next dimensional level exists. It's a specific wavelength relative to this one. Most cultures in the cosmos have this basic understanding of the universe, and they know how to move between dimensions. We've forgotten it all. God willing, we will remember.

Musicians, music theorists and physicists discovered long ago that there are places between the notes called overtones. Between each step of the chromatic scale there are twelve major overtones. (A group in California has discovered over 200 minor overtones between each note.)  •

If we show each note in the chromatic scale as a circle, we have thirteen circles [Fig. 2-30]. Each circle represents a white or black key and the shaded circle at the end would be the thirteenth note that begins the next octave. The black circle on this illustration represents the third dimension, our known universe, and the fourth circle, the fourth dimension. The twelve major overtones between any two notes, or dimensions, are a replica of the larger pattern. It's holographic. If you carry it further, between each overtone you'll find another twelve overtones that replicate the whole pattern. It goes down and up literally forever. This is called a geometrical progression, only in harmonics. If you continue to study it, you'll find that each of the unique musical scales that have been discovered *produces a different octave of experience*—more universes to explore! (This is another subject we will come back to.)

You've probably heard people talk about the 144 dimensions and how the number 144 relates to other spiritual subjects. This is because there are twelve notes in an octave and twelve overtones between each note; and 12 x 12 = 144 dimensional levels between each octave. To be specific, there are 12 major dimensions and 132 minor dimensions within each octave (though in truth the progression goes on forever). This diagram represents one octave. The thirteenth note repeats, then there's another octave above that one. There's an octave of universes below this and an octave above, and it stretches on theoretically forever. So as big and as infinite as *this* universe seems (which is just an illusion anyway), there are still an infinite number of other ways to express the one Reality, and each dimension is *experientially* completely different from any other.

That's what much of this teaching is about—reminding us that we here

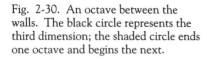

Fig. 2-30. An octave between the walls. The black circle represents the third dimension; the shaded circle ends one octave and begins the next.

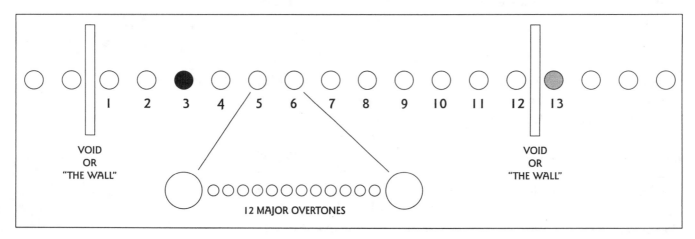

on Earth are sitting in the third dimension on a planet that is in the process *right now* of becoming fourth-dimensional and beyond. The third-dimensional component of this planet is about to be nonexistent for us after a while—we're going to be aware of this dimension for only a short time longer. First we'll go into certain overtones of the fourth dimension. Most people in the higher dimensions who are watching and helping with this process now believe that we're going to keep moving on up through higher dimensions quite rapidly.

### The Wall between Octaves

Between each whole-note universe and between each subspace or overtone universe, there is nothing—no thing, absolutely zip. Each of these spaces is called a *void*. The void between each dimension is called the *duat* by Egyptians or the *bardo* by Tibetans. Each time you pass from one dimension or overtone into the next, you pass through a void or blackness that's in between. But certain voids are "blacker" than others, and the blackest of these exist between the octaves. They're more powerful than the voids that exist within an octave. Please understand that we are using words that cannot fully explain this concept. This void that exists between octaves can be called the Great Void or the Wall. It's like a wall you have to pass through to get to a higher octave. God put these voids there in a particular way for certain reasons that will soon become apparent.

All of these dimensions are superimposed over each other, and *every point in space/time contains them all*. The doorway to any of them is anywhere. That makes it convenient—you don't have to go looking for it, you just have to know how to access it. Although there are certain sacred places in the geometries of our reality here on Earth where it's easier to become aware of the various dimensions and overtones—sacred sites, which are nodal points connected to the Earth and the heavens (we'll also talk about them later)—there are also specific places in space that are tied to the geometries of space. These places are sometimes referred to by explorers as stargates, openings to other dimensional levels where it's easier to get through. But in truth, you can be anywhere to go anywhere. It really doesn't matter where you are if you truly understand the dimensions and, of course, are capable of divine love.

### Changing Dimensions

Going back to those guys on the temple ceiling (a few pages ago), they're changing dimensions. They're making a 90-degree turn and changing their wavelength. And those wheels, as you're going to see later, are connected to the harmonics of music—and you now know that the harmonics of music are connected to the dimensional levels. Since the people on the ceiling are making this change while thinking about metamorphosis and resurrection, I believe these wheels are actually telling us exactly where they went, into which dimension. By the time we finish, you'll understand what I'm talking about.

## The Star Tetrahedron

This star tetrahedron with Leonardo's image behind it [Fig. 2-31] is going to become one of the most important drawings for this work. What you're looking at is two-dimensional, but think of it in three dimensions. A star tetrahedron, just as shown here, happens to exist around each human body. We're going to spend a great deal of time to get you to the point where you can see that you do have this image around your body. Notice especially that there's a tube running down the center of the body through which we can breathe life-force energy, and the two apexes at the top and bottom of this tube connect the third dimension to the fourth dimension. You can inhale fourth-dimensional prana directly through the tube. You

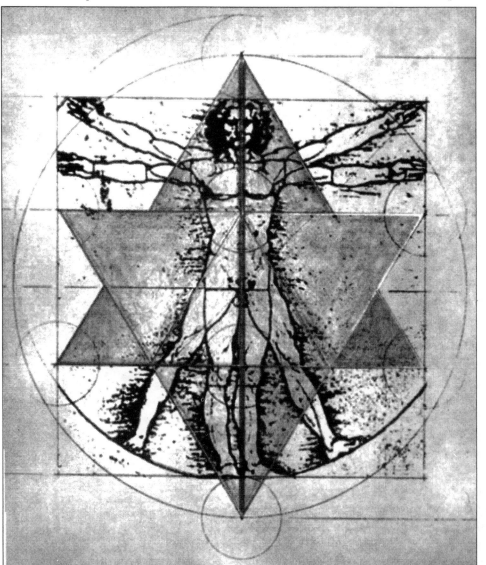

Fig. 2-31. Leonardo's canon, with star tetrahedron symbolizing the Mer-Ka-Ba, and a central prana tube.

could be in a vacuum, a total void, with no air to breathe, and completely survive if you could live the principles of this understanding.

As Richard Hoagland has shown the United Nations and NASA, we are now beginning to scientifically rediscover this field. Just as it is shown around Leonardo, it is also around planets, suns and even larger bodies. This could become the standard explanation of how some of these outer planets survive. Why? The planets are radiating off the surface far more energy than they're receiving from the Sun, a lot more. Where is it coming from? With this new understanding, if Leonardo were a planet instead of a person, the points at the north and south poles would be bringing in huge amounts of energy from another dimension (or dimensions). Planets literally exist in more than one dimension, and if you could see the whole Earth in all its glory—the various fields and energies around a planet—you'd be astounded. Mother Earth is far more intricate and complex than we at this dense level can perceive. This channeling of energy is actually how it works for people, too. And the particular dimension (or dimensions) that this energy comes from depends on how we breathe.

On Leonardo's drawing, the tetrahedron pointing up to the Sun is male. The one pointing down toward the Earth is female. We're going to call the male one a *Sun* tetrahedron and the female one an *Earth* tetrahedron. There are only two symmetrical ways that a human being can look out of this star-tetrahedral form with one point of the star above the head and one point below the feet and with the alignment of the human body looking toward the horizon: For a male body looking out of his form, his Sun tetrahedron has a point facing forward, and the opposite flat face is behind him; his Earth tetrahedron has a point facing out the back, and the opposite flat face is in front [Fig. 2-32a].

For a female body looking out of her form, her Sun tetrahedron has a flat face forward, and a point facing out the back; and her Earth tetrahedron has a point facing forward, and the opposite flat face is behind her [Fig. 2-32b]. We'll explain the Mer-Ka-Ba meditation through the fourteenth breath in volume 2. First I would like to introduce other aspects so that you

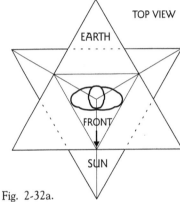

Fig. 2-32a.
Male in his star tetrahedron.

can begin to remember and prepare yourself for the eventual reactivation of your lightbody, the Mer-Ka-Ba. Beginning soon, we'll start talking about yogic breathing, which probably many of you are already familiar with. Then we'll learn about mudras after that. We're going to keep going step by step until we are ready to experience spherical breathing, the state of being from which your Mer-Ka-Ba can come to life.

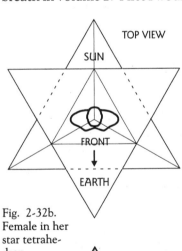

Fig. 2-32b.
Female in her star tetrahedron.

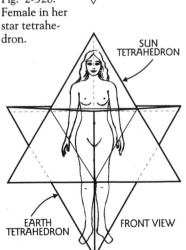

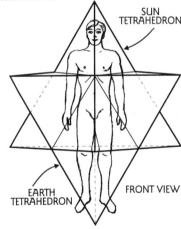

### Threeness in Duality: The Holy Trinity

To understand the situation here on Earth, we will offer another piece of information to refer to as we proceed. In nature, the law of opposites appears to be manifesting throughout our reality, such as male and female or hot and cold. In truth, this is incomplete. Actually, every manifestation in our reality has *three* components. You hear people talk about male and female polarity and about polarity consciousness; that isn't the full truth. There has never been a polarity in this reality without a third component, with one rare exception we will talk about in a moment.

There is a trinity in almost every situation. Let's think of some examples of what we usually call polarity. How about black and white, hot and cold, up and down, male and female and Sun and Earth? For black and white, there's gray; for hot and cold, there's warm; for up and down, there's the middle; for male and female, there's a child, for the Sun and the Earth (male and female), there's the Moon (child). Time is also in three components: past, present and future. The mental relationship of how we see space is with the x, y, z axes—front and back, left and right, up and down. Even in each of these three directions there's a middle or neutral point, creating three parts.

Probably the best example is the fabric of matter itself in this third dimension. Matter is made of three basic particles: protons, electrons and neutrons. On the next higher level of organization from the three basic particles you will find atoms, and on the next lower level, finer particle divisions. In a similar manner, consciousness perceives itself in the middle between the macrocosm and the microcosm. If you look closely into either level, you will always find threeness.

There is a special exception, as there almost always is. It relates to the beginning of things. Primal aspects usually *do* have twoness, but they are extremely rare. An example is found in number sequences. Sequences such as 123456789 . . . , or 2-4-8-16-32 . . . , or 1-1-2-3-5-8-13-21 . . . —and in fact all sequences known—strangely enough need a minimum of three successive numbers of the sequence in order to calculate the entire sequence, with one exception: the Golden Mean logarithmic spiral, which needs only two. This is because that spiral is the source of all other sequences. In the same manner, atoms all have three parts, as mentioned before, with the single exception of the first atom: hydrogen. Hydrogen has only one proton and one electron; it has no neutron. If it has a neutron, which is the next step up, it is called heavy hydrogen, but the very beginning of matter has only two components.

Since we mentioned numbers exhibiting threeness, we might as well bring up color. There are three primary colors from which the three secondary colors are created. This means that the universe as we now know it—all created things—is composed of three primary parts except in its rare primal areas. In addition, the very nature of how the universe is perceived by human consciousness is through the three major ways we just spoke of: time, space and matter, all of which are reflections of the sacred holy trinity.

## An Avalanche of Knowledge

Most people by now are aware that something unusual is going on here on Earth. We are in extremely accelerated time, and many events are happening that have never been seen before. There are more people on the planet than have ever been known before, and if we continue at the same rate, in a few more years we will double our population to about eleven or twelve billion people.

Regarding our human evolutionary learning curve, the supply of information on the planet is growing far faster than the population. Here's a fact according to the *Encyclopedia Britannica*. From the time of our oldest known human civilization, the ancient Sumerians (circa 3800 B.C.), continuing for almost 5800 years until about A.D. 1900, a certain number of bits of information had been collected, a certain number of so-called facts that were added up to determine precisely how many things we knew. Fifty years later, from 1900 to 1950, our knowledge had doubled. That means it took 5800 years to learn a certain amount, then it took fifty years to double it—amazing! But then in the *next twenty years*, by about 1970, we doubled it again. It took only ten more years, to about 1980, to double *that!* Now it's doubling every few years.

Knowledge is coming in like an avalanche. The information was coming so fast in the mid-eighties that NASA couldn't put it into their computers fast enough. I heard that in approximately 1988 they were eight or nine years behind in simply entering the incoming data. At the same time this avalanche of knowledge is building up, the computers themselves, which are boosting the acceleration, are about to make a huge change. Approximately every eighteen months computers are doubling both speed and memory. First we came out with the 286, then the 386; then we had the 486, and now the 586 is out [this was 1993], which makes the 486 obsolete. We didn't even know how to use the 486 yet, and here's the 586. And we've already got the 686 planned. By the turn of the century or soon afterward, a home computer will be so powerful and fast that it will surpass all of the present (1993) computers of NASA and the Pentagon combined.

A single computer will be so fast and powerful that it can actually watch the whole Earth and give constant weather data for every square inch of the planet. It will do things that now seem absolutely impossible. And we're beginning to speed up our ability to enter the data: Now huge amounts of information are entered directly from other computers and scanners and direct voice. So with this incredible amount of knowledge entering into human consciousness, it becomes obvious that a major change for humankind is being birthed.

For thousands of years spiritual information was kept secret. Priests and priestesses of various religions or cults would give their lives to keep the rest of the world from knowing about one of their secret documents or piece of spiritual knowledge, making sure it remained secret. All the various spiritual groups and religions around the world had their secret information. Then suddenly, in the mid-sixties, the veil of secrecy was lifted. In unison, almost all the spiritual groups of the world opened their archives at the same moment in history. You can browse through books in your neighborhood bookstore and see information that has been sealed and guarded for thousands of years. Why? Why now?

**Update: The Pentagon has just announced in the spring of 1997 that they have a computer that requires only one second to compute what would take a 250-MH, 3-GB PC 30,000 years. In one day it can compute what would take the PC 2.6 billion years! I would call this something more than a quantum leap.**

Life on this planet is accelerating faster and faster and faster, obviously culminating in something new and different, perhaps just out of the reach of our normal imagination. We are always changing. What does this mean for the world? Why is it happening? Better yet, why is it happening *now*? Why didn't it happen a thousand years ago? Or why didn't it wait to happen 100, 1000 or 10,000 years from now? It's really important to understand the answer to this question, because if you don't know why this is happening now, then you probably will not understand what's happening to you in *your* life or be prepared for the coming changes.

Though I don't want to get into the real meaning of what this is about right now, one of the answers lies in the fact that the computer is made out of silicon and we're made out of carbon. It's tied into the relationship of silicon and carbon, but I'll leave that for a while and continue with the unusual nature of what's happening here on Earth.

Fig. 2-33. Earth's location in the solar system.

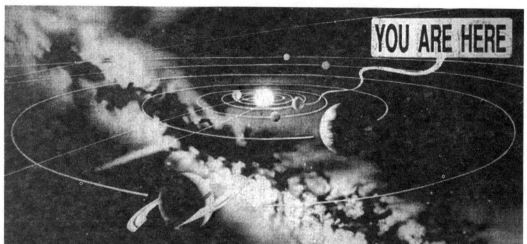

## Earth's Relation to the Cosmos

Let's talk about Sirius and the Earth again. You are here [Fig. 2-33], and this is where we begin in the big picture. From where we are on this third planet out from the Sun, Earth's intimate connection to Sirius cannot be understood very easily. You have to go out into deep space to things like this [Fig. 2-34], which you might not recognize—at least most people don't. This is a quasar, and it's enormous. It defies all the laws of physics, and we don't know what the heck it's doing. But that's not really what I want you to notice.

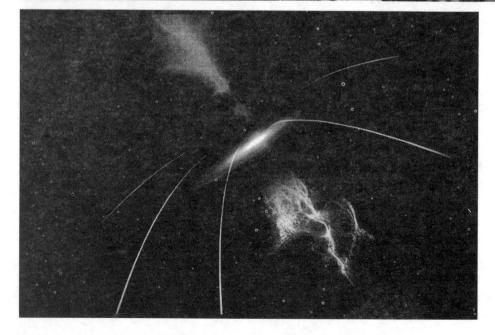

Fig. 2-34. Quasar (quasi-stellar radio source) believed to be the most distant and luminous objects in the universe.

## Spirals in Space

This next photo is a little closer and more familiar to us [Fig. 2-35]. This is a galaxy, obviously not us, because it's pretty hard to take a picture of yourself from within yourself. (The cluster at the bottom right is a nebula, and it is almost certainly much, much closer than the galaxy; they are not connected.) Notice the stars coming out of the galaxy in a white spiral. At exactly 180 degrees opposite one of the spirals is another emerging spiral. I believe there are eight known forms of galaxies—though all of them are functions of each other—and this is the primary model.

Fig. 2-35. Spiral galaxy.

For a long time astronomers pretty much thought that what you saw out there was it; if you could see it, it was there. They were either totally oblivious to the invisible side of Reality, or they didn't feel it was that important. But the invisible side of our Reality is actually much greater than the visible side, and probably more important. In fact, if the full electromagnetic spectrum were a line about two yards long, then visible light, with which we see objects, would be a band about 1/32 of an inch wide. In other words, the visible part of the Reality is far less than one percent of the total—almost nothing. The invisible universe is really our true home.

There's much more. There are things even *beyond* the electromagnetic spectrum that we're just beginning to understand. For example, they've discovered that when an old sun explodes and dies, like the one in the bottom right of the picture, it seems to occur only in the dark area of the spiral (shown by arrow A), indicating that there is a difference between deep space (arrow B) and the inner space between the light spirals. So they're beginning to realize there's a distinct difference between the two areas of space as well as between the dark and the light areas of the galaxy. There's something different about the dark areas of the spiral that seems to be related to the light areas.

## Our Sirius Connection

Observing these characteristics of a galactic spiral led to another discovery. Other scientists noticed that as our solar system moves through space, it's not moving in a straight line, but in a helical pattern, a spiral. Well, such a spiral is not possible unless we are gravitationally connected to another large body, such as another solar system or something larger. For example, many people think the Moon rotates around the Earth, right? It does not. It never has. The Earth and the Moon rotate *around each other*, and there's a third component between them approximately one-third of

**Update:** This update will not make complete sense until you fully understand the Mer-Ka-Ba, but this is the most appropriate place to put it. Astrophysicist William Purcell has just discovered (reported May 12, 1997, in *Time* magazine) that "a colossus of antimatter," a tube at 90 degrees to the plane of the galaxy, "is spewing out from the center of our galaxy and reaching trillions of kilometers into space." This resembles the same geometries of the Mer-Ka-Ba on a galactic level.

At the same time, Cornell astronomers have discovered that about 80 percent of the stars in the galaxy NGC 4138 (mostly older stars) are rotating in one direction, whereas about 20 percent of the stars (mostly younger stars) are rotating in the opposite direction along with a huge cloud of hydrogen gas. Their findings were presented on January 18, 1997, at the American Astronomical Society. This is a

Fig. 2-36. Spiral galaxy, overhead view (top) and on edge (bottom).

the distance from the Earth to the Moon, which is the pivotal point, and the Earth and Moon rotate around this point in a helical pattern as they also move around the Sun. This happens because the Earth is connected with a very large body, which is the Moon. Our moon is huge, and it's causing the Earth to move in a particular pattern. And since the entire solar system is spiraling in the same manner through space, then the whole solar system must be gravitationally connected with some *other* very large body.

So astronomers started searching for this body that was pulling on our solar system. They first narrowed it down to a certain area of the sky that we were linked with, then they narrowed it down further and further, until just a few years ago they finally pinned it down to a specific solar system. We are linked with the star Sirius—with Sirius A and Sirius B. Our solar system and the Sirius system are intimately connected through gravitation. We move through space together, spiraling around a common center. Our fate and the fate of Sirius are intimately connected. We are *one system!*

Ever since scientists have known about the dark area inside a spiraling galaxy being different, they have discovered that stars don't just move out along the curved arm of a spiral. If someone spun a water hose over his head and you viewed the scene from above, you would see droplets that appeared to move in spirals. Can you envision that? Each individual drop, though, is not moving in a spiral, but is moving radially away in a straight line from the center; it only *appears* to be moving in spirals. It's the same way in a galaxy. Each of these stars is actually moving radially away.

At the same time the stars are moving radially away from the center, they are also moving, independent of the system as a whole, from one arm through the dark light into the white light, orbiting the whole galactic system. It probably takes billions of years—I don't know—for one cycle to complete itself.

Imagine that Figure 2-36 is a galaxy viewed from above and that the dark color represents the black-light spirals and the light color represents the white-light spirals. From the edge it looks like a flying saucer. The orbit we make around the center of the galaxy has within it a spiral motion similar to a coiled spring. In addition to our solar system, the same spiral motion is seen between Sirius A and Sirius B [see Fig. 1-4 in chapter 1]. The spiral of the Earth and the Moon, I believe, is different. This spiraling motion of the two Sirian stars just happens to be identical to the geometries of the DNA molecule, according to an Australian scientist. This makes you suspect that perhaps there's a relationship in the unfoldment of things, that events happen according to some kind of larger plan, similar to the unfoldment of a human body guided by the information within the DNA. Of course, it's only speculation, but because of the principle "as above, so below," this is highly probable.

So we have two related questions to answer. One is why Sirius is so important, which has been explained by our gravitational connection to it. Another is, why is this extremely rapid pattern of evolution we are experiencing on Earth today taking place at this moment in history? Let's keep looking in the heavens. First, here are two incidental pieces of information to share.

### A Galaxy's Spiral Arms, Surrounding Sphere and Heat Envelope

Figure 2-37 is out of *National Geographic*, showing what they've now discovered. They've found that spheres of energy surround galaxies. Notice the tiny galaxy with its spiraling arms, along with a bunch of loose stars, all enveloped in the sphere of energy. Then outside that sphere is another enormous sphere of energy, shown here as a hexagonal grid. So there's a huge sphere inside a smaller sphere, with a tiny galaxy inside it. As we progress, you're going to see that you have exactly the same field around *you*.

Figure 2-38 is a picture of the heat envelope of a galaxy, slightly tilted,

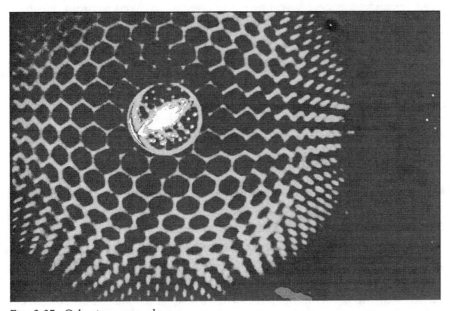

Fig. 2-37. Galactic energy spheres.

taken with an infrared camera. It looks like a flying saucer. It has a big circle around the outer edge, which is dark because the outer edge is moving very, very fast. This heat envelope is in exactly the same proportions as the Mer-Ka-Ba around your body when it's activated through breathing and meditation. When you follow a certain breathing procedure, you'll find that a field about 55 feet wide will form around your body that looks like this heat envelope. With the proper equipment, you could see it on a computer screen, since it does have an electromagnetic component in the microwave range. This is very real stuff. It is the same shape of the Mer-Ka-Ba that, if you so choose, you will activate around your body.

### Precession of the Equinoxes and Other Wobbles

Going on to why this change is happening at this moment: Our Earth currently tilts approximately 23 degrees to the plane of its orbit around the

counterrotating field. Not only do galaxies look like Mer-Ka-ba fields, but they appear to have the same internal dynamics! (Of course, I personally believe that galaxies are living beings, and that they are really nothing *but* a huge living Mer-Ka-Ba field.) In addition, physicists at the University of Rochester and the University of Kansas have found evidence that changes the long-held belief that space is the same in all directions. Researcher John Ralston reported that "there seems to be an absolute axis, a kind of cosmological North Star that orients the universe." This work is published in the April 21, 1997, issue of *Physical Review Letters*.

They have also discovered that light travels differently along this axis than anywhere else. There are now two known different speeds of light! The *axis* is the key to the living Mer-Ka-Ba field, and this finding may eventually prove that the entire universe is really just a giant living Mer-Ka-Ba field. After you are aware of your own Mer-Ka-Ba field, reread this section and you will understand.

Fig. 2-38. Galactic heat envelope.

Sun, and as the Earth orbits the Sun, the angle that the light hits the surface of the Earth changes, depending on where it is in its orbit. This is why we have four seasons.

*Within* this yearly rotation there's another very slow wobble, which most people know as the precession of the equinoxes, which takes almost 26,000 years to complete. To be more accurate, it's about 25,920 years—it depends on who you read, because everybody comes up with a few years' difference. There are other wobbles, too. For example, that +23-degree angle to the Sun is not fixed; there's a wobble of about 40,000 years where it changes about three degrees—from about 23 to about 26 degrees. Then there's another wobble inside the little three-degree wobble that completes a cycle about every fourteen months. And they've discovered another one that completes about every fourteen years. Now they say they've discovered yet another one. If you read the ancient Sanskrit writings, *all* these wobbles are profoundly important for consciousness on the planet. They're tied directly to specific events and to the time these events happen on the planet—just as our DNA is tied to the various phases in the growth of the human body.

For now I just want to look at the main wobble, which is called the *precession of the equinoxes* [Fig. 2-39]. This wobble moves in an oval pattern, and the large oval in Figure 2-40 is the wobble itself. The right end, on the long axis of the oval, is called the apogee, which points toward the center of the galaxy. The bottom half of the oval shows when the planet is heading *toward* the center of the galaxy, and the top half shows when the planet has come back around and is heading *away* from the center. This movement away from the center of the galaxy is also called *going with the galactic wind*. The Sanskrit writings say that the ancient beings—who somehow knew about the precession—say that it's not at the far ends of this oval when great change takes place, but slightly *after* these extreme points are passed—at the points indicated by the two small ovals at A and C. Great

Fig. 2-39. Precession of the equinoxes (the point at which the Earth's celestial equator intersects its ecliptic) is due to the slow rotation of the Earth's axis around a perpendicular to the ecliptic.

Fig. 2-40. Traveling through the time period marked by the cycle of the precession of the equinoxes. The large oval is the path of the Earth's axis.

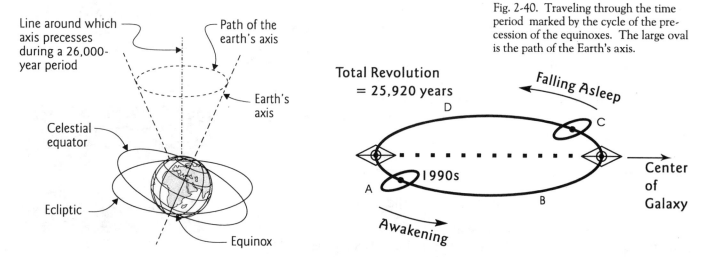

change takes place at those two points. There are two other points sitting halfway between the small ovals, shown at B and D, which are also very important places, though change is not as likely as at A and C. Right now in the 1990s we are positioned at A, the lower small oval, which indicates that this is a time of tremendous change.

According to the ancient writings, when we reach the upper small oval at C [Fig. 2-41], moving away from the center of the galaxy, we begin to fall asleep and keep losing consciousness and falling through the dimensional levels until we come to the place at the lower small oval, when we start to wake up and begin to move up through the dimensional levels. We wake up in definite stages until we get to the upper oval again, when we fall asleep again. But this is not a closed pattern, because we're moving through space. It's a helical, open-ended pattern like a spring, not a repeating cycle as within a circle. Because of that, each time around we fall asleep a little less than the time before and wake up a little more. A similar cycle occurs on Earth each day. If you look at the Earth from space, it is half dark and half light at any moment, and the people on the dark side are pretty much asleep and the people on the light side are pretty much awake. Even though we have day and night, we don't repeat the same things over and over, but hopefully we wake up and become more conscious each day. Even though we fall asleep and wake up, we keep going further each time. This precession of the equinoxes is just the same, only it's a much longer cycle.

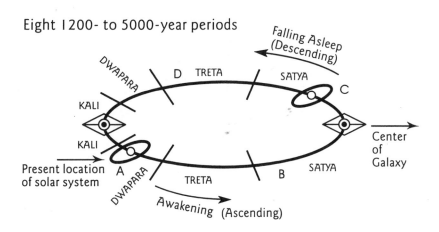

Eight 1200- to 5000-year periods

Fig. 2-41. The four Hindu yugas, ascending and descending.

### Yugas

The Tibetans and the Hindus called these particular time periods *yugas*, which are simply ages. Each yuga has both a descending and ascending phase, so if you use the Hindu system, the age around the top oval at C is called the descending satya yuga. Then comes the descending treta yuga, dwapara yuga, and kali yuga at the other end. In the kali yuga you have both descending and ascending. Then you enter the ascending dwapara and so on. We're now in the ascending dwapara yuga. We're out of the kali yuga by about 900 years, and *right now* is the time when amazing things are predicted to happen. The world is now rediscovering for itself that these are periods of enormous changes on Earth.

This diagram [Fig. 2-42] was made by Sri Yukteswar, Yogananda's guru. He did this in the late 1800s. Though he did not know the true time duration of the precession of the equinoxes, he put it at 24,000 years. That was very close, because most Hindus had no idea of what they were doing when working with the yugas. (I don't mean to put them down, but they

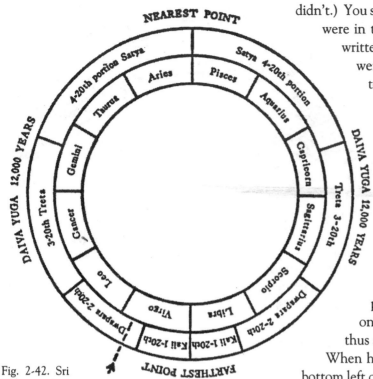

Fig. 2-42. Sri Yukteswar's yuga diagram.

didn't.) You see, when we were coming through the kali yuga, we were in the darkest most-asleep times. Most of the books written in the last 2000 years were written by people who were asleep, relatively speaking, and were trying to interpret books written by people who were much more awake. They didn't understand what the older books were saying. So, as with any book written in the last 2000 years, you've got to be a little bit careful because of the time it was written in. Many Hindu scholars were putting the precession of the equinoxes at hundreds of thousands of years, and some said one yuga is around 150,000 years. They were wrong and just did not understand.

Yukteswar knew better, but he wasn't quite right either. What he did in this diagram was to put the different yugas around the outer edge, and on the inside he put the twelve signs of the zodiac, thus showing which yugas corresponded with what sign. When he made this chart we were in Virgo, shown in the bottom left quadrant. At the moment we're between Virgo and Leo. Depending on what astrologer you talk to, we're close to the third eye of the virgin right now and passing into Leo—that's physically. That means the planet physically is between Virgo and Leo. But if you look 180 degrees across the heavens, you see the *sky* moving from Pisces into Aquarius. At this moment we're right on the line between Pisces and Aquarius, about to head into the Age of Aquarius. But physically it's a whole different point of view. You need to understand that, because when we look at the works in Egypt, some of their writings don't make sense without knowing this perspective.

## Modern Views on Pole Shifts

In the 1930s, Edgar Cayce was channeling answers for a geologist when, in the middle of a question, Cayce stopped and said something like, "You know, there's something a little more important going on with the Earth that maybe you should know about," and started talking about how the poles of the Earth are going to shift soon. He said the year it would happen would be the winter of 1998, but things have changed since then in a psychically unpredictable manner. The poles still may shift, but then again, they may do it in a way slightly different from Cayce's prediction. We do have free will, and we can change the fate of the world simply through our being.

Edgar Cayce was an extraordinary human. He was a man people listened to when he spoke. The statement by Cayce that the poles were going to shift in the near future was almost unbelievable by most of the world. But because it was Edgar Cayce predicting this outrageous event, scientists and other interested persons began to study the possibility. Geologists would not believe his statement because they thought it would probably be millions or hundreds of millions of years between pole shifts, that this kind of change took a very long time. But because of Cayce's prediction, certain scientists began to search anyway. A string of major pieces of evidence came forth that lent tremendous weight to what Cayce was saying, and they have now changed the world's view on this subject. The scientists suspected that if there were a change in the physical poles, then there would also be a change in the *magnetic* poles. One of the ways they decided to study this possibility was to examine the ancient lava beds of the world. This started taking place, I believe, in the 1950s or early '60s. They wanted to study lava beds because (1) they figured there would be tremendous volcanic action if such a shift took place, and (2) lava has a characteristic that could verify and date previous magnetic pole shifts.

### Iron Pilings and Core Samples

Iron pilings are found in most lava, and these pilings have a different melting point than the lava itself. The pilings harden while the lava is still flowing and, being iron, line up with the magnetic poles. Through this observation, geologists can see exactly where the magnetic poles were at the time the lava hardened. They needed to get samples from only three locations to be able to triangulate and know exactly where the magnetic north pole was at the time the pilings hardened. Then, of course, they could radiocarbon-date it, which was the best they could do back in those days. There were other approaches to this problem, which we will look at in a moment.

So they discovered an earlier magnetic north pole that was not where it is now but a long way away, centered in Hawaii. That last shift took place right at the upper oval—a little less than 13,000 years ago. They then did another test and found that the poles had shifted before *that* at the lower oval. This opened up a whole new area of investigation into the Earth's magnetics.

The Geological Society of America published a summary of findings gathered from ocean-floor core samples (*Geology* 11:9, September 1983). The samples were six inches in diameter and eleven feet long, and the researchers analyzed the sediment. They discovered that sometimes the poles simply reverse themselves. The north becomes the south and the south becomes the north. This was another thing Edgar Cayce talked about that people had a hard time believing. But when they analyzed these core samples, they found it was true.

Going back hundreds of millions of years, they discovered a cycle where the magnetic north pole would remain in place for a long time—then in a single day, less than 24 hours, magnetic north switched to the south. It stayed that way for a long time, then switched again. But toward the ends of these long cycles were shorter periods where the magnetic poles would reverse themselves again. This flip happened every once in a while. And as we come closer into present times, the flips are starting to happen closer together—from north to south, south to north, and at the same time moving to new locations. This has happened hundreds of times over the last several hundred million years. A whole new viewpoint of the Earth's magnetics, called *geomagnetics*, is beginning to be understood. From space, would this not appear as a pulse?

## Pole-Shift Triggers

By now there have been many people trying to figure out what could cause a pole shift. What are the dynamics? What's the trigger that makes it happen? There's a book by John White—who's also an Edgar Cayce advocate—who has compiled almost all the information in the world on this subject, though he does not mention, I believe, the particular information on the last magnetic shift being in Hawaii. His book is called *Pole Shift*, of course. It's a very scientific and interesting book. If you read it, you'll get an excellent understanding of this subject, which is vast and amazing.

There are two main theories right now about what the trigger could be that would cause the poles to move. One of them is obvious and the other more subtle. The obvious one is called the Brown theory, named after Hugh Auchincloss Brown, who conceived this idea. His theory is that for some reason the south pole begins to form off-center (which is exactly what's happening now), then it builds up quite rapidly toward the end of the cycle (which is also exactly what's happening now), until one day it breaks free from the centrifugal force of the Earth's rotation. It's just like any spinning object: When something is off-center, it throws the whole object off-center and forces it to find a new equilibrium. If the weight of the ice keeps building and building, eventually something's going to happen. The Earth can't keep spinning in the same rotational position. It will find a new pole that is centered. Yet there are some scientists who believe that the mass of ice at the South Pole is not enough to trigger a pole shift.

As a matter of fact, the ice at the South Pole in some places is over three miles deep and building, especially rapidly over the last 20 years, faster than ever expected, probably because of the greenhouse effect. And today there are three enormous volcanoes underneath the icecap that can be seen from our satellites. It's melting the underside of the icecap, and huge rivers are flowing out from beneath it at this very moment. Perhaps this fact was not entered into the equation by the doubting scientists. If that icecap, which is twice the size of the United States, were to break free, it's been calculated that it would move toward the equator at 1700 miles an hour to find balance, according to John White. That would obviously cause some problems here and there. Brown's theory appears to be happening, but it is not a certainty.

However, someone has offered another theory, one which even Albert Einstein considered seriously, that holds a possible answer to the equations that unbelieving scientists have used. His name is Charles Hapgood. He, and other scientists who worked with him, discovered at least two layers of unusual rock underneath the Earth's crust which liquefy under certain conditions. Other scientists have demonstrated this in laboratories where they've put the same kind of rock into a miniature Earth and duplicated the conditions of the inner earth. From this experiment, they found that the surface or crust of the Earth can slip over the main mass of the Earth, which continues its rotation as if nothing had happened. It's a fact. It *can* happen, but of course we do not know if it will actually happen in real time. They don't know the specifics of how this would work—such as what trigger could cause this slippage. Charles Hapgood wrote two books, *Earth's Shifting Crust* and *The Path of the Pole*, that will probably eventually change our view of our world dramatically.

Albert Einstein wrote the foreword to Charles Hapgood's first book, *Earth's Shifting Crust*. I feel it is important enough to reprint here directly:

> I frequently receive communications from people who wish to consult me concerning their unpublished ideas. It goes without saying that these ideas are very seldom possessed of scientific validity. The very first communication, however, that I received from Mr. Hapgood electrified me. His idea is original, of great simplicity, and—if it continues to prove itself—of great importance to everything that is related to the history of the earth's surface.
>
> The author has not confined himself to a simple presentation of this idea. He has also set forth, cautiously and comprehensively, the extraordinarily rich material that supports his displacement theory. I think that this rather astonishing, even fascinating, idea deserves the serious attention of anyone who concerns himself with the theory of the earth's development.

It is a given that Albert Einstein was one of the most brilliant humans who has ever lived, yet few geologists even yet believe such an outrageous theory. Only in more recent times has proof begun to accumulate that such things could be true. The same scientific world didn't believe Mr. Einstein either when he said how much energy was contained within a very small amount of matter.

It is my belief that the trigger to the pole shift is connected with the geomagnetism of the Earth. This would take a long time to explain, which I am not prepared to do here at this time. What is known is that for the last 500 years the Earth's magnetic field has been continually weakening, and in the last few years it has been doing absolutely bizarre things. According to Gregg Braden in *Awakening to Zero Point: The Collective Initiation*, the Earth's magnetic field actually began to weaken about 2000 years ago. Then around 500 years ago, the weakening really began to accelerate. (Could it be 520 years? This would match the Mayan Calendar, which predicted a huge change at that time.) In recent times the magnetic field is making unheard-of changes.

Fig. 2-43. Magnetic flow around Earth.

## Magnetic Flow Changes

The idealized lines of magnetic flow [Fig. 2-43] you see coming out in a torus around the Earth are *not* what geologists have found. The reality is that the magnetic lines look rather like straight weaving patterns [Fig. 2-44]. They're fixed, but they're not precise in that idealized kind of way. And there are certain areas where they're stronger and other areas where they're weaker. These lines normally do not move, but because the field is getting so weak, they are beginning to move and change. The birds, animals and fish, and the dolphins and whales and other creatures use these magnetic lines for their migration patterns. So if the magnetic lines change, their migration patterns go off, which is what we're seeing all over the world right now. Birds are flying to places they're not supposed to be, and whales are beaching themselves on land, where it's supposed to be water as far as they're concerned. They're simply following the magnetic line they've followed for centuries, and they're running into land that wasn't on that line before.

When these magnetic fields pass through zero point and completely change—which they may do very soon—we'll have another subject to talk about, about what happens then. You see, we believe your very memory is tied to those fields. You can't remember anything without these magnetic fields. In addition, your emotional body is tied powerfully to the magnetic fields, and if they change, your emotional body is radically affected. It's easy to understand that the Moon affects the tides of the world through the pull of gravity. We also know that the magnetic fields of the Earth are slightly affected by the phases of the Moon. When the Moon is full and passes overhead, we get a slight bulge and change in the magnetic field of the Earth. Just look at what happens in big cities during a full moon. The day before, the day of, and the day after the full moon, we have more rapes and murders and killings and weirdness of this nature than we do for the rest of the entire month. The police blotter of any major city will verify that. Why? Because these fields especially affect people who are right on the edge of emotional instability, who are barely able to cope during normal times. They're right on the edge, then the Moon comes along and moves the magnetic field just a little bit, and the person experiences an emotional dip and does things he or she normally wouldn't do.

So imagine what would happen if the geomagnetic field of the Earth starts destabilizing. I heard in October 1993 from someone who's involved in aviation that in the last two weeks of September, major landing strips had to recalibrate their guidance systems because the magnetic fields made a unilateral shift all over the planet. It seemed to be temporary, lasting about two weeks. At that time you might have remembered an incredible emotional outburst within yourself and people around you. In my world I'm on the phone with people from all over the world. People were freaking out everywhere. That's why I suspected that maybe what I heard might really be true. If it *is* true, then we are beginning to proceed almost certainly into the next phase of this work. These breakdowns in the magnetic field of the Earth will begin to come closer and closer together until there is a total collapse of the field and a shifting of the poles. This is one of the signs of the very end times.

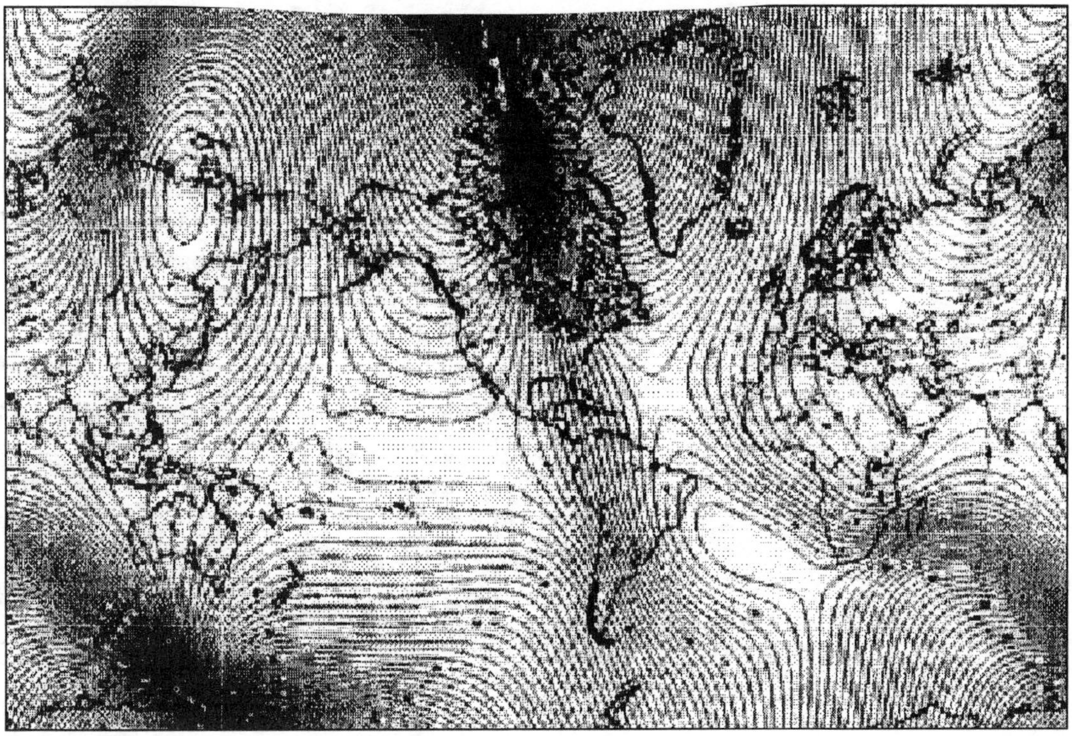

There's no reason to get into fear about any of this. Even though what's happening is unusual, we've all been through these kinds of things many, many

Fig. 2-44. Sample of complex model of Earth's main magnetic field, generated by the USGS for the year 1995.

times before. This is not unusual for you, though most of you have very little memory of it. When you actually start going through the dimensional shift and get into the feel of it, you'll say, "Oh, yeah, I remember this now. Here we are, going through this birthing again." So it's not a big deal, yet it is.

You came from somewhere else when you were born as a baby, right? You came from some other dimension and you passed through a void and came out through the womb to Earth. You traveled this path before, and we're about to do a similar kind of thing, only it's a really unusual one this time. There's no reason to fear it when you know all of it and remember who you are. In fact, what's occurring is extremely positive. It's very, very beautiful.

## Harmonic and Disharmonic Levels of Consciousness

The Sanskrit literature talks about how when we approach the lower oval at A [in Fig. 2-40] in the precession, we become aware of electrical energies. We can fly in the sky. We can do many unusual things. The world becomes extremely unstable, and in a *single day* we get rid of the old way of viewing the world and make a huge transformation in consciousness. But as we approach this transformation, given the particular level of consciousness we have, we tend to destroy everything we touch. It's a natural part of who we are. We're not doing anything wrong; it's just the way we are. We're doing it exactly right. We destroy everything, we cause everything to go into disharmony. I'll be talking about this later, but I think it would be appropriate to tell you this much now:

On Earth, according to Thoth, there are five totally different steps or levels of life that each human is going to pass through. When we reach the fifth level, we will make a transformation that transcends known life itself. That's the normal pattern. Each one of these levels of consciousness has many aspects that are different from the other levels. First, they have different chromosome levels. The first level of human consciousness has 42 + 2 chromosomes; the second level has 44 + 2 chromosomes; the third one has 46 + 2; the fourth, 48 + 2; and finally 50 + 2. Each level of human consciousness has a different body height associated with it. (This might sound kind of funny if you've never heard it before.)

The first level of 42 + 2 has a range of height somewhere between four and maybe six feet. The people who fall into that category specifically are the Aborigines in Australia, and I believe that certain tribes in Africa and South America also do.

The second level of consciousness has 44 + 2 chromosomes, and that's us. Our band of height is about five to seven feet. We're a little taller than the first group. The third level's height goes up considerably. The 46 + 2 chromosome level interrupts the Reality through what you could term unity or Christ consciousness. That range of height is from about ten to sixteen feet tall.

Then there's another range for the fourth level of consciousness—the 48 + 2s—who have a height of about 30 to 35 feet.

The final band, the perfected human, is between 50 and 60 feet tall. They have 52 chromosomes. I suspect that the reason there are 52 cards in a deck is related to those 52 chromosomes of the potential of man. For those of you who are Hebrew, you might remember that Metatron, the perfect man—that which we will become—was blue and 55 feet tall. (We'll talk about this again when we get into the subject of Egypt.)

There are states between the consciousness levels, like Down syndrome, for example. Down syndrome happens when a person transitions from this second level of consciousness, which we are on, into the third level, but didn't quite make it. The person didn't get all the instructions right, and where he almost always fails is in the left-brain instructional aspect of the chromosomes. A Down syndrome person has 45 + 2 chromosomes—he got one of them, but not the other. He or she got the emotional one—the heart one—all right. If you know any Down syndrome children, they are pure love, but they don't understand how to make the transition into the third level of human consciousness. They are still learning.

The second and fourth levels of consciousness are *dis*harmonic, and the first, third and fifth levels are harmonic. You'll understand this when we see it in the geometries. When you look at human consciousness from a geometrical point of view, you can see the harmonic levels, and you can see that the disharmonic levels are simply out of balance. That's where we are right now—out of balance. These disharmonic levels are absolutely necessary. You can't get from level one to level three without passing through level two. But two is a totally disharmonic consciousness. Does not chaos bring change?

Whenever a consciousness gets into the second or fourth level, it knows it can be there for only a short time. These levels are used as stepping stones—like a stone in the middle of a river, one you jump on and get off of as soon as you can to get to the other side. You don't hang out there, because if you do, you fall in. If we were to hang out here on Earth even just a little bit longer, we would destroy our planet. We would destroy it by just *being* who we are. Yet we are a sacred and necessary step in evolution. We are a bridge to another world. And we are living this bridge by just being alive in this incredible time.

THREE

# The Darker Side of Our Present and Past

We are about to enter negative subjects for a bit. You could say, "There he goes getting into that fear stuff just after he said not to get into fear," but I want us to observe all the facets, both positive and negative, of life here on planet Earth. I don't want to look at only the positive ones; I want you to see the whole picture. And when you look at the whole picture, both the good and the bad, you'll see that the chaos is just part of the truth and part of the birth. A phenomenal change in human consciousness is occurring at this moment, though if you take any tiny segment of what's happening or look out in the world and see all the wars, famines and human emotional garbage that's filling our newspapers, the future does not look good. But when you get the whole image of life, you'll see that beyond all the negative, there's something much greater and vast and sacred and holy occurring at this moment in history. It becomes clear: Life *is* whole, complete and perfect now!

## Our Endangered Earth

However, the most conservative scientists in the world that I can find don't give our planet more than 50 years—50! The most conservative scientists on the planet say there will be no life or almost none on this planet within 50 years if we continue the way we're going. Many scientists give us only three or more years; some of them give us ten. Most don't give us more than fifteen years. It depends on who you read. Even if it were a hundred or a thousand years, would that be acceptable?

You would not be hearing any of this information today if it were not for some changes in our government that have taken place in the last eight years that have *allowed* this information to be presented. Although they're not allowing you to know everything, there has been a change in the powers that be where they're beginning to cooperate with life. They simply can't

In 1992 the world nations met at an "Earth Summit" in Rio de Janeiro to discuss Earth's environmental problems. The largest gathering of heads of state in the history of the world was called because of the danger of losing our planet. Most of the world came, but the United States, the largest polluter in the world, didn't even want to participate. It was obvious that the political administration felt that money, jobs and the economy were more important than whether the Earth survived.

Five months later, on November 18, 1992, a document titled "World Scientists' Warning to Humanity" was released. More than 1600 senior scientists from 71 countries,

Fig. 3-1. Allowing the truth to be known.

including over half of all living Nobel Prize winners, signed this document. It was the most alarming warning the world has ever received from such a powerful body of researchers. You would think that this document would hold great credibility and that the world would carefully listen. It began:

"Human beings and the natural world are on a collision course. Human activities inflict harsh and often irreversible damage on the environment and on critical resources. If not checked, many of our current practices put at serious risk the future that we wish for human society and the plant and animal kingdoms, and may so alter the living world that it will be unable to sustain life in the manner that we know.

let you know the full extent of the situation, because they believe that most of the world would just quit their jobs and say, the heck with everything, leading to complete chaos. Instead of quitting, is not this the time to focus? Human consciousness is powerful. We will know what to do. We are more than the ordinary world knows. Do you remember?

Okay, now let's talk about the dark side. This is a January 2, 1989, issue of *Time* magazine [Fig. 3-1]. In 1988 the secret government of the world decided to allow us to know some of what was going on around environmental problems. This was the first major publication on the subject in the world. *Time* magazine declared the Earth to be the "planet of the year." Instead of featuring a man or woman of the year, they broke away from their tradition. The entire magazine was devoted to our endangered Earth and its problems. If you were to read the problems as they were presented in 1989 and then read the problems as they're being presented in articles today, you'll realize that what they gave us in 1989 was a ultra-watered-down version of the truth. It wasn't even close. But at least it was a beginning for our world to see the truth about what we have done to Mother Earth.

We're going to discuss only four or five different problems the Earth has, though there are multiple different scenarios going on. If *any one* of these scenarios were to break down, all life on the planet would eventually die. And at the moment they're *all* about to break down—it's just a matter of which one breaks down first. And whenever one system goes, then all the rest of them will go eventually, and that's it, there won't be any more human life. It will be over with, and we'll end up just like Mars or the dinosaurs.

A few years ago, around the turn of this century, there were 30 million species of life forms on Earth—30 million *different* species of life. In 1993 there were about 15 million. It took billions of years to create these life forms, and in less than a blink of an eye, a mere hundred years, half of the life on this dear Earth is dead. Around thirty species a minute are now becoming extinct somewhere. If you were to watch this planet from space, it would appear to be dying very, very rapidly. Yet we're going on as though nothing's happening and everything's great. We're sticking money in the bank and driving our cars and just wiggling right on. Yet from an honest point of view, we have a real life-and-death problem going on here on Earth, and few people seem to be really serious about it.

When they tried to get the entire world to come together in Rio in the early '90s to discuss the worldwide environmental problem, our president didn't even want to go. Why not? Because the problems are so serious that if we were to fix them, another problem would happen that would be an even more serious problem, from the president's point of view: We would be plunged into a worldwide financial breakdown, after which a large portion of the Earth's population would die from starvation and other problems. In essence, we cannot afford to repair the environment. On the other side of the coin, can we afford not to?

## Dying Oceans

It was in the August 1, 1988, issue [Fig. 3-2] that *Time* magazine focused its attention on the oceans and what was happening there. Jacques Cousteau wrote a book about this around 1978. He was a very respected person, but when he wrote this book, he lost credibility in scientific circles because he made a statement that nobody could believe. He founded his statements on pure science, but people simply could not or would not accept the truth. Specifically, he said that the Mediterranean Sea would be a dead body of water by the end of 1990 and that the Atlantic Ocean would also be dead by the turn of the century. People thought, "This guy's nuts. It's never going to happen."

Well, it is happening. The Mediterranean Sea is now somewhere around 95 percent dead. It's not 100 percent, so he was not exactly right. Nevertheless, it's still going to be a dead sea if people continue to live the way they do. And the Atlantic Ocean is rapidly doing the same. Maybe it won't happen in the year 2000, but it will happen very soon after that. Unless something changes dramatically, it will die—no fish, no dolphins, no life in the Atlantic.

We can't live without the oceans. The bottom of the food chain, the plankton, will be gone, and if they go, we go. When we don't take this seriously, it's like saying, "Well, I don't really need my heart." This is a major component in the ecosystem on Earth, and it's going fast. This is not debatable, this is scientific fact. The only part that is debatable is when. It is *really happening*. Nobody believed it would happen because they just couldn't accept this truth.

New York City, for instance, has pipes that go twenty miles out and dump all their human feces into the oceans. They figured, Well, the oceans will take care of it. But for the last 60 years or so it's been building up into a huge mountain. Now, there's a mountain range of shit out in the ocean that is moving toward New York City. It's now up against and actually coming into the harbor, and they don't know what to do about it. It would take more money than New York has to fix it. This is the kind of foresight that we as humans have demonstrated.

The human manure approaching New York is an Atlantic Ocean problem. However, the problem is not limited to the Atlantic or the Mediterranean. The Pacific Ocean is Earth's largest body of water, and it will probably take longer, but it is also having tremendous problems, especially in certain areas.

The red tide [Fig. 3-3] is the first deadly sign of the pollution. It's an algae that destroys everything that lives underneath it—it kills everything. And these red tides are beginning to sweep all over, especially around Japan where there's so much pollution. We've made lots of mistakes all over the Earth because we don't have the consciousness to know how to live in harmony with our own body, Mother Earth. This is like a symptom of cancer or some other dreaded disease.

Fig. 3-2. Divulging the status of our seas.

Fundamental changes are urgent if we are to avoid the collision our present course will bring about."

The warning document then began to list the crises: polluted water, oceans, soil, atmosphere, diminishing plant and animal species and human overpopulation. (More than half of the life on this planet is now extinct and continuing to die.) The words became stern:

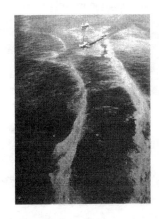

Fig. 3-3. Red tide.

## Ozone

Here's another problem. Figure 3-4 shows the ozone hole above the South Pole. Ozone forms a thin layer about six feet thick. It's a really thin, fragile layer, a living layer that's constantly being rebuilt. We know very little about it, though we know more than we would if it weren't for the UVC light (ultraviolet light, band C) that's coming through the holes right now. When they began to detect huge amounts of UVC, especially as shown here coming into the South Pole, they couldn't understand how there got to be so much, because their computers didn't show it. Then they found out that their software programming was set up in such a way as to override this sort of thing. After they reprogrammed their software, they found out the hole was really there. This was some years ago.

What they actually were looking for was chlorine monoxide, the molecule shown in the far right of Figure 3-5. They figured that the ozone hole is caused by various chemicals, one of which are CFCs. CFCs react with the ozone in such a way that when the chlorine connects with the ozone, the ozone molecule breaks apart, thus forming oxygen and chlorine monoxide.

Scientists figured, given the speed they thought the CFCs were moving toward the ozone, that the chlorine monoxide up there would be about 30 times over normal, and they were very worried about it. So the world governments tried to get the companies that were producing the CFCs—Freon and various other chemicals that cause this problem—to stop producing those products and find other answers. In reply, the companies all said in unison, "We're not doing it. That's a natural phenomenon. We have nothing to do with it."

So the world governments had to prove in court that the companies were at fault, which they did. To get the proof they needed, for the first time in the history of the Earth every single country on the planet cooperated in a single venture. This had never happened before. They flew high-altitude planes over the South Pole for about two years collecting data, and

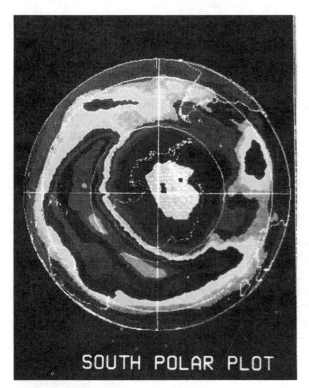

Fig. 3-4. Ozone hole above the South Pole.

"No more than one or a few decades remain before the chance to avert the threats we now confront will be lost and the prospects for humanity immeasurably diminished. We the undersigned, senior mem-

Fig. 3-5. Ozone reaction in molecules.

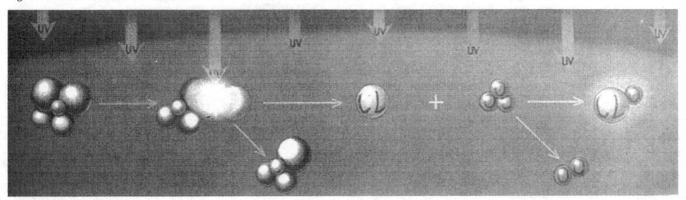

they finally came up with something that *really* scared them. The destructive ingredient, chlorine monoxide, *wasn't* 30 times over normal—it was 500 times over normal and moving much faster than they had believed.

This article came out in 1992, I believe [Fig. 3-6]. It first says that the EPA predicts 200,000 more skin cancer deaths from the ozone hole. But up in the right column they have a tiny section reporting that the EPA says that the *fatality* estimates they had originally given were incorrect, and are *21 times* worse than they had estimated. Twenty-one times—now, that's a lot. It's not like saying, "Well, it's a little bit more."

This is what the government has been doing; they give out little bits of information in little articles that don't tell you much. They don't make it a big deal. By law they *have* to announce it, so they announce it in little articles and then let it go. Then they up the ante in another insignificant article—as in this article here, for example, where they said the danger was 21 times higher than their first estimate; then two weeks later the same paper comes back and says, "Oh, by the way, we were off two weeks ago, it's actually double that." Well, double doesn't sound like much—except that means it went from 21 times to 42 times worse than their first report, which is an incredible amount. If the truth had been told in the first place, it would have sounded terrible and created fear.

This is what's been going on all over the world for a long time. The only way the world governments know how to deal with the situation is by letting it out little by little, admitting to more and more and more. They know

bers of the world's scientific community, hereby warn all humanity of what lies agead. A great change in our stewardship of the Earth and life on it is required if vast human misery is to be avoided and our global home on this planet is not to be irretrievably mutilated."

Yet most of the world rejected this statement even though it was created by one of the most respected scientific bodies ever assembled on Earth. You would think we would pause and say, "If this is true, what can we do? Let's drop everything and do whatever is necessary." But the governments

## ENVIRONMENT

# A Bigger Hole in the Ozone

## EPA predicts 200,000 more skin-cancer deaths

The nations of the world have never agreed on how to halt the destruction of rain forests or save endangered species. But when it came to saving the ozone layer, which screens out the sun's harmful ultraviolet rays, they knew just what to do. Or so it seemed. In 1987, 24 nations meeting in Montreal pledged that, by the year 2000, they would halve their production of chlorofluorocarbons (CFCs), chemicals that destroy ozone. That was when the only ozone hole that had been noticed was over Antarctica. But soon after, satellite data showed that ozone above the United States had dropped 1.5 percent. That persuaded more than 90 countries last June to agree to ban CFCs entirely by 2000. Developing nations were given until 2010 to stop producing ozone-damaging chemicals; wealthier countries promised them up to $240 million to help make the switch.

Now it seems that the problem is far graver than anyone thought. Last week Environmental Protection Agency chief William Reilly announced that ozone loss over the United States since 1978 has amounted to a "stunning" 4 to 5 percent. The preliminary satellite data, which scientists have

### Danger: Sunlight

■ Every 1 percent drop in ozone allows 2 percent more ultraviolet light to reach Earth's surface.

■ Every 1 percent reduction in ozone raises the incidence of skin cancer by 5 to 7 percent.

■ The 5 percent loss of ozone over the U.S. is expected to cause 4,000 more skin-cancer deaths a year.

■ The ozone loss is greater at higher latitudes. Over Leningrad, it is as much as 8 percent.

been analyzing since last autumn, show that Europe, the Soviet Union and northern Asia experienced similar losses, while areas at the latitude of Sweden and Hudson Bay saw losses of 8 percent. "Past studies had shown about half that amount," said Reilly. "As a result, there could be 200,000 deaths from skin cancer in the United States over the next 50 years" in addition to the 400,000 otherwise expected over that period. The fatality estimate was 21 times what the EPA had forecast earlier. Ultraviolet radiation can also cause cataracts, weaken the immune system, damage crops and disrupt the reproduction of plankton that anchor the marine food chain.

And the ozone loss is almost certain to get worse. CFCs stay in the atmosphere for decades. The EPA's Eileen Claussen told Newsweek that the agency's models show ozone loss of 10 to 12 percent over the next 20 years—"and we've already thrown out those estimates because they are far too conservative."

Reilly vowed that the EPA would intensify its efforts to find substitutes for ozone-eating substances. Researchers have made progress in finding benign chemicals that do the job of chlorine-based solvents, but they have been less successful in replacing the CFCs used in refrigerators and air conditioners. If substitute chemicals can be found, developing nations might be persuaded to phase out CFCs by 2000 rather than 2010. Right now, countries such as China and India believe that abandoning CFCs too quickly would cripple their economies. Eliminating CFCs before 2000, though, would not make much difference, because so many of the chemicals are already on their way to the stratosphere. In effect, regulators are running out of ideas. "Because such aggressive steps have already been taken," Claussen says, "it's hard to come up with anything more that can make a difference."

Fig. 3-6. Upping the ante.

know that if we are to avert this crisis, we must change the way we live, and that would not be politically comfortable. No politician wants to be the one to introduce this unpopular change. To the governments, the economy would suffer and perhaps even collapse if we were to stop polluting. So it has become a war of money against life—terrible but true.

The *New York Times* and the *Washington Post*, two of our most respected leaders in reporting the news, rejected this document as not newsworthy. This gives you a good idea of the importance we place on the planet itself. (You can read about all this and much more in *The Sacred Balance, Rediscovering Our Place in Nature* by David Suzuki.

Think for a moment: This warning document gives us "one or a few more decades" to avert this crisis—and it was written seven years ago. This Earth is billions of years old. It has taken millions of years for mankind to reach this level of awareness, yet in a mere 10 to 30 years, a geological blink of an eye, if we do not act in a positive manner, we may become "irretrievably mutilated." The word "extinct" was avoided, but we all know it is a possibility.

they have to tell you the truth (for reasons you'll learn later), but they're afraid to say we're in real trouble. They just say, "Well, it's not so bad, but it's getting worse," and statements like this.

Well, not only is there an ozone hole at the *South* Pole, but there's one at the North Pole now, and the rest of the ozone is swiss cheese. In 1991 or 1992 there was a major television production on the ozone hole. It brought together all the major people who were involved in studying this, and they discussed all the pros and cons. They interviewed a particular husband-and-wife team—I don't have their names, but they also wrote a book on this very subject several years ago, predicting that the ozone hole was going to happen. Before we even knew about it, they had studied it all, according to this program. And the ozone is now undergoing changes exactly like they said it would and at exactly the rate they predicted.

This couple was brought on TV as the experts, and the interviewer asked, "Well, what do you think?" This interviewer was kind of puppylike, asking, "What are we going to do? You guys know everything about it, so what are we going to do about the ozone?" The husband said, "There's nothing we can do." I don't believe they like to hear statements like that on major channels. The interviewer asked, "What do you mean, there's nothing we can do?" The authors said, "Well, suppose we get the entire world to cooperate?"—which is the first thing that would have to happen, and we can't even do that *now*, some fifteen years later! "Suppose we do get the entire planet to say, 'Okay, we'll stop it all today. No more of these chemicals that are destroying the ozone will ever be used again.'"

The author said, "Okay, suppose we did it. Suppose we got the whole world to stop. That still doesn't solve the problem." And the interviewer said, "What do you mean? Wouldn't it just heal itself?" The author answered, "No, because the spray can that you sprayed yesterday sits on the surface of the ground and the CFCs take 15 to 20 years to rise to the ozone layer. This layer that's slowly rising and eating the ozone will continue for 15 to 20 years even if we stop everything today. And it will continue to eat it faster and faster, because we've used more and more of these chemicals in recent years." He said, "There won't even be an ozone layer"—I think he said in ten years. "I see no solution at all."

If we lose our ozone, we're in big trouble. All the animals of the world will go blind. You won't be able to go out during daytime without a space-suit on, meaning every square inch of your body will have to be covered—special UVC goggles and everything. In a short time the UVC light would eventually kill you. And we're rapidly approaching that. If you don't think so, read what the *Wall Street Journal* reported in January 1993.

The *Journal* was reporting what's happening in southern Chile, which is close to the ozone hole at the South Pole. The animals are starting to go blind. The people who live there have thick, dark skin, and they've spent all their lives outside, but now they're getting burned in the course of everyday living. And it's spreading north from Chile and starting to happen everywhere. Because of the swiss cheese aspect of the entire ozone layer, places all over the Earth are becoming unsafe. You never know where these spots are going to be because they move over the face of the Earth from year to year. This ozone problem is happening now, not tomorrow or later or maybe someday. It's occurring at this very minute. Given another few years, we're going to be in really serious trouble.

They knew about the ozone problem at least as far back as when Reagan was president. When the environmental agencies asked him, "What will we do about this ozone problem?", Reagan was really flippant about it. He said something like, "Aw, we'll just issue raincoats and dark sunglasses to solve the problem." Just like that, what the heck? We're talking about our very lives here, our very existence, and the governments are continuing as though it doesn't even matter.

### The Greenhouse Ice Age

In the first seven days in office, President Bush was approached by 700 environmental groups—700 of them in unity and agreement. They said to Bush, "We have an even bigger problem than the ozone and the oceans; the biggest problem that we know of is the greenhouse effect. If the greenhouse effect is not checked very soon, it's going to destroy the planet." This is what they had agreed on and what they believed was the truth. For a while Gorbachev and the world's governments were talking about how they were going to put space stations up there to monitor the environment and move with responsible action. Gorbachev was gung ho on the whole thing. Then I guess they gave up on it, just quit, though they're still watching these things very carefully. It's a pretty hopeless situation.

Figure 3-7 is a satellite photograph of the oceans taken from above Australia. That dark blotch above Australia and New Guinea reached the hottest ocean temperature in recorded history in 1992. It was 86 degrees Fahrenheit in that spot. That's 86-degree ocean water. If that continues to spread across the equator, it's going to do exactly what John Hamaker has predicted. If you're familiar with Hamaker and his theories, he has powerful evidence that as this water heats up, something very different from a hot planet will happen: it's going to be a

Update: Since June 1996 a new possibility has been given to us. Perhaps we have found a way to heal the Earth of her environmental problems. This is the work of the new workshop we call the Earth-Sky. As much as I would love to tell you where the work of the Flower of Life has taken us, this is not the time. A new book will have to be written because this new information is too vast to discuss in a simple update. All I can say is that I am very optimistic for the 3D survival of Mother Earth at this time.

Fig. 3-7. Hottest ocean in history.

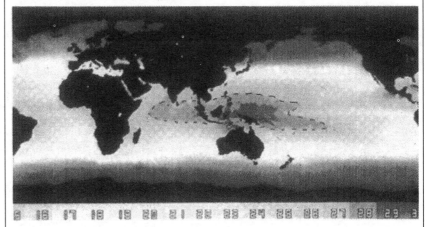

**The Heat Is On**

A hot spot in the sea could mean global warming is finally here

THE RED BLOTCH ABOVE AUSTRALIA AND NEW GUINEA in this satellite image, released last week, represents the ocean's hottest water, at 30°C (86°F). That's unusually steamy, and it may be partly a result of the global warming that scientists think is on its way. The good news: NASA reports that the ozone hole feared over northern latitudes this spring never showed up, but only because the winter was warmer than usual. A cooler season next year, which is quite possible, and goodbye ozone.

*cold* one—very, very cold. Dr. Hamaker predicts an ice age descending upon us within a few short years.

I won't go fully into the dynamics of the so-called greenhouse effect, but an intimate part of it is tied to rocks, minerals and trees. One average acre of trees holds within it 50,000 tons of carbon dioxide. When trees are cut down, burned or just die, all that carbon dioxide gets released into the atmosphere, and when the atmosphere contains a certain level of carbon dioxide, it activates the beginning of an ice age. Hamaker found proof that this is what triggered the last few ice ages on this planet. He found his evidence primarily from studying core samples taken from ancient lake beds. The core samples show, by simply looking at the pollen count, that the Earth for millions of years had a cycle of 90,000 years of ice followed by a temperate period of 10,000 years, followed by 90,000 years of ice, followed by 10,000 temperate years. That particular cycle has been going on for a long, long time.

In addition, Hamaker has discovered—and other people have verified it —that the length of time it takes to go from a warm age into an ice age is a mere 20 years! People who have been studying this for a long time believe that we're possibly now around 16 or 17 years into that 20-year cycle, but of course no one really knows. And they say that when the end of the 20 years or so is reached, [snaps fingers] in a *single day*, less than 24 hours, it'll all be over. The clouds will back up over the Earth, the average temperature will drop to about 50 below zero, and most areas of the world won't see the Sun again for 90,000 years. If those guys are right, we've got only a few more years of sunshine. It'll keep getting warmer and warmer and hotter and hotter until that day hits, then snap! it'll be all over. I'm not going to give all the details of Hamaker's work, but I suggest you do the research yourself if you want to know about it. He has powerful evidence. Study what he has to say. His book is called *The Survival of Civilization*.

## Ice Age to Warmth, a Quick Switch

Scientists have just discovered another surprise, which has some of them shocked and barely able to believe it. They thought that when an ice age recedes, it would take thousands of years to warm back up again. But they now have evidence that it takes only *three days*, says an article written in *Time* magazine. It takes 20 years to go from warm to cold and three days to go from cold to warm. So the greenhouse effect is a major and serious problem. No one knows the answer, but what's scary is that they're trying to instigate supposed answers that are totally untested. They're all fighting about whose answer is the best and who wants to do what—but nobody *knows*. It's like the ozone—they've got maybe 15 different ideas about what to do to fix the ozone, and any one of them might make it better—or worse. No one knows what these things are going to do, because we have never done them before. We seem to be willing to experiment on ourselves to find out if we're going to make it or not.

## Underground Atomic Bombs and CFCs

On top of that, all kinds of other problems are occurring. Some things are so scary that governments are afraid to tell you anything at all. They won't tell you about one thing that I simply have to talk about, because it's so important that somebody *has* to say something! I know they don't want me to talk about this, but I don't think they'll stop me.

We're finding CFCs in the upper atmosphere. Now, "authorities" in the government have been saying that CFC products like Freon will float up there because they're lighter than air. But guess what—and you scientist types can check this out: CFCs are not lighter than air, they're *four times heavier than air*. They *sink*, they don't rise! So how did they get up there? It might have been the 212 *aboveground* atomic bombs that our governments have blown off in the world. Many people suspect that's how all those CFCs got up there in the first place, and that it really wasn't *us* who caused most of the problem with our air conditioners. It was the atomic *governments of the world*.

At one point they all went underground with their bombs, and we thought, That's okay, they're bombing underground; nothing will happen now. It's not okay, folks. It's probably the most dangerous thing that's going on in the world today, even more than HAARP, and they're still doing it. I cannot prove what I am about to say, so do not believe it until you can prove it.

Adam Trombly, a famous scientist who has accomplished important work in science, has been monitoring the underground atomic bombing around the world. He probably knows more about this than any other person in the world—even the governments recognize this. Trombly explains what happens when these atomic bombs are exploded underground. The energy doesn't just sit there; it has to go somewhere, so it goes shooting through the Earth, bouncing off its insides, ripping apart the plates and doing incredible damage as it goes bouncing around like a ping-pong ball. This bouncing effect inside the Earth continues for about 30 days after the explosion.

Trombly, much like Jacques Cousteau and others, now has a theory that predicts all kinds of things that will happen—and *they're all happening now!* Things like the Indian Ocean dropping 23 feet over a very short period of time was predicted by Trombly at least ten years ago—just as Jacques Cousteau had predicted the death of the Mediterranean Sea in ten years. Many brilliant people are speaking out their truth, but few people are listening. If Trombly is correct, we're only a few more atomic bombs away from the whole planet literally splitting apart in little pieces. The governments around the world have been on red alert since about 1991 over the changes happening to the Earth that were predicted by Trombly. They're scared to death. Yet I believe China just blew up another one—and the U.S. is talking about blowing one up just because China did!

**Update:** Remember that Professor Einstein did not know *for sure* that when the first atomic bomb was ignited, the nuclear chain reaction would stop when the original fuel sample was expended. Our government knew that when this first bomb exploded, it might be the end of the world—all life over in a matter of minutes. But we did it anyway! This is spiritual incompetence!

We are faced with another moment in history where our government has decided to take another chance with our lives. When HAARP was turned on in the spring of 1997, they did not know for sure if the atmosphere was going to be destroyed. They still do not know for sure what the long-range effects will be, just as they did not know during World War II with the Manhattan Project.

What is HAARP? You need to know. HAARP stands for High-Frequency Active Auroral Research Project. It is a weapon massively more powerful than the atomic bomb. They intend to beam more than 1.7 gigawatts (billion watts) of radiated power into the ionosphere and actually boil the upper atmosphere in order to create a mirror and/or an artificial antenna to transmit huge amounts of power to any specific area on the Earth. This energy would be used to manipulate global weather, hurt or destroy ecosystems, knock out electronic communication, *and* change our moods and mental states. Not to mention that it could be used to try to destroy or manipulate the new Christ grid around the world. Read *Angels Don't Play This HAARP* by Jeane Manning and Dr. Nick Begich. You will learn more.

✧

Update: In 1995 and 1996, the secret government exploded six atomic bombs in an area near Mooréa Island, part of the French Tahitian Islands. France, along with several other countries, placed these bombs into a sacred physical place of Mother Earth's body. If they had done this to your mom, you would have called it violent rape. They were neutron bombs, which do not destroy structures, but "merely" destroy all life in the region.

If the Earth were a woman, the area where they deliberately placed the bomb would be her perineum. Going straight through the Earth from there would be Earth's crown chakra, which just happens to be the Great Pyramid region in Egypt. This became the focus of attention, for the secret government shut down the entire

Anyway, life goes on. It's a good thing there are other levels to our spirit than just the physical. If it weren't for the ascended masters and our higher aspect, we would be in a hopeless situation. But because of the work of other great souls, you and humanity are just beginning to live. You will soon be birthed into another new, clean and beautiful world, thank God, and there's no one else to thank but God. We're going to be okay through all of this. And yet I will continue . . .

### The Strecker Memorandum on AIDS

Here's one last drama. Actually, there are many other perilous situations (I could go on for hours), but I'll just give you this last one about AIDS. I suggest you try to find the Strecker Memorandum material if you haven't read it or watched the video. The governments are really trying to suppress it. Dr. Strecker made a video memorandum of what he believed happened around AIDS. He is a brilliant person. He has worked with retroviruses and is an expert on this subject. He showed the video on television, and the governments threatened him. They allegedly killed his brother and the senator who was sponsoring it. But they didn't get Strecker—that would have been too obvious, I guess. Dr. Strecker has distributed many of his videos. He got them out to the world, though you don't hear about it anymore.

Dr. Strecker shows on his film how the United Nations was trying to solve an environmental problem. They knew that the biggest environmental problem in the entire world was the human population, and at the rate it was going, the world would double its population by 2010 or 2012. But because of what the Chinese did, allowing only one child per couple, and other strenuous work around the world, they slowed it down. But they believe that it's still going to happen. It is now estimated that somewhere around 2014 the world population will have doubled. If that happens, computer models have shown that all life on Earth will die or wish they were dead, according to the United Nations, because we can barely keep it together with almost six billion people. Can you imagine what it would be like with 11 to 12 billion people in the world? There's just no way, at least under the present system.

So, if *you* were in the United Nations and knew this potential disaster was going to take place and had to make a decision, what would you do? I'm not judging the people who did this—just put yourself in their position of great power. You see that the Earth is coming to a solid wall, that it's going to be totally destroyed if something is not changed. So they made a decision—and Dr. Strecker showed the memorandum right on television. The United Nations decided that, rather than hit that wall of 11 billion people, right then and there they were going to create a virus or a disease that would kill specifically three-quarters of the people on Earth. In other words, instead of *increasing* to 11 billion, they wanted to *reduce* the current population by three-quarters. He showed the ac-

population by three-quarters. He showed the actual U.N. document that planned to eliminate three-quarters of the world's population.

Dr. Strecker showed scientifically exactly how the U.N. did it. They took a virus from a sheep and a virus from a cow and blended them together in a certain way to make the AIDS virus. But before they ever distributed it, they also made a cure for it. The governments have the cure right now, according to Dr. Strecker. The people who were doing this—and history will verify this—were obviously prejudiced, because they singled out two groups: the Blacks and the homosexuals.

In Haiti there was an epidemic of hepatitis B moving through the homosexual community, and they all needed to be injected with the hepatitis B vaccine. So U.N. agents took the AIDS virus, put it in the hepatitis B vaccine and injected it into everyone. That's how the virus started, according to Dr. Strecker. The other evidence that this is true is that throughout the rest of the world, the virus was *not* given exclusively to homosexuals. In Africa, where at least 75 million people have AIDS, the ratio of male to female infection is almost exactly 50-50, from the beginning until now. Only in Haiti, and eventually in the United States, did it spread almost exclusively through the homosexual population. If you look at the figures for this country, females are now getting AIDS faster than anyone else. Soon nature will balance it out, and you'll see exactly the same thing you see everywhere else around the world, which is that equal numbers of males and females have AIDS. It isn't a gay disease at all—it has nothing to do with it. It has to do with the prejudice of the people who created it.

According to Dr. Strecker, the World Health Organization, which has been instrumental in creating this disease, has also been concerned about other diseases—and so have doctors pretty much everywhere. For instance, let's take cancer: Doctors have been concerned that someday cancer will become contagious, not by pollution or foods or things like this, but that it will become airborne or waterborne, like a cold. You'd just walk by somebody with cancer and you'd get it. But the number of different kinds of cancer viruses is so small that the likelihood of that ever happening is pretty slim. It still could happen, but it's not likely. But for AIDS, *there are 9000 to the 4th power or 6,561,000,000,000,000 totally different kinds of AIDS viruses*—that's a huge number. And every time someone gets AIDS, a brandnew virus is created, one that has never been seen before, ever. This means that it's *inevitable*, mathematically speaking—it's just a matter of time— that AIDS will spread rapidly, just like a cold, throughout the world.

There is a story going around that the World Health Organization believes that this rapidly spreading form of AIDS may have already begun. Around 1990 or 1991 the WHO checked an African tribe of 1400 members, including everyone from little babies to old people, who obviously had all different kinds of sexual practices (you know, little babies aren't into sexual things), and they found that *every single member*, without exception, had AIDS. That's when the WHO announced secretly that the virus was

Great Pyramid, not allowing anyone to come near for three days so they could test the results in the consciousness of the planet. They were trying to destroy a specific field of energy that has grown to enclose the Earth. You could call it one of Earth's memory banks. You and I call it Christ consciousness. They, the secret government (which is still you and me), were fearful of this new consciousness, but I believe now it has been mostly resolved.

The polarities of the Earth are slowly merging. At the time of this transcript in 1993 we were living in a period of planetary insight. Now, in 1997, we are on the edge of planetary unity based on understanding. The great test is still ahead, especially if the secret government decides to use HAARP to try to destroy the Christ grid.

Update: On the positive side, doctors at UCLA began about five years ago examining a young boy who had been born with AIDS. He had been checked at birth, at six months and again at one year. He still had AIDS. He wasn't checked again until he was about five. When they checked him this time, all traces of the AIDS virus were gone. It was as though he had never contracted AIDS. They didn't know how his system became immune; all they knew was that it did. They checked everything they could think of, including his DNA. It was here where they found a change. This young boy did not have human DNA!

We have 64 codons in our DNA, but in normal humans only 20 of these codons are turned on. The rest are inert or not working, except for three, which are the stop and start programs. This young boy had 24 codons turned on—he had found a way to mutate that made him immune to AIDS. In fact, when they were testing him, they found that he was immune to everything. They found that his immune system was 3000 times stronger than a normal human's.

Then they found another child with the same situation, coming out of AIDS and turning on the same 24 codons,

probably now airborne or waterborne, and that it might eventually spread like wildfire, like a common cold. There would be a few years' lag as with any other new disease. If this were to happen, would you *know* that you are safe? You need to know the truth—*you are more than you know!*

## A Perspective on Earthly Problems

If we were not multidimensional beings, if we were only physical bodies connected to the Earth and had nowhere to go, we would be in a very serious situation. But because of who we are, what is about to happen on Earth could become a vehicle for enormous growth. Remember, life is a school. Maya is maya!

But still, if we realize the incredibly dangerous situation we're in, we might awaken to who we are. The only reason I'm even saying these words and not keeping it secret is because we're like a group of people in a sinking boat. It's got a big hole in it and the water's pouring in. *It's not time to sit there and play games and do business as usual and think along the normal ways of thinking.* If you didn't know the truth about our environment, you might just go along with your life and not act.

I'm not suggesting to act environmentally, though that is not wrong. What I'm much more concerned with is an internal form of acting, a meditation, a meditation that consciously reconnects you to all life everywhere. It is what the Taoists say: *The way to do is to be.* There's nothing wrong with acting externally, but there's another kind of acting that's required here, I believe. It requires a state of mind where we realize the situation, we begin to take it seriously and work in a way where we can make some real changes in our consciousness. This inner thing we need to focus on and understand will slowly unfold as we continue. Whoever understands the other side of this coin of life will realize that these environmental issues are not a real problem when higher consciousness enters into the 3D world, though from a 3D point of view, it does look like the end of life.

## The History of the World

We're going to open a new subject: the history of the world and how it relates to the present. Each one of these pieces of the puzzle widens the view. The situation in which we find ourselves in this world didn't develop at random. Events occurred that we need to remember. Many of us were here in past lives, and we have these memories within us. But that's beside the point. We need to know exactly what occurred in order to understand how it developed into this situation today. This history, of course, will not be found in history books, because history books of human "civilization" go back only 6000 years, and we need to go back about 450,000 years to begin.

This information was first given to me by Thoth around 1985. Then after Thoth left in 1991, I became aware of Zecharia Sitchin, read his works, and found out that Sitchin's and Thoth's information were almost *perfect* fits—so perfect it just couldn't be a coincidence. It was amazing how close they were. Many things that Thoth had mentioned—such as giants in Atlantis, which he didn't explain further—were explained in Sitchin's books. And many things that Sitchin appears to have overlooked were deeply explained by Thoth. So the combination of these two sources gives a very interesting viewpoint. You don't have to accept this viewpoint; you can just listen to it like a legend, think about it and see if it's workable for you. If something doesn't feel true to you, then of course don't accept it. But I believe this is as close as I can get to the truth, and I offer it to you. Remember, I had to translate the geometrical and hieroglyphic images of Thoth into English. Something is bound to get lost, but I do feel it is close enough to trigger your memories.

First you must realize something about written history. Somebody has to hold the pen and write it down, so written history is always the viewpoint of the person or people who wrote it. Written history began only in the last 6000 years, but would that history be the same if it had been written by different people? Consider that in most cases it was the winners of the wars who wrote the history books. Whoever won a war said, "This is what happened." The losers didn't get to put in their two cents. Look at any of the major wars, especially World War II, which was a very emotional war. If Hitler had won World War II, our history books would be completely different. We'd be examining a totally different set of "facts." We would be the bad guys, and they would have shown good reason for doing in the Jews etc. But we won, so we wrote it from our perspective.

Well, everything's like that all the way through history. Nobody ever talks about this subject, yet it's obvious. Even Thoth was very aware of this; he said, "I'm giving you my viewpoint. I have watched the centuries go by, but I'm only one person. This is what I believe is true, but you must realize that other people may hold different viewpoints on history." So even he was not saying, "This is it—take it or leave it." So with that observation, we'll proceed.

### Sitchin and Sumeria

I'm going to begin first with Zecharia Sitchin's work. If you haven't read his books yet, you have a great treat in store if you want to read about this firsthand. His primary book is called *The 12th Planet*, though I recommend two others, *The Lost Realms* and *Genesis Revisited* (in that order). He writes about many cities that were described in the Christian Bible, such as Babylon, Akkad and Erech, which for a long time people thought were myths because nobody could prove their existence. There wasn't even the slightest sign that they existed. Then they finally found one city, which led to another, which led to another, which led to another. They eventually found all of the cities mentioned in the Bible.

Realize that all these ancient cities have been discovered in the last 120 years or so, most of them more or less recently. As they've dug down into

becoming immune to AIDS and other diseases. They found 100, then 10,000. UCLA now believes that 1% of the world has made this change. They now believe that 55 million children and adults are no longer human, by DNA definition. There are so many people doing this now that science believes that a new human race is being born at this time and that it seems to have come out of AIDS. It is almost impossible for these people to become sick.

It is also interesting that in November 1998, it was announced that in 1997, AIDS dropped off by 47%, which is the biggest drop in history for any major disease. Could this be one of the reasons?

Further, in *Cracking the Bible Code* by Jeffrey Satinover, when they ran the word "AIDS" into the code, they found all the usual associated words. They saw the words *in the blood, death, annihilation, in the form of a virus, the immunity, the HIV, destroyed,* and many more. However, there were certain other words that did not make sense to those researchers but that only now can be understood in the light of the previous information. They found the words, "the end to all diseases."

This is perhaps the single most important event in the world today.

the layers of these ancient cities, they've pulled out thousands of cylindrical clay tablets upon which the history of Sumer *and* the history of the Earth is recorded in great detail, going back hundreds of thousands of years. Their written language is called cuneiform. What I'll be telling you is not just Sitchin's interpretation. Many other scholars now know how to read cuneiform, and as they translate these works, it's changing our whole viewpoint of the world, of what we think is true—just as John Anthony West's work with the Sphinx is also influencing modern thinking about human history.

We'll come back around full circle later to explain how the Sumerians received their information. The Sumerian records are the oldest written records on the planet, 5800 years old, but they describe things that happened billions of years ago, and in great detail things that happened after 450,000 years ago. Whether you're using scientific knowledge or Thoth's, our race is about 200,000 years old. Sitchin says that we're older than that, maybe 300,000 years or so, but the records and Thoth do not say that—and neither do the Melchizedeks. We've been here slightly more than 200,000 years, but there were civilizations on the Earth—long before this cycle and long before the Nefilim—that were far more advanced than the Nefilim or anything we've seen since. They left without a trace. By the end of this book you'll understand why there was nothing left when they departed. This is the planet's past. It's part of who we are, in a way. We have access to all that information. There's a component within each one of us that has all this information recorded. It's easily accessible, but most of us are just not aware of it.

Normally we give greatest credence to the oldest source of an historical event because it is closer in time than a scribe further removed from the event. These are the oldest writings we have, with the possible exception of the geometrical language that predates Egyptian hieroglyphics. The ancient Sumerians were telling us a story of history that's very difficult to accept because of our certainty that what we now know about the past is correct. The story is so outrageous on so many levels that scientists are having a very difficult time accepting it even though they know it must be true. It *is* the oldest source! If it weren't so outrageous, we would have accepted it at face value long ago because it came from such an ancient source.

On the other hand, if they were crazy, making up stories without any real knowledge, how do we explain that they knew so many facts about nature that, from our point of view of history, would have been impossible for them to know? For example, not only did the Dogons know about all the outer planets, but so did the Sumerians—from the very beginning of their culture! The oldest known culture in the world, the Sumerians, extending back to around 3800 B.C., knew exactly what it looked like to approach our solar system from outer space. They knew about all the outer planets, and counted them from outer to inner, as though coming in from outside the solar system. Just as the Dogons showed on the cave wall, the Sumerians described the relative sizes of different planets and described them in detail, as if they were actually passing them in space—what they looked like, the water on them, the color of the clouds. The whole experience was described in detail 3800 years B.C.! This is fact. How is this possible? Or is the truth of our beginning unknown to us?

Before NASA sent our space probe into outer space past the outer planets, Sitchin sent them a Sumerian description of all the planets viewed from space. And when the satellite reached them one by one, sure enough, the Sumerian descriptions were exactly right. Another example: *They knew of the precession of the equinoxes from the very beginning of their existence as a culture.* They knew that the Earth was tilted on its axis at 23 degrees to its orbital plane around the Sun and that it rotated in a circle that took approximately 25,920 years to complete. Now, that's a tough one for a straight historian to understand, especially a scientific type who knows that it takes 2160 years of continuous observation of the night skies to even know that the Earth wobbles. The minimum length of time is 2160 years, yet the Sumerians knew about it on day one of their civilization.

How did they know it? There is so much extraordinary evidence coming out of these clay tablets that it's not being absorbed into the general thinking very quickly. As I was taught in school and understood it, Moses wrote Genesis around 1250 B.C., which is about 3250 years ago. That's what I've always read. Yet Sumerian tablets exist that were written at least 2000 years before Moses lived, and they have the same account as the first chapter of the Bible almost word for word. These tablets even have Adam and Eve and the names of all their sons and daughters, the whole spectrum of events described in Genesis. *It was all written down before Moses ever received it.* This proves that Moses was not the author of Genesis. Obviously, this truth will be hard to accept by the Christian community, but it is true. I can understand why this knowledge is taking so long to sink into our modern culture, because it's a huge deviation from the accepted history of the Earth, and this minor/major truth about Moses is only a tiny part of the whole truth.

### Tiamat and Nibiru

Even deeper than any of these exceptional and impossible bits of information they knew (and there is much more) is the actual story the Sumerians wrote about the beginnings of the human race before Adam and Eve. They're talking about a time that goes way, way, way back. The story begins several billion years ago when Earth was very young. It was then a large planet called Tiamat, and it rotated around the Sun between Mars and Jupiter. Ancient Earth had a large moon, which their records say was destined to become a planet itself someday in the future.

According to the records, there was one more planet in our solar system that we are only vaguely aware of in these modern times. The Babylonians called this planet Marduk, and this name has sort of stuck, but the Sumerian name for it was Nibiru. It was a huge planet that spun retrograde compared to the other planets. The other planets are in a more or less flat plane moving in one direction, but Nibiru moves in the other direction, and when it comes close to the other planets, it passes through the orbit of Mars and Jupiter [Fig. 3-8].

They said that it passes through our solar system every 3600 years, and when it came, it was usually a big event in our solar system. Then it would go way out past the outer planets and disappear from our sight. NASA, by the way, has probably found this planet. At least it is the most probable possibility. They used two satellites and located it at an enormous distance from the Sun. It's definitely there, but the Sumerians knew about it thousands of years ago! Then, according to the records, as fate would have it, on one orbital pass Nibiru came in so close that one of its moons struck Tiamat (our Earth) and tore about half of it off—just ripped this planet right in half. According to the Sumerian records, this big chunk of Tiamat, along with her major moon, got knocked off course, went into orbit between Venus and Mars, and became Earth as we now know it. The other chunk broke into a million pieces and became what the Sumerian records call "the hammered bracelet," which we call the asteroid belt between Mars and Jupiter. This is another point astronomers have marveled at. How did they know about the asteroid belt, because you can't see it with the naked eye?

This is how far back the Sumerian records go. The records continue to talk about earlier events, until at one point they tell more about Nibiru. It was inhabited by conscious beings called the Nefilim. The Nefilim are very tall: the females are about 10 to 12 feet and the males are about 14 to 16 feet. They're not immortal, but their lifetime is about 360,000 Earth years, according to the Sumerian records. Then they die.

### Nibiru's Atmosphere Problem

According to the Sumerian records, approximately 430,000—perhaps as much as 450,000—years ago the Nefilim started having a problem with their planet. It was an atmospheric problem very much like the ozone problem we're having right now. And their scientists decided on a solution similar to what *our*

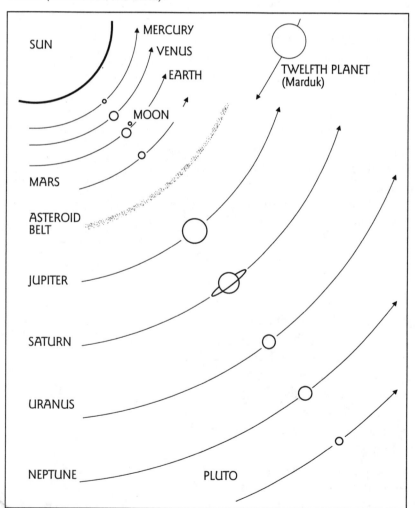

Fig. 3-8. Solar system including Marduk/Nibiru and the remains of Tiamat (asteroid belt and Earth).

scientists have considered. Our scientists have considered putting dust particles into the ozone layer to filter out the Sun's damaging rays. Nibiru's orbit takes it so far away from the Sun that they needed to hold in the heat, so they decided to put gold particles into their higher atmosphere, which would reflect the light and temperature back like a mirror. They planned to get large quantities of gold, pulverize it and suspend it in space above their planet. Yes, it is true that they talked about subjects that seem contemporary—ancient humans talking about ETs and sophisticated science. This is not *Star Trek* or science fiction; it is real. What they said is pretty amazing, and that's why it's been so slow coming out into the general public's knowledge.

The Nefilim had the capability of space travel, though they weren't at that time much further advanced than we are right now, it appears. The Sumerian records show them in their spaceships with flames coming out the back—rocket ships. This is beginning space travel, not sophisticated. In fact, they were so primitive that they had to wait until Nibiru got near enough to Earth before they could even make the trip between the two planets. They couldn't just take off any old time, but had to wait until they were close. I believe that since the Nefilim weren't able to leave the solar system, they searched through all the planets that were here and found that Earth had large quantities of gold. So they sent a team here over 400,000 years ago for one purpose only—to mine gold. The Nefilim who came to Earth were headed by twelve members who were like bosses, about 600 workers who were to actually dig the gold, and about 300 who stayed in orbit in their mothership. They first went into the area of present-day Iraq and began to establish themselves and build their cities, but that's not where they mined the gold [Fig. 3-9]. For the gold, they went to a specific valley in southeast Africa.

Fig. 3-9. Original Nefilim settlements and gold mines.

SETTLEMENTS

One of the twelve, whose name was Enlil, was the leader of the miners. They went deep into the Earth and dug large quantities of gold. Then every 3600 years, when Nibiru/Marduk came around, they would shuttle the gold to their home planet. Then they'd continue their digging while Nibiru traveled its orbit again. According to the Sumerian records, they dug for a very long time, about 100,000 to 150,000 years, and then the Nefilim rebellion took place.

I don't quite agree with Sitchin's dating on when this happened. He got it, not directly through the Sumerian records, but by calculating how long he *thought* it should be. He came up with the time of about 300,000 years ago when the rebellion took place. I believe it was closer to 200,000 years ago.

### The Nefilim Rebellion and the Origin of Our Race

Somewhere between 300,000 and 200,000 years ago the Nefilim workers rebelled. The Sumerian records wrote about this rebellion in great detail. The workers rebelled against their bosses; they did not want to keep digging in the mines. You can imagine the workers saying, "We've been digging this gold for 150,000 years, and we're tired of it. We're not going to do this anymore." I would probably have lasted about one month.

The rebellion presented a problem for the bosses, so the twelve leaders came together to decide what to do. They decided to take a certain life form that already existed on this planet, which was, as I understand it, one of the primates. Then they would take the blood of the primates, mix it with clay, then take the sperm of one of the young male Nefilim and mix these elements together. The tablet actually shows them with what looks like chemical flasks, pouring something from one flask to another to create this new life form. Their plan was to use the DNA of the primates and their own DNA to create a more advanced race than Earth had at that time so that the Nefilim could control this new race for the sole purpose of mining gold.

According to the original Sumerian records, we were created to be miners, as slaves to mine gold. That was our only purpose. And when they mined all the gold they needed to save their own planet, their intention was to destroy our race and leave. They weren't even going to allow us to live. Now, most people hearing that would think, That can't be us; we're too noble for something like that. But that is what the oldest written records on Earth state to be the truth. Remember, Sumerian is the oldest known language in the world, older by far than works such as the Holy Bible and the Koran. It now appears that the Holy Bible was birthed out of the ashes of Sumer.

What science has discovered is almost as interesting. In the exact place where the Sumerian records say we mined gold, archaeologists have found gold mines. These ancient gold mines are dated back as far as 100,000 years. What is really incredible is that *Homo sapiens* (that's us) were mining gold in these mines. Our bones were found there. Those gold mines had been worked at least 100,000 years ago, and they have dated humans in these mines as early as 20,000 years ago. Now, what the heck were we doing mining gold 100,000 years ago? Why did *we* need gold? It's a soft metal, not something you could use like certain other metals. It wasn't found very often in ancient artifacts. So why were we doing this, and where was it going?

## Did Eve Come from the Gold Mines?

Then there's the so-called Eve theory that people have been trying to put down for a long time.

Scientists took a certain component in the DNA molecule and overlapped it to show which one came first, and they figured out that the first person of humanity lived somewhere between 150- and 250,000 years ago. And that first person, whom they called Eve, happened to come from the exact valley the Sumerians claim that we were mining gold [Fig. 3-10]! Since then one scientist has discarded this theory because there are many other ways to look at the DNA origins. But I still find it remarkable that this theory just happened to point at the same valley where the Sumerian records say it all started.

Fig. 3-10. Tracing human descent back to a genetic Eve.

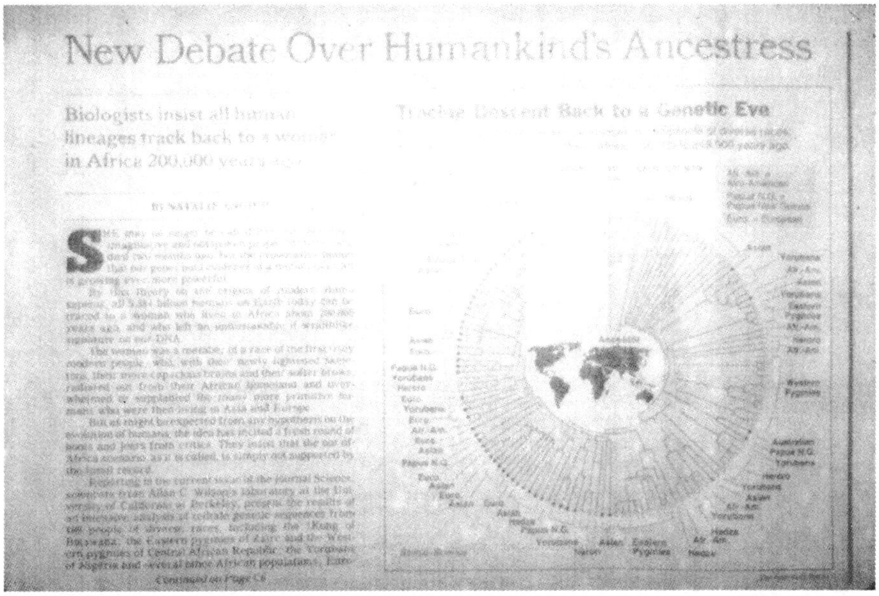

### Thoth's Version of the Origin of Our Race

Now, let's see how similar Thoth's version is. He agrees with the Melchizedek tradition that our particular race didn't start 350,000 years ago as Sitchin says, but exactly 200,207 years ago (from 1993), or 198,214 years B.C. He said that the original people of our race were placed on an island located off the coast of southern Africa, called Gondwanaland.

I don't know if this is the right shape for Gondwanaland [Fig. 3-11]; it's not important, but it was in that area. They were placed here primarily so that they could be contained and not leave. When they evolved enough to be useful to the Nefilim, they were transported to the mining area in Africa and to various other places where they were used to mine gold and perform other services. So this original race, our ancestors, developed and evolved there on the island of Gondwanaland for about 50- to 70,000 years.

Fig. 3-11. Gondwanaland.

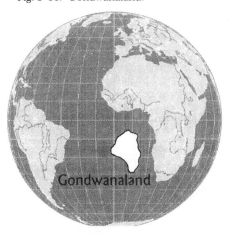

You can see on this map how the various landmasses could have fit together at one time, and this is what scientists now suspect is true. They call this one landmass, before it divided, Gondwanaland. They got the name from the creation stories of the tribes in western Africa. If you read the various creation stories of these tribes, they all have different ideas about how creation took place, but one thread runs through all of them exactly the same. They all say they came from the west, from an island off the western shore of Africa, and that it was called Gondwana. They all agree on that one piece of information, with the one known exception of the Zulus, who claim to have come from space.

The Sumerian records actually picture humans as about one-third the height of the Nefilim. The Nefilim were definitely giants compared to us. They were 10 to 16 feet tall, if you believe the records. I don't see any reason for them to lie. Thoth said that there were giants on the Earth, but he didn't say who they were or anything more about them. The Bible says the same thing. Here it is in chapter six of Genesis:

"And it came to pass, when men began to multiply on the face of the earth, and daughters were born unto them"—that's an important statement, "when men *began* to multiply" (I'll talk about that in a moment)— "that the sons of God" (think about that one for a moment; it's saying the "sons of God" plural) "saw the daughters of men, that they were fair; and they" (the *sons* of God) "took them wives of all which they chose. And the Lord said, 'My spirit shall not always strive with man, for that he also is flesh' " (this indicates that "the Lord" is also flesh), "yet his days shall be an hundred and twenty years. There were *giants* in the earth in those days and also after that; when the sons of God came in to the daughters of men and they bare children to them, the same became mighty men which were of old, men of renown."

That part of the Bible has been interpreted in a lot of ways. But when you see it in the light of what the Sumerian records are saying, it takes on a completely different aspect, especially when you read the older Bibles that tell what the giants were called. They were called the "Nephilim" in the Christian Bible, exactly the same-sounding word as the Sumerian records give. There are over 900 versions of the Bible in the world, and almost all of them talk about giants, a large percentage of them specifically calling them the Nefilim.

### Conceiving the Human Race: The Sirian Role

Thoth says there were giants here on Earth. That's all he said. He didn't say how they got here or where they came from. He said that when our race was created, these giants became our mother. He said that seven of them came together, dropped their bodies by consciously dying, and formed a pattern of seven interlocking spheres of consciousness, exactly like the Genesis pattern (which you'll learn about in chapter 5). This merging created a white-blue flame, which the ancients called the Flower of Life, and they placed this flame into the womb of the Earth.

The Egyptians call this womb the Halls of Amenti, which is a fourth-dimensional space that's located third-dimensionally about a thousand miles under the surface of the Earth and is connected to the Great Pyramid through a fourth-dimensional passageway. One of the primary uses of the Halls of Amenti is for the creation of new races or species. Inside it is a room, based on Fibonacci proportions, made from what appears to be stone. In the middle of the room sits a cube, and on top of the cube is the flame the Nefilim created. This flame, which is four or five feet tall and about three feet in diameter, has a whitish blue light. This light is pure prana, pure consciousness, which is the planetary "ovum" created for us to begin this new evolutionary path that we call human.

Thoth says that if there's a mother, there's got to be a father somewhere. And the nature of the father—the father's sperm—must come from outside the system or body. So when the Nefilim were setting up their flasks and preparing for this new race to develop, another race of beings from a far-distant star—from the third planet out from Sirius B—were preparing to travel to Earth. There were 32 members of this race, 16 males and 16 females who were married into a single family. They were also giants of the same height as the Nefilim. Though the Nefilim were primarily third-dimensional beings, the Sirians were primarily fourth-dimensional.

Thirty-two people marrying each other probably sounds strange, too. On Earth, one male and one female marry because we're reflecting the light of our sun. Our sun is a hydrogen sun, which has one proton and one electron. We duplicate that process of hydrogen, and that's why we marry the way we do, one on one. If you were to visit planets that have helium suns, which have *two* protons, *two* electrons and *two* neutrons, then you would find two males and two females joining together to make children. When you go to an old sun like Sirius B, which is a white dwarf and highly evolved, it has a system of 32 (germanium).

So the Sirians came here and knew exactly what to do. They entered directly into the womb of the Halls of Amenti, right into the pyramid and before the flame. These beings had the understanding that all things are light. They understood the connection between thought and feeling. So they simply created 32 rose-quartz slabs that were about 30 inches high, 3 or 4 feet wide and roughly 18 to 20 feet long. They created them out of nothing—absolutely nothing at all—around the flame. Then they lay down on these slabs, alternating male and female, facing upward with their heads toward the center around this flame. The Sirians conceived, or merged with the flame or ovum of the Nefilim. On the third-dimensional level, the Nefilim scientists placed the laboratory-created human eggs in the wombs of seven Nefilim women, from which the first human being was eventually born. Conception in human terms happens in less than 24 hours—the basic process through the first eight cells. But conception on a planetary level is very different. According to Thoth, they lay there without moving for approximately 2000 years, conceiving with the Earth this new race. Finally, after 2000 years, the first human beings were born in Gondwanaland, off the western shores of southern Africa.

### Enlil's Arrival

Now, the part of the story where the Sirians are the father doesn't seem to completely correlate with what the Sumerian records say, at least according to the story given by Zecharia Sitchin, until you look at a sequence of events that Sitchin didn't seem to understand. Enlil, who was the first one to come to Earth and was the boss in southern Africa—did not land on

*land* when he arrived on Earth. He landed in the waters. Why did he go into the waters? Because that's where the dolphins and the whales were. The dolphins and whales were the highest level of consciousness on this planet, and still are. In simple galactic terms, Enlil had to go into the ocean to get permission to live and mine gold on Earth. Why? Because this planet belonged to the dolphins and whales, and it is galactic law that permission must be granted before an off-planet race can enter into a different consciousness system. According to the Sumerian records, Enlil stayed with them a very long time, and when he finally decided to come onto land, he was *half human and half fish!* At one point Enlil became all human. This was described in the Sumerian records.

You see, the third planet out from Sirius B that some call Oceana happens to be the home planet of the dolphins and whales. Peter Shenstone, leader of the dolphin movement in Australia, has channeled an unusual book, *The Legend of the Golden Dolphin*, which came from the dolphins and describes exactly how they came from another galaxy, how they came to be on the little star around Sirius B, and how they traveled to Earth. The entire planet there is almost completely water; there's an island about the size of Australia and another about the size of California, and that's all. On those two landmasses there are human-type beings, but not very many. The rest of the planet, which is all water, is cetacean. There's a direct connection between the human-type beings and the cetaceans, so when Enlil (a Nefilim) came here, he first connected with the dolphins (Sirians) to receive their blessing. *Then* he went onto the land and began the process that led to the creation of our race.

### Nefilim Mothers

To recapitulate and clarify: After the rebellion, when it was decided to create a new race here on Earth, it was the Nefilim who became the mother aspect. The Sumerian record says seven females stepped forward. Then the Nefilim took clay from the earth, blood from the primate and sperm from the young Nefilim male, mixed this together and put it into the wombs of the young female Nefilim who were chosen for this. They gave birth to human babies. So seven of us were birthed at once, not just one Adam and Eve, according to the original stories—*and we were sterile*. We could not reproduce. The Nefilim continued procreating little humans, making an army of little beings—us—putting them on the island of Gondwanaland. If you want to believe this story, which is part Sumerian record and part Thoth, our race's mother is Nefilim and our father is Sirian. Now, if it were not for the Sumerian records concerning the Nefilim, this would all seem absolutely outrageous—and it still does. But there's a tremendous amount of scientific evidence that this is true if you read the archaeological records—not about the Sirian father, but definitely about the Nefilim mother.

Science doesn't understand how we got here. You are aware that there's a "missing link" between the last primate and us. We seem to come out of nowhere. They *do* know that we're somewhere between 150- and 250,000 years old, but they have no idea where we came from or how we developed. We just stepped through some mystical doorway and arrived.

### Adam and Eve

Another interesting part of the Sumerian records was that after they mined gold for a while in Africa, the cities in the north, near modern-day Iraq, became quite elaborate and extremely beautiful. They were in rain forests and had huge gardens around them. It was finally decided, according to the Sumerian records, to bring some of the slaves from the southern mines to the cities to have them work the gardens. Evidently we made great slaves.

One day Enlil's younger brother, Enki (whose name means *snake*), went to Eve—and the records used that name, Eve—and told her that the reason his brother didn't want the humans to eat of that tree in the center of the garden was because it would make them like the Nefilim. Enki was trying to get even with his brother for a dispute they were having. (The whole story is much more involved than this, but you can read it in the records.) So Enki convinced Eve to eat of the apple tree, the tree of the knowledge of good and evil, which, according to the records, included more than just a dualistic point of view. It gave her the power to procreate, to give birth.

So Eve found Adam and they ate of this tree and had children, each of which was listed by name on the Sumerian tablets. Now, think about the Adam and Eve story from here on—both stories: the one in Sumerian records and the one in the Bible. God walks through the garden—he's *walking*, he's in a body, in flesh, which was suggested in Genesis. He's walking through the garden calling for Adam and Eve. He doesn't know where they are. He's God, but he doesn't know where Adam and Eve are. He calls for them and they come. He doesn't know that they ate of the tree until he sees them trying to hide themselves because they're ashamed. Then he realizes what they've done.

Here's another thing: The word for God, *elohim*, in the original Bible—in fact, in all the bibles—was not singular but plural. Was the God who created humanity a race of beings? When Enlil found out that Adam and Eve had done this, he was furious. He especially didn't want them to eat of the other tree, the tree of life, because then not only would they be able to procreate, but they would become immortal. (We don't know if these are really trees or not. It might have been symbolic for something bound to consciousness.) Therefore, at that point Enlil removed Adam and Eve from his garden. He put them somewhere else and monitored them. He had to have monitored them because he wrote down the names of all the sons and daughters; he knew everything that was going on in the whole family. It was all written down over 2000 years before the Bible was ever written.

From the time of Adam and Eve, our race developed in two strains: one that could procreate and were free (though monitored), and the other that could not have children and were slaves. According to modern scientists, this latter strain continued to mine gold until at least 20,000 years ago. The bones of this second strain that were found in the mines were identical to ours; the only difference is that they couldn't have children. This strain was completely destroyed at the time of the Great Flood, roughly 12,500 years ago. (There is much more to this subject, which we will give to you at the right moment.)

We will be talking about four Earth pole shifts in this work—when Gondwanaland sank, when Lemuria sank, when Atlantis sank (which is the Great Flood) and the one that is now about to happen. This side note is important to understand: According to Thoth, the degree of tilt of the Earth's axis and the degree of the pole shift—which happens on a pretty regular basis, according to science—have a direct relationship to the change in consciousness on the planet. For example, the last time the pole shifted at the time of the Great Flood, the North Pole was in Hawaii (I realize this is debatable)—at least that's where the *magnetic* pole was—and now it's practically 90 degrees from there. That's a big change. It was not a positive change, but a negative one—we went down in consciousness, not up.

### The Rising of Lemuria

According to Thoth, after Adam and Eve there was a major shift of the axis, which submerged Gondwanaland. Thoth says that when Gondwanaland went down, another landmass came up in the Pacific Ocean, which we call Lemuria, and the descendants of Adam and Eve were taken from their homeland and brought to Lemuria.

Figure 3-12 is not exactly what Lemuria looked like, but it's close in a certain way. It extended from the Hawaiian Islands all the way down to Easter Island. It was not a solid mass, but a series of thousands of islands that were closely linked. Some of them were big, some of them little, and there were a whole lot more than this picture shows. It was like a continent that was barely above water—a water continent.

Adam's race was brought there and allowed to develop on its own without the Nefilim interfering, as far as I know. We remained on Lemuria for 65- to 70,000 years. While we were on Lemuria, we were very happy. We had few problems. We were accelerating through our evolutionary path and moving very well. We did lots of experiments on ourselves and implemented many physical changes to our bodies. We were changing our skeletal structure, working on the base of our spine a great deal, working on our skull size and shape. We were mostly right-brained, feminine in nature. An evolutionary cycle has to choose whether it's going to be male or female, just like you did when you came to Earth. You've got to make that decision. So our race was becoming female. By the time Lemuria sank, as a race we were equivalent to about a 12-year-old girl.

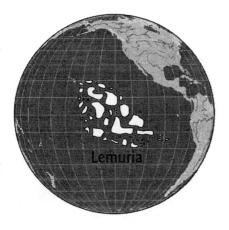

Fig. 3-12. Lemuria.

## Explorations of Lemuria in 1910

The fact that Lemuria probably existed was established in our society as far back as 1910. We don't remember much about this knowledge, because in 1912 something happened to change our course of evolution. In 1912 experiments took place that were similar to the Philadelphia Experiment of 1942 and '43, which we'll talk about later. They actually did the experiment in 1913, but it turned out to be a huge catastrophe, and I personally believe that this experiment is what caused World War I in 1914. After that we were never the same.

Before World War I the spiritual growth pattern of the United States was similar to what's happening right now. People were extremely interested in spiritual and psychic work, in meditation, in understanding the ancient past and in everything else of that nature. People like Colonel James Churchward and Augustus Le Plongeon from France were studying Atlantis and Lemuria, and there were many similar thought patterns compared to the present. Then when World War I came along, we fell asleep and didn't start waking up again until the 1960s. But the proof they had in 1910 about the existence of Lemuria was pretty remarkable, and it had to do with coral. Coral can grow underneath the surface of water only to a depth of 150 feet. In 1910 I suspect the Pacific floor was higher than it is now, because they were able to see coral rings on the surface of the ocean floor heading away from Easter Island for a great distance.

By the way, the ocean floor *does* rise and fall. You might not know it, but the Atlantic Ocean floor rose over two miles in December 1969; you can look this up in the January 1970 issue of *Life* magazine. In the Bermuda area many islands suddenly began to break the surface. Some are still there, but most of them sank again. The ocean floor had been over two miles deep prior to that time.

At the time that Plato described Atlantis and the Atlantic Ocean, the Greeks were having a difficult time navigating their ships into the Atlantic Ocean outside the Straits of Gibraltar because the water in that area was only 10 or 15 feet deep, sometimes even less. Now the water is deep again.

The coral rings they discovered in the Pacific were estimated at 1800 feet deep. This meant that the rings originally had islands inside, because the coral had to be close to the surface in order to grow. If the rings were 1800 feet deep, it meant that since coral cannot grow below 150 feet, the rings sank very, very slowly. In 1910 people could see these rings going off into the distance, so they knew there had to be a lot of islands there at one time. Probably more important, if you follow the fauna and flora from the Hawaiian Islands, you find the same features on a whole series of islands moving along an arc from Hawaii all the way to Easter Island. These islands are separated by long distances, but if you look on a map, you'll see a long string. That string used to run along the western shores of Lemuria. All those islands, including Tahiti and Borea, were part of Lemuria. All the islands in this string have exactly the same fauna and flora—not on any of the other islands, just this one string—the same trees, same birds, same bees, same bugs, same bacteria, same everything. Science can explain this phenomenon only if there were at one time much closer land bridges between these islands.

## Ay and Tiya and the Beginning of Tantra

This new civilization in Lemuria was developing quite well; everything was going along just great. But most of Lemuria eventually sank. About a thousand years before it sank, two people were there whose names were Ay and Tiya. This couple did something that no one else had ever done before, at least in our evolutionary cycle. They discovered that if you make love in a certain way and breathe in a certain way, you get different results when you have a child. Through the conception of that different kind of birth, all three of them—the mother, the father and the child—would become immortal. In other words, by having a baby in a certain way, the experience changes you forever.

Ay and Tiya suspected that they had become immortal, I'm sure, because of their experience. As time went on and everybody else started dying but they remained alive, people began to realize that they really did have something. So they finally set up a school. As far as I know, it was the first mystery school on the Earth in this cycle. It was called the Naacal, or Naakal (rhymes with McCall), Mystery School, where they simply tried to teach how to do this thing we call resurrection or ascension through tantra. Tantra is a Hindu word for yoga or union with God though sexual practices. (We have a lot to go over before we can understand exactly what they were doing.) Anyway, they did this and then they began to teach other people.

Before Lemuria sank, they had instructed approximately a thousand people, which means that about 333 families of three each were able to understand what they were doing and demonstrate it. They were able to make love in this unusual way. They didn't touch each other, actually. In fact, they didn't even need to be in the same room. It was interdimensional love-making. They taught others how to do it, and it was getting to a place where in another few thousand years they would probably have translated the whole race into a new consciousness.

But God evidently said no, it was not the right time. They had just gotten started when Lemuria sank. Lemuria, like I said, was female, and the Lemurians were very psychic. They knew that Lemuria was going to sink a long time beforehand. They knew with absolute certainty; it wasn't even a matter of discussion. So they prepared a long time in advance. They took all their artifacts to Lake Titicaca, Mount Shasta and other places. Even the great golden disk of Lemuria was removed. They got everything of value out of the country and prepared for the end. When Lemuria finally sank, they were totally off the islands. They had resettled from Lake Titicaca through Central America and Mexico to as far north as Mount Shasta.

### Lemuria Sinks and Atlantis Rises

According to what Thoth says, the sinking of Lemuria and the rising of Atlantis occurred at the same time, during another shift of the axis. Lemuria went down, and what would be called Atlantis rose.

Atlantis was a pretty large continent, as shown here [Fig. 3-13]. The southeastern part of the United States wasn't there; Florida, Louisiana, Alabama, Georgia, South Carolina, North Carolina and parts of Texas were under water. I don't know if Atlantis was quite this big or not, but it was pretty big. It actually consisted of this continent plus nine islands: one to the north, one to the east, one to the south and six to the west, which extended to where the Florida Keys are now.

Fig. 3-13. Atlantis.

**Update: On May 23, 1998, Aaron Du Val, president of the Egyptology Society in Miami, Florida, announced that ancient Atlantis has been found near Bimini, and that it can be scientifically proven beyond any doubt. They have found a huge underwater pyramid and have open hermetically sealed chambers to expose records that confirm what Plato said about Atlantis during the time of ancient Greece. Mr. Du Val said they will present their evidence to the world before the end of 1998 or soon afterward.**

# The Aborted Evolution of Consciousness and the Creation of the Christ Grid

## How the Lemurians Evolved Human Consciousness

The immortal beings of Lemuria "flew" from their homeland to a little island north of the newly risen continent of Atlantis. They waited for a long time on the island they named Udal, then they began to re-create their spiritual science. If you had watched them, you wouldn't have known what the heck they were doing; you'd have thought they were nuts. In order to describe what they were doing, I have to describe something else first

### The Structure of the Human Brain

This circle [Fig. 4-1] represents a human head, looking down from above. There's the nose (N). The human brain is divided into two components, the left side and the right side.

In Figure 4-2, the left side is male and the right side is female, and they are linked by the corpus callosum. According to Thoth, this is the nature of these two hemispheres: The left, male component sees everything absolutely logically—as it is, you might say. The right, female component is much more concerned with *experiencing* something than understanding it. The female and male perceptions are mirror images of each other—as if you had a mirror between them. If you had the word LOVE written into the male component, he would see it as shown. But the female sees its mirror image, also as shown. When the male looks at her way of perceiving, he says, "There's no logic here." She looks at him and says, "Where is the feeling?"

The brain is further divided into four lobes by another thin division. The male side of the brain has a component behind it that reflects, or mir-

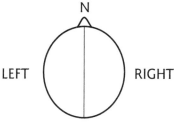

Fig. 4-1. The two hemispheres of the human brain.

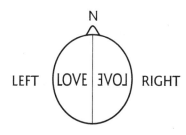

Fig. 4-2. Dynamics of the two hemispheres, reflecting side to side.

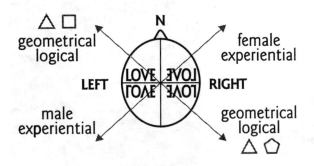

Fig. 4-3. The reflective areas, front to back.

rors the front, as shown in Figure 4-3. There's another mirror image behind the female side that reflects what's in front of it. The male logical component has a totally experiential component behind it and the female experiential component has totally logical component behind it. It's as if there are four mirrors reflecting each other in these four possible ways. When we look at the geometries later, you'll see that the forward part in the male brain, the logical component, is based on the triangle and the square (in two dimensions) or the tetrahedron and the cube (in three dimensions). The forward part in the female brain, the experiential component, is based on the triangle and the pentagon (in two dimensions) or the tetrahedron, the icosahedron and the dodecahedron (in three dimensions). There are also diagonal pathways connecting the left-front logical to the back-right logical, and the right-front experiential to the back-left experiential. Thus the mirror quality reflects side to side, front to back, and diagonal to diagonal. This is the way we're made up, according to Thoth.

### The Attempt to Birth a New Consciousness on Atlantis

When the time was right, the Naacals from Lemuria created a spiritual representation of a human brain on the surface of their Atlantean island. Their purpose was to birth a new consciousness based on what they had learned during Lemuria. They believed the brain had to come first before the body of the new consciousness of Atlantis was to emerge. With Thoth's image of the human brain in mind, you can begin to make sense of their actions. First they made a wall down the middle of the island about 40 feet high and 20 feet wide, which sealed off one side of the island from the other. Literally, you had to go into the water to get to the other side. Then they ran a minor wall across at 90 degrees to the first wall, which divided the island into four parts.

Then half of these thousand people, who were of the Naacal Mystery School, went on one side and half stayed on the other, depending on their nature. That could mean that all the women stayed on one side and all the men went to the other side, but as I understand it, where a person went did not depend on the physical body, but his or her dependency on one side of the brain or the other. In this way, approximately half became the male component of the brain and the other half became the female component.

They spent thousands of years in this physical state until they believed they were ready for the next step. Three people were selected to represent the corpus callosum, the part of the brain that links the left and right hemispheres together. Thoth's father, Thome, was one of these. He and two other people were the only ones allowed to go everywhere on the island. Otherwise, the two sides had to remain completely separate from each other. Then the three began to align their energies and thoughts and feelings and all aspects of humanness into an integrated human brain, not with human cells, but rather with human bodies.

The next step was to project onto the surface of Atlantis the form of the Tree of Life. They used the form here [Fig. 4-4] with 12 circles on it instead of 10, but the 11th and 12th circles were off the mainland; one of the points was on Udal and one was in the water to the south. So there were ten components on the mainland, which is the configuration we're familiar with. Even though it extended over hundreds of miles on the surface of this land, they projected it to the accuracy of a single atom, according to Thoth. There is an indication that even the spheres of the Tree of Life were used to designate the size and shape of the cities of Atlantis. Plato says in his book *Critias* that the main city of Atlantis was made of three rings of land separated by water, as shown in this drawing [Fig. 4-5]. He also says the city was constructed of red, black and white stones. This last statement will make sense as soon as we talk about the Great Pyramid.

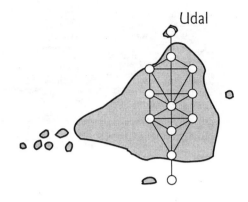

Fig. 4-4. Tree of Life on Atlantis.

### The Children of Lemuria Are Called Forth

Suddenly, in a single day, the brain of Atlantis, the Naacal Mystery School, breathed life into the Tree of Life on the surface of Atlantis. This created vortexes of energy rotating out of each of the circles on the Tree of Life. Once the vortexes were established, then the brain of Atlantis psychically called forth the children of Lemuria. Millions and millions of Lemurians, who by then had settled along the west coast of North and South America and in other places, began to be pulled to Atlantis. A great migration began, and the ordinary people of the sunken Lemuria started moving toward Atlantis. Remember, they were feminine right-brained beings and inner communication was easy. However, the Lemurian body of consciousness had reached only the age of twelve as a planetary consciousness. It was still a child, and some of its centers weren't functioning yet; they had worked with those energies and had mastered only eight of the ten. So each migrating Lemurian was attracted to one of these eight centers on Atlantis, depending on the nature of the individual. There they settled and began to build cities.

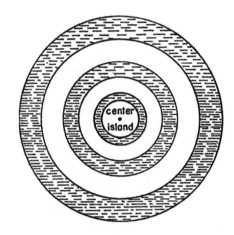

Fig. 4-5. Atlantean city of Poseidon.

That left two vortexes with nobody using them, not a single person. These two vortexes were pulling life toward them, and in life you just can't have an empty place. Life will find a way to fill it. For instance, if you're driving along the freeway following another car and you drop too far behind it, somebody will fill in the gap, right? If you leave a place empty, life will step in and fill it. That's exactly what happened on Atlantis.

Though Lemurians settled into only eight of the vortex areas, Mayan records state clearly that there were ten cities in Atlantis when it fell. In fact, you can see those records in the Troano document, which is now located in the British Museum. This document is estimated to be at least 3500 years old, and it describes in detail the sinking of Atlantis. It's Mayan, and it contains an authentic account of the cataclysm, according to Le Plongeon, the French historian who translated it. Here is what it says:

In the year 6 Kan on the 11th Muluc in the month Zak, there occurred terrible earthquakes which continued without interruption until the 13th Chin. The country of the hills of Mud, the land of Mu, was sacrificed, being twice upheaved. It suddenly disappeared during one night, the basin being continually shaken by volcanic forces. Being confined, these caused the land to sink and to rise several times and in various places. At last the surface gave way, and ten countries were torn asunder and scattered, unable to stand the forces of the convulsions. They sank with their 64 million inhabitants.

The ten countries mentioned were referring to the ten points on the Tree of Life. When you see this document, it shows an extremely sophisticated city with volcanoes going off inside and all around it, pyramids and everything else being destroyed and people getting in boats and trying to escape. It describes the incident in the Mayan language, which uses pictures.

## The Aborted Evolution

### Two Empty Vortexes Drew Extraterrestrial Races

To fill those two empty vortexes, according to Thoth, two extraterrestrial races stepped in—not one, but two completely different races. The first race was the Hebrews, coming from our future. Thoth says they came from off the planet, but I don't know specifically where. The Hebrews were kind of like a kid who went through the fifth grade and didn't make it and had to do that grade over again. They hadn't graduated to the next level of evolution, so they had to repeat that grade. In other words, they were like a child who had already been through the math stuff. They knew a lot of things that we didn't know yet. They had legal permission from the Galactic Command to step into our evolutionary path at that time. They brought with them, according to Thoth, many concepts and ideas that we had no idea about yet because we hadn't entered into those levels of awareness. This interaction actually benefited our evolution, I believe. There was no problem with their coming to Earth and settling. There probably would have been no problem at all if just this one race had come here.

The other race that stepped in at that time caused big problems. These beings came from the nearby planet of Mars. (I know this may sound strange, but it sounded even stranger when I was saying this back in 1985 before people like Richard Hoagland began to speak up.) It has become evident, because of the situation that has developed in the world, that this same race is still causing major problems. The secret government and the trillionaires of the world are of Mars extraction or have mostly Martian genes and little or no emotional/feeling body.

### Mars after the Lucifer Rebellion

According to Thoth, Mars looked much like Earth a little less than a million years ago. It was beautiful. It had oceans and water and trees and was just fantastic. But then something happened to them, and it had to do with a past "Lucifer rebellion."

From the very beginning of this experiment we are in—and all of God's creation is an experiment—experiments similar to the Lucifer rebellion (if you want to call them rebellions) have been attempted four times. In other words, three other beings besides Lucifer attempted to do the same thing, and each time it resulted in utter chaos throughout the universe.

More than a million years ago, the Martians had joined the third rebellion, the third time that life decided to try this experiment. And the experiment failed dramatically. Planets everywhere were destroyed, and Mars was one of them. Life attempted to create a separate reality from God, which is the same thing that's going on now. In other words, a portion of life attempted to separate itself from all other life and create its own separate reality. Since everyone is God anyway, this is okay—you can do that. The only thing is, it never has worked so far. Nevertheless, they tried it again.

When someone tries to separate from God, they sever their love connection with Reality. So when the Martians (and many others) created a separate reality, they cut the love bond—they disconnected the emotional body—and in so doing they became pure male, with little or no female within them. They were purely logical beings with no emotions. Like Mr. Spock in *Star Trek*, they were pure logic. What happened in Mars, and in thousands and thousands of other places, was that they ended up fighting all the time because there was no compassion, no love. Mars became a battleground that just kept going on and on and on, until finally it became clear that Mars was not going to survive. Eventually they blew their atmosphere away and destroyed the surface of their planet.

Before Mars was destroyed, they built huge tetrahedral pyramids, which you're going to see in photographs in the second volume. Then they built three-sided, four-sided, and five-sided pyramids, eventually building a complex that was able to create a synthetic Mer-Ka-Ba. You see, you can have a space-time vehicle that looks like a spaceship, or you can have certain other structures that do the same thing. They built a structure from which they were able to look ahead and behind in time and space to tremendous distances and time periods.

A small group of Martians tried to get away from Mars before it was destroyed, so they translated themselves into the future and found a perfect place to resettle before Mars was destroyed. That place was Earth, but it was about 65,000 years in our past. They saw that little vortex sitting there on Atlantis with nobody in it. They didn't ask permission. Being part of the rebellion, they didn't go through the normal procedure. They just said, "All right, let's do it." They stepped right into that vortex, and in so doing, they joined our evolutionary path.

## Martians Rape the Human Child Consciousness and Take Over

There were only a few thousand of these Martians who actually used the time-space-dimension consciousness machine, or building. The very first thing they did when they arrived here on Earth was try to take control of Atlantis. They wanted to declare war and take over. However, they were vulnerable because of their small numbers and perhaps other reasons, so they couldn't do it. They were finally subdued by the Atlanteans/ Lemurians. We were able to stop them from conquering us, but we could not send them back. By the time this took place in our evolutionary path, we were about the age of a 14-year-old girl. So what you had here was similar to a 14-year-old girl being taken over by a much older man, a 60- or 70-year-old man who simply forced himself on her. In other words, it was rape. We were raped, we had no choice. The Martians just stepped in and said, "Like it or not, we're here." They didn't care what we thought or felt about it. It was really no different from what we in America did to the Native Americans.

Once the initial conflict was over, it was agreed that the Martians would try to understand this female thing they lacked, this emotional feeling, of which they had none at all. Things more or less settled down for a long time. But the Martians slowly began to implement their left-brain technology, which the Lemurians didn't know anything about. All the Lemurians knew was *right*-brain technology, which today we know very little about. Psychotronic machines, dowsing rods and those kinds of things are right-brain technologies. Many right-brain feminine technologies would astound you if you saw them in action. You can do absolutely anything that you can imagine with right-brain technology, just as you can with left-brain technology, if they are brought to their full potential. But then we really do not need either one—this is the great secret that we have forgotten!

The Martians kept putting out these left-brain inventions, one after another after another, until finally they changed the polarity of our evolutionary path because we began to "see" through the left brain, and we changed from female to male. We changed the nature of who we were. The Martians gained control bit by bit, until eventually they controlled everything without a battle. They had all the money and all the power. The animosity between the Martians and the Lemurians—and I'm putting the Hebrews in with the Lemurians—never subsided, not even to the very end of Atlantis. They hated each other. The Lemurians, the feminine aspect, were basically shoved down and treated like inferiors. It was not a very loving situation. It was a marriage that the female component did not like, but I don't think the Martian males really cared if she liked it or not. It remained this way for a very long time, until approximately 26,000 years ago, when the next phase slowly began.

## Minor Pole Shift and the Subsequent Debate

It was about 26,000 years ago when we had another minor pole shift and a small change in consciousness. This pole shift took place at the same point on the polar wobble called the precession of the equinoxes that we have now returned to (see the lower small oval at A in Fig. 4-6). It wasn't much, though it has been recorded by science. The two small ovals on the cycle are where these changes always take place, and right now we're back at point A again.

At the time of this pole shift, a piece of Atlantis, probably about half the size of Rhode Island, sank into the ocean. That caused a tremendous amount of fear in Atlantis, because they thought they were go-

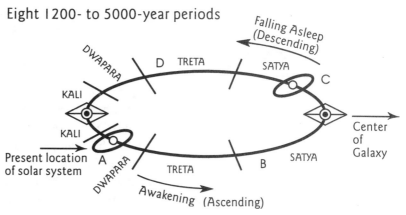

Eight 1200- to 5000-year periods

Fig. 4-6. The cycle of the precession of the equinoxes; A is the point of pole shift.

ing to lose the whole continent, like what happened to Lemuria. By this time they had lost most of their ability to see into the future. They were shaking in their boots for a long time simply because they didn't know for sure what was going to happen. They were still afraid a hundred years later, then slowly this fear began to subside. It took over 200 years for them to feel safe again.

Atlantis was a little beyond the lower oval at A when they finally relaxed their fear about Earth changes. But the memory was still there. They were going along nicely for a while, then out of the blue approximately 13,000 to 16,000 years ago, a comet approached Earth. When this comet was still in deep space, the Atlanteans knew about it because they were more technologically advanced than we are now. They witnessed its approach.

A great conflict began to occur in Atlantis. The Martians, who were in the minority even though they were in control, wanted to blow it out of the sky with their laser technology. But there was a huge movement amongst the Lemurian population against using the Martian left-brained technology. The feminine aspect said, "This comet is in divine order, and we should allow this to take place naturally. Let it hit the Earth. That is what's supposed to take place."

Of course, the Martians replied, "No! Let's blow it out of the sky. We have very little time, or we all will be killed." After lots of arguing, the Martians finally and reluctantly agreed to allow the comet to hit the Earth. When it arrived, it came screaming into the atmosphere, plunging into the Atlantic Ocean just off the western shore of Atlantis near where Charleston, South Carolina, is now, only it was on the bottom of the ocean then. The remnants of that comet are now scattered over four states. Science has definitely determined that it did hit there somewhere between 13,000 and 16,000 years ago. They're still finding pieces. Although most of the fragments were centered near Charleston, one of the two largest pieces actually struck the main body of Atlantis in its southwestern area. These left two huge holes in the floor of the Atlantic Ocean and could have been the true cause of the sinking of Atlantis. The actual sinking did not happen at that time, but took place at least several hundred years later.

## The Martians' Fateful Decision

The pieces of the comet that crashed into the southwestern area of Atlantis happened to be right where the Martians were living, killing a huge portion of their population. The Martians got hurt the worst by consenting to allow the comet to come in. Well, that was too humiliating and painful for them. This was the beginning of a great loss of consciousness for Earth. What was about to take place was the seed for a bitter tree, the same tree we live by today. The Martians said, "It's all over. We are divorcing you. We're going to do whatever we want from now on. You can do whatever you want, but we're going to lead our own lives and try to control our own fate. And we're not going to listen to you ever again." You know this whole number. We've seen it in divorced families throughout the world. And the children? Look at our world! *We* are the children!

The Martians decided to take over the Earth, of course. Control, the Martian's primary interface with the Reality, rose to meet their anger. They began to create a building complex like the one they had constructed on Mars a long time earlier, in order to create a synthetic Mer-Ka-Ba once again. The only thing is, around 50,000 Earth years had passed since they had created one, and they didn't remember exactly how to do it—but they thought they did. So they built the buildings and began the experiment. That experiment is directly tied to a chain of Mer-Ka-Bas that began with the Mars experiments a little less than a million years before. Later, one was done here on Earth in 1913, another one in 1943 (called the Philadelphia Experiment), another one in 1983 (called the Montauk Experiment), and another one that, I believe, they're attempting to do this year (1993) near Bimini Island. These dates are windows of time that open up and are tied to the harmonics of the situation. The experiments must be timed to these windows in order to succeed.

If the Martians had succeeded in setting up a synthetic harmonic Mer-Ka-Ba, they would have had absolute control of the planet, if that was their intention. They would have been able to make anybody on the planet do anything they wanted, though eventually it would have meant their own demise. No higher-order being would place this kind of control on another if they truly understood the Reality.

## Failure of the Martian Mer-Ka-Ba Attempt

The Martians built the buildings in Atlantis, set up the whole experiment, then threw their switch to begin the energy flow. Almost immediately they lost control of the experiment, like falling through space and time. The degree of destruction was more horrible and sinful than I care to describe. In this Reality, you can hardly make a greater error than to create an out-of-control synthetic Mer-Ka-Ba. What the experiment did was begin to rip open the lower-dimensional levels of the Earth—not the higher ones, but the lower ones. To give an analogy, the human body has membranes between different parts, such as in the heart, the stomach, the liver, the eyes and so on. If you took a knife and slit open your stomach, that's would be like ripping open the dimensional levels of the Earth. Various aspects are separated from other aspects of spirit by these dimensional membranes, and they're not meant to mix. You're not supposed to have blood in your stomach, but in your arteries. The purpose of a blood cell is different from that of a stomach cell.

These Martians did something that almost killed the Earth. The environmental disaster we are experiencing today is nothing in comparison, though the problems we are having are a direct result of what we did long ago. With the right understanding and enough love, the environment could be repaired in a single day. But had this Martian experiment continued, it would have destroyed the Earth forever. We would never have been able to use the Earth as a seed base again.

The Martians made a very, very serious mistake. This out-of-control Mer-Ka-Ba field, first of all, released a huge number of lower-dimensional spirits into the Earth's higher-dimensional planes. These spirits were forced into a world they did not understand or know, and were in total fear. They had to live—they had to have bodies—so they went right into people, hundreds of them into each person in Atlantis. The Atlanteans could not stop them from entering their bodies. Finally, almost every person in the world was totally possessed by these beings from another dimension. These spirits were really Earthlings like us, but very different, not coming from this dimensional level. It was a total catastrophe—the biggest catastrophe the Earth has probably ever seen.

## A Disruptive Heritage: The Bermuda Triangle

The Martians' attempt to control the world took place near one of the Atlantean islands in the area we now call the Bermuda Triangle. There's an actual building sitting on the ocean floor down there that contains three rotating star-tetrahedral electromagnetic fields superimposed on each other, creating a huge synthetic Mer-Ka-Ba that stretches out over the ocean and into deep space. This Mer-Ka-Ba is completely out of control. It's called the Bermuda *Triangle* because the apex of one of the tetrahedrons—the stationary one—is sticking up out of the water there. The other two fields are counterrotating—and the faster-rotating field sometimes moves clockwise, which is a very dangerous situation. (When we say clockwise, we mean the *source* of the field, not the field itself. The field itself would appear to be rotating counterclockwise.) You'll understand this when you learn more about the Mer-Ka-Ba. When the faster field rotates *counterclockwise* (from its source), everything's okay; but when the faster

Note: For those of you who believe that we will be out of this dimension before 2012, you are probably right. The correction to this Atlantean field, even though the Earth will probably be in at least the fourth dimension by then, will be completed in that third-dimensional year, according to Thoth.

one moves *clockwise* (from its source), that's when time and space distortions happen. Many of the airplanes and ships that have disappeared in the Bermuda Triangle have literally gone into other dimensional levels because of the out-of-control field there.

A primary cause of much of the distortion in the world—the distortion between humans such as wars, marital problems, emotional disturbances etc.—is that imbalanced field. That field is not only causing distortions on Earth, it's causing distortions way, way, way out in remote areas of space because of the way Reality is constructed. That's one of the reasons why this race of beings called the Grays, and other ET beings we'll talk about at the appropriate time, are trying to correct what happened here long ago. This is a big problem that extends way beyond Earth. What they did back in Atlantis was against all galactic law. It was illegal, but they did it anyway. It will be solved, but not until the year 2012. There's not much the ETs can do in the meantime, but they'll probably keep trying. Eventually they'll succeed.

## The Solution: A Christ Consciousness Grid

### Ascended Masters Assist the Earth

At the time of the synthetic Mer-Ka-Ba failure, there were about 1600 ascended masters on Earth, and they did everything they could to try to heal the situation. They tried to seal the dimensional levels and get as many of these spirits as they could out of people and back into their own worlds. They did everything on every level they could. They eventually got most of the spirits out and healed about 90 to 95 percent or more of the situation, but people still found many of these unusual beings living in their bodies.

The situation at that time began to deteriorate extremely rapidly. All the systems on Atlantis—financial, social and all the concepts of how life ought to be—degenerated and collapsed. The continent of Atlantis and all its people became sick. They started getting weird diseases. The entire continent went into a state of survival just trying to live through each day. The situation grew continually worse. For a long period of time it was hell on Earth, horrible. If it had not been slowed down by the ascended masters, it would truly have been the end of this world.

The ascended masters (the highest levels of our consciousness at that time) didn't know what to do to help bring us back into a state of grace. I mean they *really* didn't know what to do. They were children compared to the events that had been forced upon them, and they had no idea how to handle it. So they prayed. They called in higher levels of consciousness. They called in everybody who could hear their plea, including the great Galactic Command. They prayed and prayed. So the problem was reviewed on many high levels of life.

Similar kinds of events have happened before on other planets; this wasn't the first time. So before it actually happened, our ascended masters and galactic friends knew that we were going to fall out of grace, out of the high level of awareness we were experiencing at the time. They knew that we were going to fall way down the spectrum of life. Their concern was to figure out some way to get us back up on track after the fall, and they knew it had to be done quickly. They were looking for a solution that would heal the whole Earth, both the dark and the light. They weren't concerned with a solution where only the Martians would be healed, or only the Lemurians or only *part* of the Earth. They were looking for a situation that would heal the whole Earth and all of its inhabitants.

Higher levels of consciousness don't go along with this "us and them" point of view. There's only *one* consciousness moving through all life, and they were trying to get everybody to come back into a state of love and respect for each other. They knew that the only way they could do it was to get us back into Christ consciousness, a level of beingness where we can see the unity, and they knew we would proceed from there with love and compassion. They knew that if we were going to get back on track, we would have to be in Christ consciousness as a planet by the end of the 13,000-year cycle—which is now. If we were not in Christ consciousness by then, we wouldn't make it at all. We would destroy ourselves. Although spirit is eternal, life interruptions can be temporally lost.

The only problem was that we couldn't get back to Christ consciousness by ourselves, at least in a short time. Once we had fallen to this level it would be a very, very long time before we would be able to come back up naturally. So the problem was really one of time. We were part of a greater consciousness that loved us, and out of love it wished to assist us back into conscious immortality as soon as possible. It would be much like having a child who hit his head real hard, resulting in a concussion. You would want him to return to consciousness quickly.

It was finally decided to try a kind of standard operating procedure that usually works in these situations, though not always. In other words, it was an experiment. Earth's people were about to be subjects of a galactic experimental project in the hope of helping us. We would experiment on ourselves. It wasn't done by extraterrestrials or anything like that; they simply showed us how to do it. We were given instructions on how to proceed with this experiment, and we actually carried it out . . . successfully.

What about the Sirians? Our helpers honestly believed that we would make it, though they knew it would be close. In fact, they wouldn't have gotten permission from the Galactic Command to do the experiment if they hadn't honestly believed we would make it. You can't lie to the Galactic Command.

## A Planetary Grid

At this point, so that you'll understand the procedure they decided on, I

need to talk about grids. A planetary grid is an etheric crystalline structure that envelops the planet and holds the consciousness of any one species of life. Yes, it does have an electromagnetic component associated with the third dimension, but it also has an appropriate higher-dimensional component for each dimension. Science will eventually discover that there's a grid for every single species in the world. There were originally 30 million grids around the Earth, but now there are about 13 to 15 million, and they're decreasing rapidly. If there are just two bugs on the planet, and they're just sitting somewhere in Iowa, they have a grid that stretches around the entire planet, or they couldn't exist. It's just the nature of the game.

Each of these grids has its own geometry and is unique; there's not another one like it. Just as a species' body is unique, its point of view of interpreting the Reality is also unique. The Christ consciousness grid holds the Christ consciousness for the planet, and if that grid isn't there, we can't reach Christ consciousness. This grid was there during Atlantean times, though we were very young, and it was beginning to function at certain times during the precession of the equinoxes. They knew it would be placed into a passive state by the Martians' actions, so they decided to synthetically activate the Christ consciousness grid around the Earth. It would be a living grid, but it would be synthetically made—like creating a synthetic crystal from a living cell of a live crystal. Then at the right time, hopefully before we killed ourselves off, the new grid would be complete, and we could ascend to our previous level once again. One example of the effect of a grid is shown in the hundredth monkey theory.

### The Hundredth-Monkey Concept

You have probably read the book, *The Hundredth Monkey* by Ken Keyes, Jr., or perhaps the earlier book of Lyall Watson, *Lifetide: The Biology of the Unconscious*, who describe a 30-year scientific research project on the Japanese monkey, *Macaca fuscata*. The island of Koshima, Japan, has a wild colony and the scientists were providing them with sweet potatoes dropped in the sand. The monkeys liked the sweet potatoes, but not the sand and dirt. An eighteen-month-old female they named Imo found she could solve the problem by washing the potatoes. She taught this trick to her mother. Her playmates also learned this new way, and they taught their mothers, too. Soon all the young monkeys washed their sweet potatoes, but only the adults who imitated their children learned this behavior. The scientists recorded these events between the years 1952 and 1958.

Then suddenly, in the autumn of 1958, the few monkeys doing this on the island of Koshima reached a critical mass, which Dr. Watson arbitrarily placed at 100, and bingo!—almost every monkey on the island started washing its potatoes without any further influence. If it had happened on only that one island, they probably would have figured there was some form of communication and looked for it. But simultaneously the monkeys on the surrounding islands also started washing their potatoes. Even on the mainland of Japan in Takasakiyama the monkeys were washing their potatoes. There was no possible way these monkeys could have communicated by any way we know. It was the first time that scientists had ever observed anything like this. They postulated that there must have been some kind of morphogenetic structure or field that stretched across these islands through which the monkeys were able to communicate.

### The Hundredth Human

Many people thought a lot about the hundredth monkey phenomenon. Then a few years later a scientific team from Australia and Britain wondered if human beings possessed a grid similar to the monkeys. They did an experiment. They made a photograph that had hundreds of human faces in it, little ones and big ones, faces in the eyes. Everything was made up of these faces, but when you first looked at it, you could see only about six or seven. It took training to see the other ones. Usually someone had to first point out where they were.

These people took their picture to Australia and conducted a study there. They selected a certain number of people from a spectrum of the population, then showed each of them the picture, giving them a certain length of time to look at it. They held the photograph up to someone and said, "How many faces do you see in this photo?" During the time the subjects were given, they would generally come up with six, seven, eight, nine or maybe ten faces. Few people saw more. When they had gotten a few hundred people as their basic sampling and recorded accurately what had been observed, some of the researchers went to England—on the other side of the planet—and showed the picture on a closed-cable BBC television station that broadcasts only to England. They carefully showed where all the faces were, every single face. Then *a few minutes later* other researchers repeated the original experiment with new subjects in Australia. Suddenly people could easily see most of the faces.

From that moment, they knew for certain that there was something about humans that had not been known. Now, the Aborigines in Australia had known about this "unknown" part of us for a long time. They knew that there was an energy field connecting people. Even in our society, we've observed that somebody on one side of the planet would invent something very complex at the same moment that someone on the other side of the Earth invented the same thing, with the same principles and ideas. Each inventor would say, "You stole it from me. It was mine. I did it first." This has happened many, many times, stretching back for a long time. So after this Australian experiment, they began to realize that *something* very definitely connects us all.

### The Government's Discovery of the Grid and the Race for Control

As far back as the early 1960s, the American and Russian governments had discovered these electromagnetic fields, or grids, that stretched around the world. Human grids—yes, there are more than one—are high above the Earth, about 60 miles or more.

Remember, I told you about the five levels of consciousness on Earth that correspond to different numbers of genes and different heights? Well, there are only three levels of consciousness that Earth is actually experiencing right now. Two others are way beyond us at this time. The first level is primal, the second level is our present consciousness, and the third level is the Christ or unity consciousness, the one we're about to enter. After the Fall, about 13,000 years ago, there were only two active human grids around the Earth, the first and the second levels. The Aborigines in Australia were on the first level, for example, and we, the mutants, were on the second level. (That's what they call us—mutants—because we mutated to where we are now.) Science has done very little research on the Australian Aborigines, so our countries haven't become aware of their grid. But the governments did a lot of research on us, and they discovered exactly what our grid looks like: It's based on triangles and squares. It's a very male grid that stretches around the whole planet. Now, we have a third grid up there, which we will call the unity-consciousness grid, or simply "the next step." It's been there, completed, since February 4, 1989. Without that grid, it would be all over for us, folks. But it is there.

The governments became originally aware of our second-level grid maybe as far back as the 1940s. I realize that this statement is in contradiction to what was said above. But nevertheless I believe that the grid was discovered even before the hundredth monkey theory came out. Because of World War II, the governments were beginning to place military bases all over the world in little out-of-the-way places, on obscure islands like Guam. Why did they select these particular places for their bases? It probably wasn't for the reasons they said. When you lay out the grid and the military bases all over the world, especially those of Russia and the United States, well, son-of-a-gun, the bases are *almost always* located right on the nodal points of the grid—exactly over the top or on little spirals that come off of the nodal points. It could not possibly have been a coincidence that they just happened to spread out their empire of military bases in these precise places. They were trying to take control of this grid, because if they could control it, they knew they could control what we think and feel. A subtle war was going on between these two governments. However, the war changed its nature considerably in 1970, though I'll have to explain that later. Of course, behind both the United States and Russia was the secret government, which controlled the outer appearance and timing of this conflict.

## How the Grid Was Constructed, and Where

Now that we have the necessary background, we can continue with the drama in Atlantis. The project to rebuild the grid was begun by three men: Thoth, a being named Ra and a being named Araragat. These men flew to

Note: In the movie *Stargate,* was not given proper †. He was actually one ended masters and a ht, not evil.

107

a place in what is now Egypt, to the area now called the Giza plateau. At that time it was not a desert, but a tropical rain forest, and it was called the Land of Khem, which means the land of the hairy barbarians. The three men went to that particular place because the axis of the old unity-consciousness grid extended out of the Earth from that point. They were going to rebuild a new grid on the old axis, according to instructions given by higher consciousness.

They had to wait until the right moment—until the precession of the equinoxes passed the low ebb in consciousness—before they could act, and this low ebb was still far into their future. After that they would have a little less than half a cycle, about 12,900 years or so, to complete everything by the end of the twentieth century. We couldn't go any longer than this or we would destroy ourselves and our planet.

First they had to complete the grid on the higher dimensions, then they had to physically build the temples in this dimension before the new unity grid would manifest. Once manifested and balanced, they were to help us begin to consciously move into the higher worlds of being and begin anew our path home to God.

So Thoth and friends went to the very spot where the unity-consciousness vortex exited the Earth. This point was about a mile away from where the Great Pyramid sits in the desert today, but then it was out in the middle of nowhere, in the middle of a rain forest. Centered right over the axis of this vortex on the Earth, they created a hole extending approximately one mile into the Earth, lining it with bricks. It took only a few minutes or so, because they were sixth-dimensional beings, and whatever they thought always happened. It was that simple.

Once the hole aligned with the unity axis was created, they mapped the ten Golden Mean spirals that emerged from the hole and located where they moved above the Earth. They used the hole as the axis, starting far down, and mapped the spirals of energy as they moved up out of the hole and extended into space. One of the spirals exited the Earth not far from the present Great Pyramid. Once they found it, they built a little stone building in front of the hole; that building is the key to the entire Giza complex. Then they built the Great Pyramid.

According to Thoth, the Great Pyramid was built by himself, not Cheops. Thoth says that it was completed about 200 years prior to the shifting of the axis. The apex of the Great Pyramid, if the capstone were in place, sat exactly on the curve of the spiral. They lined up the center of the hole with the south face of the stone building and the north face of the Great Pyramid. It has amazed surveyors who have looked at this. Though these structures are a mile away from each other, the south face of the stone building and the north face of the Great Pyramid are in perfect alignment. They do not believe that we could do it any better today even with our modern technology.

Later the other two pyramids were also built directly on that spiral. In fact, that's how the hole was discovered, through aerial photography. They noticed that the three pyramids were laid out on a logarithmic spiral. Then they traced the spiral back to its source and went to that spot, and there was the hole and the stone building. That discovery was made, I believe, in the early 1980s. It was recorded in the McCollum survey that was completed in 1984 by Rocky McCollum.

I've seen the axis hole and the building with my own eyes. I consider it to be the most important place in all of Egypt and so does the Edgar Cayce A.R.E. There's also another hole about a city block away from the first spiral, and this spiral starts out a little differently, but then slowly, asymptotically, superimposes itself over the first spiral. To be able to build around this hole in this spiral pattern, the planners had to have a very sophisticated understanding of life. (I'll explain this understanding later also.) So these two completed spirals defined the axis of what would eventually become the unity-consciousness grid around the Earth.

## Sacred Sites

After starting the new grid over the existing collapsed grid and putting one pyramid on the line of the spiral, Thoth, Ra and Araragat mapped where these two energy lines curved and crossed each other in over 83,000 places on the surface of the Earth. Fourth-dimensionally, one dimension higher than this one, they constructed an entire network of buildings and structures over the whole planet, placing them on the nodes of this energy matrix. All of these structures were laid out with the proportions of either the Golden Mean or Fibonacci spirals, and all were mathematically referred back to that single point in Egypt now called the Solar Cross.

The location of the sacred sites of the world are no accident. It was a single consciousness that created every single one of them—from Machu Picchu to Stonehenge to Zaghouan—you name it, to anywhere. Almost all of them (with a few exceptions) were created by a single awareness. We're becoming more aware of this now. Richard Hoagland's work brings this forth, though he wasn't the first one. They show how one sacred site is extrapolated from another one, then another and still another. These sites go beyond time, in that they were all built at different times, and they go beyond any particular culture or geographical location. They were obviously done by one consciousness who coordinated the whole enterprise. Eventually researchers will see that this spot in Egypt is the point from which all the other sacred sites were calculated.

This Egyptian area is the north pole of the unity-consciousness grid. On the other side of the planet, out in the South Pacific in the Tahitian Islands, is a little island called Mooréa, where the south pole of the grid is located. For those of you who have been on top of Wayna Picchu for a birds-eye view, Machu Picchu, at about 9000 feet in the Peruvian mountains, seems to be surrounded in a perfect circle by mountains. It's like a female circle surrounding a phallus rising in the middle. Well, the island of Mooréa is

similar to this, only it's shaped like a heart. Each house on Mooréa has a heart with the house number on it. The phallic Mooréan mountain in the center of the heart is much bigger than Wayna Picchu in Peru, but you will still see the same ring of mountains surrounding this earthen pole. This is the precise south pole of the entire unity-consciousness grid. If you go straight through the Earth at Mooréa, you come out in Egypt. It's off only an ever so tiny bit—there's a very slight curve, which is natural. The Mooréan pole is negative, or female, and the Egyptian pole is positive, or male. All the sacred sites are connected to the Egyptian pole, and they're all interlinked through the central axis leading to Mooréa. It's a torus, of course.

### The Pyramid's Landing Platform and the Ship beneath the Sphinx

This is the Great Pyramid [Fig. 4-7]. It has a so-called "missing capstone," and there have been all kinds of speculations about it. According to Thoth, the actual missing capstone is 5½ *inches* high and solid gold; it is a holographic image of the entire pyramid. In other words, it has all the little

Fig. 4-7. The Great Pyramid.

rooms in it and everything in proportion, and it's sitting in the Hall of Records. The other two pyramids go up to a sharp point; only the Great Pyramid has a flat surface on top. That missing piece is not little—it's about 24 feet square at the base. If you get on top, it's a huge platform. This flat area is actually a landing platform for a very special airship that exists on Earth.

The Sphinx is not far away from the Great Pyramid. According to *The Emerald Tablets* and Thoth, the Sphinx is much, much older than the 10- to 15,000 years estimated by John Anthony West. One factor that many present researchers have neglected to consider is that the Sphinx has been under sand during most of its recent existence. In fact, when Napoleon went to see the Sphinx, he didn't even know it was there because all he saw was its head. It was completely buried, and it has been buried for most of the last few hundred years at least. Taking that factor into consideration, which could be a major one, the wear caused by rain and wind would have taken a lot longer than they're presently figuring.

According to Thoth, the Sphinx goes back at least five and a half *million* years. I guess eventually that will be brought forth, because he hasn't been

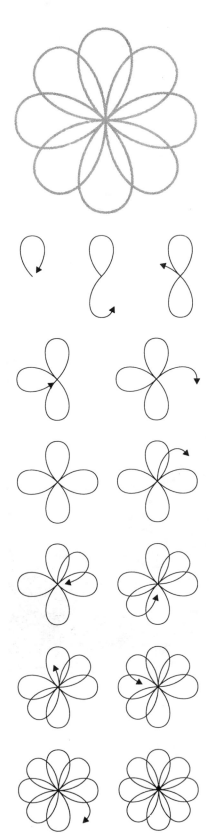

Fig. 4-8. The pattern on the disk beneath the Sphinx.

wrong about anything yet. Even John Anthony West secretly suspects that it is a great deal older than 10- to 15,000 years. He wasn't concerned with making speculations into the millions of years; he just wanted to get it well past the 6000-year mark, because that will crack our previously accepted Earth history. He and his team have now done that, and later, I believe, they'll try to push the date back further as they introduce more evidence.

According to Thoth, approximately one mile under the Sphinx there is a round room with a flat floor and a flat ceiling. Inside this room is the oldest synthetic object in the world—older than any other consciously assembled matter on Earth. According to Thoth, though even he can't prove it, this object goes back 500 million years when "that which led to human life" began. The object is about two city blocks in size; it's round like a disk and has a flat bottom and top. It's unusual in that its skin is only three to five atoms thick. Its top and bottom surfaces have a certain pattern that's shown in Figure 4-8.

The pattern itself is five atoms thick; everywhere else it's only three atoms thick. And it's transparent—you can see right through it—almost like it's not there. This is a ship, but it has no motors or visible form of power. Even though Doreal's interpretation of *The Emerald Tablets* states that this ship had atomic motors in it, according to Thoth it does not. Doreal translated *The Emerald Tablets* in the Yucatan in 1925 and could not understand the description of how the ship was powered. The idea of atomic motors was the farthest-out idea he could think of for a power source. But it is actually propelled by thoughts and feelings, and is designed to connect with and extend your own living Mer-Ka-Ba. This ship is connected directly to the spirit of the Earth, and in *The Emerald Tablets* it's called a warship. It was the protector for the Earth.

## The Vulnerability of This Period and the Appearance of the Heroine

Every single time we reach that vulnerable point in the precession of the equinoxes when our poles make these little shifts, extraterrestrials have tried to take over the planet, according to *The Emerald Tablets*. This has been going on for millions and millions of years, and it's still going on. When I read that in the *Tablets*, I didn't yet know about the Grays or any of these beings, and I thought, "Someone coming from somewhere else to take over the Earth? Naw, this is silly!" But even today, this same thing's going on. It never stops, it just keeps on. It's called, simply, the battle of the dark and the light.

Every single time a takeover seems imminent, there has always been one very pure person who figures out how to get into the next level of consciousness, then finds the ship and raises it into the air. The Earth and the Sun connect within that person and give him or her great power, then whatever that person thinks and feels will happen. That's how this airship is a warship: Whatever races are trying to take over Earth, this person just thinks them away—thinks up a situation that forces them to leave. This keeps our evolutionary process going without any kind of outside interference or influence. At least that's what is *supposed* to happen.

By now we have definitely been tampered with. That pure person has appeared, and that event has already happened here on Earth. This is why the Grays are leaving. The problems they're having is because of one single woman—one 23-year-old female from Peru (she was 23 in 1989 when she did this). She made the first ascension process up to the new grid and connected with it, connected with the Earth, found the ship and raised it into the air. First she made some basic connections that had to be done with crystals on the Earth, then performed the programming that had to be recalculated. The very next thing she did was to *think* that the Grays and others related to this attempted takeover of Earth were going to become sick if they remained here, and there would be no cure.

Within one month, all the Grays started getting sick, and the whole process she envisioned began to happen. The Grays have been forced to leave the Earth now. Their bases have been abandoned, and they have been forced to alter their plans. The presence of this entire army of beings from space has now been reduced to almost nothing, all because of one small but holy woman. It's amazing [chuckles]. We guys know what that's like—I've been reduced to nothing lots of times by my wife.

### Awaiting the Atlantean Catastrophe

Thoth and his partners finished the complex in Egypt to help rebuild the grid. Then they abandoned it in the middle of the rain forest and went back to Atlantis to prepare. It sat alone for 200 years, because they knew that at that critical point in the precession of the equinoxes, the poles would shift. They knew that Atlantis would sink, so they waited.

One day it finally happened. The catastrophe actually took only one night. Science has proven that when poles shift, it takes about 20 hours. It happens just like that [snaps fingers]. You wake up one normal day, and that evening it's a totally different world. The whole process is about three and a half days long, but the pole shift happens in about 20 hours. We're all going to experience this enormous change when we see big chunks of the United States start to drop off into the water—then you'll know it's for sure. There are other early signs that will tip you off that the change is about to happen. When enough information has been given, I'll remind you of what you already hold in your memories.

When they saw the very first signs of the shift coming on, Thoth, Ra and Araragat returned to the Sphinx and raised the warship into the sky. All they did was raise the vibration of the molecules only one overtone higher than the Earth exists on. This allowed them and the ship to pass right through the Earth into the sky. Then they moved to Atlantis, lowered the ship to the surface, and picked up the people of the Naacal Mystery School, which included the original immortals from Lemuria as well as those who became enlightened during the time of Atlantis (by that

time about another 600 people had ascended). So the original thousand from Lemuria and the 600 from Atlantis had increased the number of ascended masters to about 1600, the only occupants of the ancient airship.

Now, the people on this ship were not only passengers, they were creating a living group Mer-Ka-Ba that surrounded the ship with a very large field in the shape of a flying saucer—the same shape that's around the galaxy and around your body when your Mer-Ka-Ba is spinning. They had a very powerful protective field around themselves as they headed for Khem, soon to be the new Egypt. Thoth said that they had risen about a quarter mile off the planet with the members of the mystery school on board when they watched the island of Udal sink. This was the last piece of Atlantis to disappear into the water, with the exception of a few small islands. Then they flew the ship to Egypt and landed it on top of the Great Pyramid. From the side it looked like the middle drawing in Figure 4-9.

If you were to extend the Great Pyramid up to where the capstone

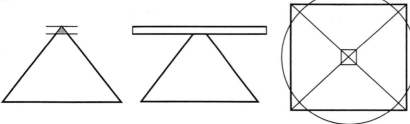

Fig. 4-9. Warship atop the Great Pyramid.

would naturally terminate, you would find that the ship and the pyramid were built for each other. If you were to look at this from the top, it would look like the right-hand view in the figure. The circle is the ship and the square is the Great Pyramid. The perimeter of the Great Pyramid and the circumference of the ship are the same. It's debatable if that's possible or not, but they can get very, very close. Whenever that mathematical relationship happens, life appears. It's the basic relationship of life throughout the universe. (We'll describe this geometrically soon.) If the ascended masters had not had spinning Mer-Ka-Ba fields around them, they wouldn't be here today (and probably neither would we), because their Mer-Ka-Bas protected them from all that happened next.

After they landed on the pyramid, the poles began to shift and the human consciousness of the Earth began to plummet. Simultaneously, the electromagnetic and magnetic fields of the Earth collapsed, and all life on this planet went into the Great Void, the three and a half days of absolute blackness described by many cultures around the world.

### The Three and a Half Days of the Void

*The Emerald Tablets* say that every single time we go around the precession of the equinoxes and our poles go through these changes, we go through a void space for about three and a half days. The Mayas described the Void in the Troano document. At one point in the story, three and a half stones are painted black. This refers to the time when we go into what we now call the *electromagnetic null zone*. As the poles shift, a phenomenon takes place (we'll go into great detail about this later) where for about three and a half days we're in darkness (it could actually be anywhere from two or two and a half days to a little over four days). The last time, it was evidently three and a half days. It's more than just blackness; it's nothing, it's void. And, by the way, when you are in the Void, you will realize that you and God are one, that there is no difference at all. We'll talk about the Void again at the right moment.

### Memory, Magnetic Fields and Mer-Ka-Bas

If the people on the warship hadn't been protected by the Mer-Ka-Ba during that change, they would have completely lost their memories. You see, our memory is held together primarily by a magnetic field that exists around the brain—inside the skull and around the head. That field is further connected to every cell in the brain by individualized magnetic fields within each cell. Science first found the internal magnetic particles within each cell and then found the larger outer field. This was the first new find in human physiology in the last 300 years. Memory is dependent on a steady, living magnetic field, very much like a computer. Its connection to the Earth's magnetic field is not understood by science at this time. If you don't have a means of protecting your memory, it will be erased, gone. It'll be like unplugging a computer in the middle of a file. It's just gone. That's exactly what happened to the Atlanteans and others who survived the catastrophe but who didn't have spinning Mer-Ka-Bas. Those very sophisticated people, who were more advanced than you and I, suddenly found themselves in a situation where they didn't know anything. They had high-tech bodies and high-tech minds, but it was like having a great PC sitting on the table with no software, nothing there.

So the population that survived, and there were a few, had to start all over again. They had to begin at square one to figure out how to stay warm, how to make fire and so on. This loss of memory was the result of their forgetting how to breathe, forgetting their Mer-Ka-Bas, forgetting everything—falling down through the dimensions, going into a totally unprotected state and ending up in this very dense world—having to eat food again, doing all kinds of things that hadn't been part of our experience for a very long time. They were slammed into a very dense aspect of the planet and had to learn to survive all over again. This was all a result of the synthetic Mer-Ka-Ba experiment that had taken place on Atlantis.

Without that small group of ascended masters, we would not have survived at all—we definitely would all have left human experience. The whole Earth experiment would have been over forever. But they kept the field alive, just barely, while everything else crashed around them. Besides the ascended masters, there were also two other groups on Earth who had Mer-Ka-Ba fields intact at the time. The Nefilim and the Sirians, our mother and father, kept their fields alive. I don't know where the Nefilim retreated to within this planet's dimensional worlds, but the Sirians remained in the Halls of Amenti, inside the inner earth. Both of these groups are still here on the planet, hidden within the dimensional worlds.

## What the Thoth Group Did after Light Returned

After the three and a half days of darkness, the Earth reappeared, light reappeared, the fields stabilized themselves, and we were down in this third-dimensional world where we are now. Everything was new and different—everything. It had totally changed experientially. When we consider the landmass of Atlantis, the Atlanteans had really been on a much higher level of interpreting that landmass. They didn't experience it like we do. It was experienced in a totally different way that's pretty hard to explain from our third-dimensional point of view.

After they landed on top of the Great Pyramid, Ra and about a third of the people from the ship went down through a tunnel that goes into a room at the two-thirds level, which will someday be discovered. (They've discovered four new rooms in the Great Pyramid in only the last few years.) When this room is discovered, they'll find that it's made with red, black and white stones, which were the primary architectural colors of Atlantis. This is what Thoth told me to say. From this room is a channel they used to descend to a city or a temple far below the pyramid, which Thoth and friends built when they built the pyramid. It was designed to hold approximately 10,000 people because they knew a large number would ascend over the next 13,000 years, until the Day of Purification.

After the fields stabilized and a third of the people followed Ra into the room made of red, black and white stones, from there they entered the underground city and began the root of our present civilization. Another part of the root was being formed at the same time in Sumer (another story). At the same moment in time, the remaining 1067 or so ascended masters lifted the warship off the Great Pyramid and flew to the place now called Lake Titicaca, where they landed on the Island of the Sun (in Bolivia). Thoth got off there, along with about a third of the people. Then they took off again and flew to the Himalayan mountains, where Araragat got off with the remaining third of the people. Seven people, however, remained with the ship, flew it back to the Sphinx and lowered it into that room, where it has remained for the last 13,000 years—until recently when the young woman from Peru raised it again into the open blue skies of Mother Earth's atmosphere.

## Sacred Sites on the Grid

Egypt became the male component of the grid. That is where the male structures were laid out. There's hardly any femaleness there compared to female areas of the world. Of course, the polarity to maleness does exist—Isis is that counterpart—but the overall energy flow is male. South America, especially Peru, Central America and also parts of Mexico became the female component of the grid. However, ultimately the entire female aspect of the grid became centered at the complex in Uxmal, in the Yucatan, where many survivors from Atlantis had found refuge.

Starting at Uxmal, seven temples are laid out in a spiral, probably a Fibonacci spiral, and they are the seven primary temples of the female component of the grid. These are chakra centers, just like the chakra centers that are laid out down the length of the Nile. These feminine centers begin with Uxmal, then go to Labna, then to Kabah, then over to Chichén Itzá, then over to Tulum near the ocean, then way down near Belize to Kohunlich, curving back inland to Palenque. Those seven places created the primary spiral of the feminine aspect of the grid being created for our new Christ consciousness, which we are only now able to access.

From Palenque the feminine aspect of the grid splits north and south. Here we see another polarization of the energy. The feminine component of the female spiral of the grid heads south and jumps over to Tikal in Guatemala, and that begins a new octave. When we relate it to music, the seventh site bridges to the eighth note, or the beginning of the next octave of the next spiral. And the spiral keeps going south through the feminine component of the grid. Eventually it moves through places like Machu Picchu and Sacsayhuaman near Cuzco, Peru. One of the main spirals ends in a place called Chavín, in Peru, which was the primary religious center of the Incan empire. From there it goes to Lake Titicaca to a place about a half a mile off the Island of the Sun in Bolivia. Then it makes a 90-degree turn and heads out toward Easter Island and finally to Mooréa, where it anchors into the Earth.

Heading north from Palenque is the male component of the female aspect of the grid. It goes through the Aztec ruins and up through the American Indian pyramids. (The American Indians made physical pyramids, some remains of which can be seen in and around Albuquerque, New Mexico.) Then the spiral continues to Blue Lake near Taos, New Mexico, which is the counterpart of Lake Titicaca. This is one of the most important areas in the United States, protected for a long time by the Taos Indians. Again, there's a 90-degree turn at Blue Lake. From there the spiral heads out across the mountains, going through Ute Mountain (on the New Mexico side of the Colorado border) and through many mountains and structures that have been built.

In conjunction with the sacred sites, the creators also used mountains because of their vortex energy. Finally, before the spiral leaves the coast of California, it passes through Lake Tahoe, Donner Lake and Pyramid Lake. From there it goes through underwater mountain complexes until it reaches the Hawaiian Islands, where Haleakala Crater is one of the primary components, then heads south again. It goes through the Hawaiian Island chain that connects for thousands of miles all the way back to Mooréa.

So it's a huge open circle that comes around the Earth, starting at Uxmal and connecting at the south pole of the Christ grid. The feminine component of the grid is a massive circle of complexes. Understand that in between each of the major sites mentioned above are literally hundreds of smaller sites—churches and temples of many religions, sacred sites of nature such as mountain peaks and ranges, lakes, canyons and so on. If you could see the greater plan, you would see how they form perfect spirals, first moving clockwise, then moving counterclockwise until they reach their destination, Mooréa, in the South Pacific.

The pyramids built in the Himalayan mountains were primarily crystalline in nature, meaning they were constructed by using third-dimensional crystals at the corners, aimed to form a pyramid. They built physical pyramids there, too—lots of them. Most of them are not known, though some are. The largest known pyramid in the world so far is in the western mountains of Tibet. It's a solid-white pyramid that's in almost perfect condition, with a huge, solid-crystal capstone. At least two teams of scientists have been there, and it has also been photographed from the air. It's visible only three weeks out of the year when its crystal capstone peers out of the deep snow to view a valley long deserted from human endeavor.

I talked with the leader of the team that went into this pyramid. He said it looks like a brand-new pyramid and that there's nothing written on the walls. It's white, smooth and hard, like marble. When they entered it, they went down a long tunnel, where they found a large room in the center. There's no writing anywhere, no designs, no nothing—except that in the middle, high up on a wall, there is one inscription—the Flower of Life! That's it. If you want to say everything, all you have to do is put that on a wall. That says it all. By the end of this book you'll understand why.

All the sacred sites on Earth, with a few exceptions, were planned on a fourth-dimensional level by higher consciousness, and by now most have third-dimensional counterparts connected to them—in other words, real buildings on real sites. However, there are still some very important sites that have *only* fourth-dimensional structures. Those fourth-dimensional pyramids primarily represent the neutral or child energy of the Christ grid. Altogether there are three aspects of the Christ grid that surround the Earth—Mother, Father and Child. The Father is in Egypt, the Mother is in Peru-Yucatan-South Pacific and the Child is in Tibet.

### The Five Levels of Human Consciousness and Their Chromosomal Differences

According to Thoth, there are five different levels of human consciousness possible here on Earth. These are people who have different DNA, completely different bodies and different ways of perceiving the Reality. Each level of consciousness grows from the last one, until finally on the fifth level humanity learns how to translate into a whole new manner of expressing life, leaving Earth forever.

The primary visual difference between these types is their height. The first-level people are about 4 to 6 feet tall. The second-level people are about 5 to 7 feet tall, where we are at now. Third-level people are about 10 to 16 feet tall, which we are about to translate to. The fourth-level being is about 30 to 35 feet tall, and the last is about 50 to 60 feet. These last two levels are for the distant future.

This may seem strange at first, but do we not begin as a microscopic egg and get larger and larger until we are born? Then we continue to grow taller and taller until we are adults. According to this theory, the human adult is not the end of our growth pattern. We continue through DNA steps until we are 50 to 60 feet tall. Metatron, the Hebrew archangel who is the perfection of what humanity is supposed to become, is 55 feet tall! Remember the giants who lived here on Earth referred to in chapter 6 of Genesis? According to the Sumerian records, they were about 10 to 16 feet tall. When we look at a three-year-old and a ten-year-old, we know that they have different levels of consciousness, and it is primarily by their height that we make this judgment.

According to Thoth, each level of consciousness has different DNA; however, the primary difference is the number of chromosomes. Using this theory, we are now on the second level and have 44 + 2 chromosomes. An example of the first level is certain aboriginal tribes in Australia where they have 42 + 2 chromosomes. On the third level, which we are about to move to, people have 46 + 2 chromosomes. The next two levels have 48 + 2 and 50 + 2, respectively.

We will discuss this in depth in the second volume of this book and show the sacred geometry around this understanding, which will make it clear.

## The Evidence in Egypt for a New Look at History

We're now going to focus on Egypt because Egypt happens to be where the main mystery school was located and where evidence of the different-sized humans, and levels of consciousness, still remain, though generally unrecognized. Egypt was the area they chose where they would ultimately restore our consciousness, and the primary area where survivors from Atlantis and the ascended masters were in one place. We could discuss the history of those other areas, and we will a little, but the focus for this work will be on the Father, because it is through the Father that the primary information of the Mer-Ka-Ba must be remembered.

This is an Egyptian statue of Tiya [Fig. 4-10]. Tiya and her husband Ay were the first two to create a baby by interdimensionally connecting through the sacred tantra, which led to immortality for all three, the father, the mother and the child. You can get a pretty good idea what Lemurians looked like from looking at her. She and her husband are still alive, and they're still on the planet today even after tens of thousands of years. They're two of the oldest beings in the world and two of the most respected of all the ascended masters because of all they've done for human consciousness.

Fig. 4-10. Bust of Tiya.

Fig. 4-11. Abu Simbel.

### Giants in the Land

This is Abu Simbel [Fig. 4-11] in Egypt, which is located at the base of the spine in the chakra system of the masculine aspect of the Christ grid. Notice how very tall these statues are; this was the *actual height* of these beings! Compare it to the size of the tourists near the bottom right in the photo. If these stone folks were to stand up, they would be in that 60-foot range, which indicates that they were at the fifth level of consciousness.

These beings [Fig. 4-12], on a different wall at Abu Simbel, would be about 35 feet tall, representing the fourth level of consciousness. They built rooms for these different heights. This doorway is made for the Venusians—the Hathor race—who are on the third level of consciousness. I'll tell you more about the Hathors later.

These third-level beings [Fig. 4-13] are about 16 feet tall, indicating they are male, as the females of this race are about 10 to 12 feet tall. In their section of the building the rooms are around 20 feet high, with ceilings and beams in proportion to 10- to 16-foot-tall beings. Next to that room, through a little doorway (you can't see it here) that looks like it's

Fig. 4-12. Abu Simbel and the Hathor doorway.

made for us, is a little room with a much lower ceiling. The Egyptians didn't make these statues arbitrarily—they never did *anything* arbitrarily. There isn't a single scratch on a single stone; there is not even one, I believe, that was done unconsciously. There was a reason and a purpose for everything. And usually it was created on many, many different levels. *The Emerald Tablets*, for example, are written on one hundred levels of consciousness. Depending on who you are, you'll understand something utterly and completely different from other people. If you should go through a consciousness change, go back and reread *The Emerald Tablets* again. You won't believe it's the same book, because it'll talk to you in a different way, depending on your understanding.

Fig. 4-13. Inside Abu Simbel; third-level beings.

Fig. 4-14. King and queen on different levels of consciousness.

These are Earth beings [Fig. 4-14] passing through the various levels of consciousness. In this photo you see a huge 55-foot-tall being with a statue our size standing by his leg. This is the king and queen. Archaeologists don't know how to interpret this, so they just say that the kings were more important than the queens, and that's why they made her little. But it didn't have anything to do with that. The statues are showing the five levels of consciousness. Every king and pharaoh who ever lived in Egypt had five names, representing the five levels of consciousness.

Some of the kings and queens were able to translate between the different levels in order to guide the population into the spiritual realms. One special example of this still exists. In Egypt there's an ancient round house. I didn't get to see it, but it was described to me by the famous archaeologist, Ahmed Fayhed, so I know it's real. This was Ay and Tiya's house for a long time (though they're obviously not using it now). This round house has a wall down the middle. You can't get from one side of the house to the other without going outside, walking around, and coming in the other side. Does this sound like the island of Udal in Atlantis? On one side of the middle wall is a picture of Ay, who looks very Egyptian with his angled skirt, beard and various Egyptian paraphernalia. He appears of normal height. On the other side of the wall Ay's image is about 15 feet tall. He looks very different, but you can see that his face is the same. He has a huge skull going way back like the higher-level races do (I'll show you some soon). These two pictures of Ay show that he could go back and forth between these two different levels of awareness by changing consciousness.

## Stair-Step Evolution

According to Melchizedek knowledge, both the Sumerians and the Egyptians emerged onto the surface of the Earth at almost the same moment, complete, whole and perfect, with their language totally intact, with all their skills and understanding and knowledge, with almost no evolution prior to that time (at least none that science knows of). They simply appeared at one moment in history in their most perfect state. The writing that came out at that moment was extremely sophisticated and clear, and has never been improved on since. After that initial impulse, these cultures became less and less clear, until finally these advanced civilizations degenerated away. You would think they would get better and more sophisticated as time advanced, but that's not what happened. This is scientific fact. No one in conventional archaeology knows how this happened or can even explain how it *could* have happened. It's a great mystery.

Egypt and Sumer are placed into a special category called *stair-step evolution* by archaeologists. They were given this classification because of how they seemed to gain information and knowledge. What happened was, one day Egypt got its language, full and complete, then that knowledge leveled off; then a little while later they would know everything you could possibly imagine about, perhaps, building a certain kind of moat or water system. A little more time would go by, and then they would suddenly know everything about hydraulics. It would keep going on and on like that. How did the Egyptians and the Sumerians get this information? How did they suddenly, in one day, know everything? I'll give you Thoth's answer.

First I need to make this clear on the precession drawing, repeated below [Fig. 4-15]: Point A is where we are now, and point C is when the fall of Atlantis happened. Point C is also when the poles shifted; science has determined that's when it happened. That's also when the Great Flood of Noah happened, and the melting of the icecaps because of all the changes that were occurring on Earth. Point C is when the destruction occurred. Remember, I mentioned earlier that there were two other points, B and D, when change could also take place and be assimilated most easily. For a 6000-year time span, from point C where the destruction happened to point D where new teachings could be given, the ascended masters had to sit and wait while the Atlanteans, who were now hairy barbarians in Egypt, slowly returned to the state where they could accept this new, yet ancient, knowledge. These approximately 1600 ascended masters had been living under the Great Pyramid since the Fall, and they had to wait 6000 years before they could start teaching and building the new culture.

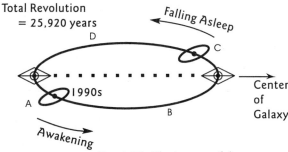

Fig. 4-15. The journey of the precession.

### The Tat Brotherhood

Thoth's son Tat remained in Egypt with Ra after the Fall. Later this group became known as the Tat Brotherhood. Even today there's an external brotherhood in Egypt called the Tat Brotherhood, physical people who are the protectors and keepers of the sacred temples. Hidden behind the current Tat Brotherhood are the ascended masters.

So the immortal aspect of the Tat Brotherhood sat there waiting and waiting, observing and waiting, until the time when the Egyptians could receive their teachings. When that day finally came, which was the birth of Sumer and Egypt, the Tat Brotherhood watched until they found either a person or a group of Egyptians who were ready for the ancient knowledge. Then one, two or three members of the Brotherhood appeared in bodies looking just like the people they were about to teach. They would go up to the surface, approach the person or group and give them the information outright. They flat-out said, "Hey, look at this. Did you know that if you did this and this and this, that *this* is what will happen?" The Egyptians would say, "Wow, look at that!" They would use the knowledge, thus creating a new "step" in their evolution.

Then the men and women from the Brotherhood would go back under the pyramid, the Egyptians who were given these teachings would give it to the rest of the culture, and the culture would quickly ascend to the next step. The Egyptians would assimilate that for a while; then the Brotherhood would look for another group that was ready for the next subject. They'd go to the surface again and say, "Look, here's everything you want to know about this." They simply gave it to them. The ascended masters gave the people this information over a short period of time and their evolution simply shot up and up in stair steps.

### The Parallel Evolution in Sumer

This same evolutionary pattern was also occurring in Sumer. Though the present historical line says that Egypt began in approximately 3300 B.C. and Sumer began 500 years earlier, in about 3800 B.C., I believe they both started at almost the same moment. I think that if historians would get their dates accurate, they'd discover that both Sumer and Egypt started only a few years apart. However, the evolution in Sumer was led by the Nefilim, the mother aspect, and the one in Egypt was led by the Sirians, the father aspect. That's the primary difference. I think the mother and the father agreed, "Now is the time for our children to remember." I believe it was a parental decision, and that when researchers look very carefully, they'll find that both countries started to blossom at the same moment in time, which was tied to the point in the precessional orbit (point D) when it was most likely to be successful.

This is also how the Sumerians knew about the precession of the equinoxes. It takes 2160 years to recognize that there is a precession of the equinoxes, but the reason the Sumerians knew about it was because the Nefilim said, "Do you know there's a precession of the equinoxes?" Very simple. It's not a complicated thing. They just explained it all and the people wrote it down. The Sumerians knew about events that went back 450,000 years because they were given the information. They simply wrote it down and applied it.

But after these ancient cultures got all this brilliant information, they degenerated. Why would they degenerate instead of going higher? Because they were in the *sleep* cycle, the "falling asleep" portion of the precession. They were falling more and more asleep with each breath, right into the kali yuga, the most asleep moment of the cycle. In the middle of the kali yuga—2000 years ago—was the time of Jesus, and humans were sound asleep and snoring. People in the kali yuga who read books and other studies written in the earlier, more-awake period had a difficult time fully understanding what was being written about. Why? Because they were relatively unconscious. This is why cultures all over the world, not just in Egypt and Sumer, degenerated until they ceased. Right now we are about to awaken fully and know the truth of our beingness.

## Well-Kept Secrets in Egypt, Key to a New View of History

This is Saqqara [Fig. 4-16]. According to the linear archaeological belief, this is where the Egyptian culture began. This pyramid was the first to be built in Egypt, by their way of thinking. When it was first created, it was covered with beautiful white stones. In fact, this whole city stretches for miles and miles and into the Earth hundreds of feet, including buildings and complexes *under* the ground. This would have been amazing if you could have seen it when it was brand new—especially since only a short time in history before it was built, we were supposedly all hairy barbarians. There was a jump from hairy barbarians to this supersophisticated culture in only a second of archaeological time.

This is a pyramid [Fig. 4-17] that I think destroys the belief that Saqqara is where it all began. This pyramid is at least 500 years older than Saqqara. If this is true, the time when the Egyptians emerged on the Earth is identical to the time the Sumerians emerged— which I believe is exactly what happened. This pyramid is called Lehirit (a phonetic spelling), and it's one of the few unguarded pyramids in this category. There are quite a few of these stepped pyramids, called *mastabas*. The Egyptians have taken almost all

Fig. 4-16. The pyramid at Saqqara.

Fig. 4-17. The pyramid that destroys the Saqqara theory. One of the two flat blocks in foreground has a carved Star of David inside a circle (✡).

these pyramids that approach or exceed 6000 years of age and put military bases and huge electrical fences around them. In some cases they've got soldiers on guard with machine guns. If you try to approach these pyramids, they would probably try to kill you. They don't want anyone to know about these pyramids, and they especially don't want you to examine them. If you try to talk to an Egyptian about them or ask to see them, they play it down.

I went through this. They would say, "Aw, it's not important. They're just made out of little adobe bricks by primitive people. They're nothing, nothing to them." And I'd say, "Well, can I go see one?" "Nah, it's just a waste of time. Don't do it." I had to keep pushing and pushing because I wanted to see one. I was brought in to various governmental offices, and I kept saying, "Please, can I just go see one?" And they would say, "No, no, no." Finally I had to give bribes to get into these places. One government official wanted $8,000 to sneak me in there at night without any cameras, just to look at it for fifteen minutes, then get away. This is how closely they protect these structures.

Finally, after a long ordeal, I found out about one of these pyramids that was not on a military base because there was a little village around it about a half an hour from Saqqara. Once I realized that I didn't have to go through any government red tape, I finally found a person who was connected with that village. I had to pay him a lot of money—it wasn't thousands, but it was hundreds—to go there. So we drove into the little village; I had to go to the leader to ask permission and pay *him* money, too. Then I was allowed to go there for thirty minutes but not take any pictures. I managed to get this one photograph, and that was all.

Not only was this pyramid there, but *there were pyramids all over the place everywhere,* for what I estimated to be ten miles around! At one time this was a major complex. They're not doing anything to take care of it because they know that this pyramid is probably older than 6000 years. So I found out that these "unimportant" pyramids were not so unimportant after all. The stones that covered this pyramid, like the slanting ones shown in Figure 4-17, probably weigh 60 to 80 tons apiece. They were very sophisticated even though the internal part of the pyramid was made with adobe bricks.

On top of a block beside the base was a circle with a Star of David—the key to the Mer-Ka-Ba experience. A ramp goes down maybe 200 feet to the river below, and the pyramid is still working, still functioning—it's pumping water. Pyramids pump water; they've demonstrated this in the United States now. If you build a pyramid right, it'll pump water with no moving parts. So this pyramid fills up with water and has to be pumped dry before anyone can enter.

To top all this off, I just happened to sit next to an American linguistics team when I was flying back home (pure luck, of course), who happened to have just entered this pyramid! Very few people can go in there, but this was a team of 30. He told me about the writing inside that was definitely older than Saqqara. There is geometrical writing all over the walls. I would *love* to see that. This guy was very excited as he told me that this team of 30 linguistics experts who got to see the inside now believe that *the key to all languages in the world* is in that pyramid. I believe he's probably correct. He understood sacred geometry, and as you will soon discover, sacred geometry is the root of all language in the universe.

F I V E

# Egypt's Role in the Evolution of Consciousness

## Introduction to Some Basic Concepts

### Egyptian Tools and Symbols of Resurrection

The ancients used certain symbols to represent the three aspects of consciousness we use for our sojourn here on Earth. You'll see representations of these symbols all over the world. These depictions have one animal that lives underground, one that walks on the Earth, and one that flies over the Earth. The animal that lives under the ground represents the microcosm; the one who flies through the air represents the macrocosm; and the one who walks the Earth represents the middle level between the two—like us. The same symbols are everywhere. In Egypt you'll see a vulture on the left, the right eye of Horus in the middle, then a cobra on the right [Fig. 5-1]. In Peru it's the condor, the puma and the rattlesnake. For the American Indians it's the eagle, the mountain lion and the rattlesnake. In Tibet it's a chicken, a pig and a snake.

Fig. 5-1. Symbols representing the three aspects of consciousness.

Fig. 5-2. Tools of resurrection.

Fig. 5-3. Geometric images from the Old Kingdom.

This photo [Fig. 5-2] shows the tools and symbols of resurrection the Egyptians used. The object at point A is a shortened form of a rod that's usually about four feet long and has a little tuning fork on one end and a 45-degree angle on the other end. This was used at the back of the head to transfer vibration into the body. Along with that they used the hook and the flail, which we'll see in just a moment. Arrow B points to the oval, which is usually a red-orange color, that you see over the initiates' heads. This was the symbol for the metamorphosis that happens when we go through resurrection or ascension, when we literally change the shape and chemistry of our body.

Arrow C shows a power generator they sometimes use to increase the vibration. Unfortunately, Thoth left before I could fully understand the use of this object. Arrow D indicates the ankh, which I understand more, and I'll give you my understanding. It's the most important tool of understanding they possessed. From an Egyptian point of view, it's the key to eternal life. Arrow E points to a triangle within a triangle, which is the Egyptian hieroglyphic for the star Sirius, the symbol for Sirius A and Sirius B. Point F is just a name, called a cartouche. The bird at the top right is a vulture, which is sacred to the Egyptians and associated with the movement from one level of consciousness to another. I'm not going to go into the other things in the picture, but these are some of the tools the early Egyptians used.

### The Difference between Dying, Resurrection and Ascension

These geometric images [Fig. 5-3] come from the Old Kingdom. The little Flower of Life patterns are associated with Lehirit—the pyramid that I believe destroys the Saqqara theory.

Figure 5-4 is a picture of Osiris (on the left). He's holding a crook (A); a 45-degree rod with a tuning fork on the end (B); and a flail (C), which are the three primary instruments used for resurrection. These tools were connected with resurrection, not ascension. There's a difference between the two. What is the difference? First of all, there's dying, a process where you go into the void state immediately after death. You're unconscious, unaware of the dying process to the degree that you have no control over the images. This way of dying takes you into the third overtone of the fourth dimension, which results in your cycling back into this Earth existence again and again—reincarnation. Because you're unconscious in this cycle, you're not using your Mer-Ka-Ba except unconsciously, so once you get to the other side, you don't have any memories of this side. When you reincarnate back to Earth again, you don't have any memories of where you just came from, either. So the reincarnating just keeps going on and on. It's a lot of energy moving very slowly. You eventually get through it, but it's a very slow process.

When you go through resurrection, you're aware and conscious of your Mer-Ka-Ba, though usually you don't become fully aware of it until after you die. You die, you drop the body and *then* you become aware of your Mer-Ka-Ba. Then you re-create your body and go through a process that leads you into either the tenth, eleventh or twelfth overtone of the fourth dimension. From there you don't go through reincarnation anymore. Your memory is never blocked again and you continue on into eternal life.

There's a big difference between dying and resurrection, but there's an even greater difference in ascension—which is now possible, since the grid was completed in 1989. Ascension was highly unlikely until this grid was complete. In ascension you don't die at all; there's no death process involved as we know it. Of course, it is true that you no longer are on Earth, and from that point of view, you die. What happens is, you simply become aware of your Mer-Ka-Ba one way or another—either remembering it on your own, being taught it or however it happens to you. This means you become aware of your body as light. Then you're able to pass through the Void totally consciously—from the Earth side through the Void to the higher dimensions, aware the whole time. In this way you simply walk out of this life without going through the death process, which involves reconstructing your human body. When a person ascends, he/she simply disappears from this dimension and reappears in the next, passing through the Void.

Ascension is now completely possible, and this book is one possible set of instructions on exactly how to accomplish this process. You personally might not pass through ascension; you might actually die or go through resurrection. It doesn't make much difference at this point in the game of life on planet Earth, because if you die in the normal manner, you'll go into the third overtone and into a holding pattern for a while. Then when the rest of the Earth cycles through this coming change, all people on that third

Fig. 5-4. Resurrecting Osiris.

overtone will also rise to the same dimensional level as those who resurrected or ascended. Even the Bible refers to this, saying that at this time the dead will rise. There is no such thing as death; there are just different states of being. It's a little like water, which can be a liquid, solid (ice) or gas (fog), but it is still water.

Right now very few human reincarnations are occurring on Earth except under certain conditions. This is probably your last life, folks—this is it! Of course, there are exceptions to almost all rules, so there may be a few on this Earth who have decided to reincarnate. Time is running out. If we make it to the end of this century, I'll be amazed. I seriously doubt if the third dimension will still be available for human life by that time. Only God knows for certain. Where are the people coming from who are being born on Earth today? Not from here! I'll explain when I talk about the new children.

### When the Sun Rose in the West

As Egypt began to evolve, it developed into two countries, Upper Egypt and Lower Egypt. Upper Egypt was south and Lower Egypt was north. Egyptians named Upper and Lower Egypt in this sort of reverse way of thinking because in their earlier life as a country during Atlantis, the Earth was rotating in the opposite direction and the magnetic poles were reversed. Our present north was then south and vice versa. Not only did the poles shift their position after Atlantis, but the Earth actually rotated in the opposite direction. Thoth said that he's gone through five pole shifts: He's seen the Sun rise in the east and he's seen it rise in the west, then in the east, the west and again the east—five times!

Fig. 5-5. The Egyptian zodiac, shown flowing in the opposite direction even though this depiction was done in the present age.

On the ceiling of the temple at Dendera, which is the heart chakra of the male aspect of the Christ grid, is an astrological zodiac that demonstrates this reversed polarity. The zodiac rotates in the opposite direction, as if the Sun rose in the west instead of the east [Fig. 5-5]. The River Nile flows from south to north, whereas almost all the other rivers in the world flow from north to south. This indicates to me that the Egyptians held onto the older energy flow even in the Earth.

We are the creators of our universe. People involved in Sufism may remember Sufi Sam, also known as Murshid Sam Lewis. He was buried—in the early '70s, I believe—at the Lama Foundation in New Mexico. There's a plaque over his grave that reads: "On that day the sun will rise in the west, and all men seeing will believe." He was referring to the time that's coming. When the poles shift this next time, there will be a reversal of the Earth's rotation, thus the way we move in relation to the Sun.

## Osiris, the First Immortal

Prior to Egypt, during Atlantis, existed the Naacal Mystery School headed by Ay and Tiya and a thousand members from Lemuria. It was located on the island of Udal, north of the mainland. They were trying to teach the Atlanteans how to become immortal. The only thing is, either they weren't very good teachers then, or the people just couldn't get it, because it took 20- to 30,000 years before one person finally achieved the immortal state of being. The first person to make it was Osiris, who was not Egyptian, but Atlantean. The story of Osiris didn't happen in Egypt, even though it talks about the Nile, but in Atlantis. Though most of you know this story, I'll tell it anyway, in a condensed form.

There were two brothers and two sisters from the same family. Their names were Isis, Osiris, Nephthys (or Nefus) and Set. Isis married Osiris and Nephthys married Set. At the point where this story begins, Set killed Osiris. He put Osiris' body in a box and floated it down the Nile, though it was really another river in Atlantis. This killing disturbed Isis, and she and her sister, Set's wife, went out to look for Osiris. They found his body and brought it back, intending to bring Osiris back to life. When Set found out, he cut Osiris' body into fourteen pieces and spread them all over the world so that his sisters could not bring him back to life. Isis and Nephthys then went out looking for these pieces to put him back together. They found thirteen of the fourteen and assembled the pieces, but they never found the phallus, the fourteenth piece. It was Thoth (who was in Atlantis as well as Egypt) who, through magic, restored the fourteenth piece. This restored the creative energy flow, brought Osiris back to life and, in addition, gave him immortality.

From the Egyptian point of view, it was through sexual energy that immortality was reached. (Remember, it was through sexual energy, tantra, that immortality took root in Lemuria.) I'm going to leave the last element of this story until another appropriate moment, because a certain understanding needs to come first. But notice that Osiris was first alive, walking around in a body in the first level of consciousness. Then he was killed and his body was cut into pieces. He was separated from himself—this was consciousness level two, our level. Then his pieces were brought back together and he was made whole again, which put him into the third level of consciousness, which is immortality.

He went through three levels of consciousness. The first one was whole, the second one was separated from itself, and in the third level all the components were brought back together. This made him whole again and also made him immortal; he would no longer die. When Osiris finally got through all this, he came back as an immortal being, the first resurrected master of Atlantis. So they used Osiris's understanding of how he became immortal as the template for how other people could reach the same state of consciousness. This became the religion of Atlantis and later on the religion of Egypt.

## The Transpersonal Holographic Memory of the
## First Level of Consciousness

Atlanteans, because of the way their brains functioned, had complete memory. They remembered everything that had ever happened to them. And their memory was *transpersonal*, which means that anything one person remembered, the others in their race could remember. The Aborigines in Australia have this type of memory right now. When anything happens to one Aborigine, any other can reexperience it anytime he or she wants. If an Aborigine were to walk into this room right now, he or she would in effect be giving the experience to all of their race anywhere on the planet.

You see, they're on the first level of consciousness where they're not separated from themselves. We're on the second level and are very separated from ourselves. Like the Atlanteans, Aborigines don't have memory like our vague kind of recollection; they have full-tilt 3D holographic memory. They could reconstruct this room moment by moment through the entire workshop, and all the rest of them could walk around in here and look at it. They could walk up to your table and look into your eyes. It wouldn't be real time; it's what they call Dreamtime, like in a dream, but it's an absolute replica of the Reality. Their memory is perfect; they don't have any mistakes or flaws. Obviously, in that kind of culture the Atlanteans had no reason to write anything down. Why try to describe something with words when you've got the real thing?

They didn't need it; however, the Martian aspect did need it, so they had a written language. Even after the Fall, the Egyptians (and others) had an amazing ability to remember. At that point they had lost their holographic and transpersonal memory, but they still had *photographic* memory. When the mystery school students were doing the complicated kind of training we'll be doing soon, they could do it all in their head. With our less efficient memory, we cannot do this in the same way they did; we have to struggle just to remember someone's name. The complexity will increase as we progress, making it difficult to remember from photo to photo, but the ancient ones could do this completely in their head. There is something about doing this in your head that's important, so later I'm going to show you some illustrations that will assist you to do this yourself.

This experience holds a primary key for understanding the nature of creation. Re-create the illustrations that follow as if you were actually in the Void moving through the geometrical movements. Experiencing it gives you the understanding that the circles on the page represent actual movements, and that these geometrical movements of spirit in the Void are the beginning and end of creation.

## The Introduction of Writing, Which Created
## the Second Level of Consciousness

*The Forty-Two Books of Thoth* record that after the Fall, when the Atlanteans got into Egypt and were no longer experiencing full memory, writing was introduced. In fact, it's written right in the Egyptian records that it was Thoth who introduced writing to the world. This one act completed the "fall" and threw us out of the first level of consciousness and fully into the second, because it changed the way we accessed memory. It sealed our fate.

This act of learning how to write caused us to grow the top half of our skull from our eyebrows up. The simple act of introducing writing changed many factors in the way we perceive our Reality. To get at our memory now, we have to go in and pull out the desired information with a code. We go in with a word or a concept to bring back the memory of whatever it is. In fact, we can't even remember something without having certain eye movements. Our eyes have to move in certain ways in order for the memories to flow out. The Egyptian memory system was vastly different from the way it was before the Fall. Comparing this change of memory to the Osiris saga, the Egyptians had entered the stage where they were in separate pieces, where they were inside their bodies, thinking they were separate from the rest of Reality. This feeling of being separate was, of course, destined to change many aspects of how human beings live.

### The Roadblock of Polytheism: Chromosomes and Neters

Now the plot thickens. Things were going well with the stair-step evolution plan. After a while Upper and Lower Egypt combined into one country under King Menes and the First Dynasty began. But as time went on, a serious problem developed which, if it had not been solved, would have caused major catastrophes for us in the twentieth century—in fact, we would not have survived as a planet. We wouldn't have had a chance. It seems like a not-so-important thing, but it was very important for some who watch over this planet. It had to do with the religious beliefs of the Egyptians.

As I said, the Egyptians no longer had full holographic transpersonal memory anymore, so they had to write down what their religion was. This writing is called *The Forty-Two Books of Thoth*. Donald Beaman, who lives in Boston, is the man who reconstructed this book. There were 42 books, with two more books set aside from the main body. Forty-two plus two represents the number of chromosomes of the first level of consciousness. Your chromosomes, as you are about to see, are geometric images and patterns that describe the entire Reality—not just your body, but *everything* in the Reality, from the most distant planet to the smallest plant and every single atom.

Inside his book you'll see what are called *neters*. Neters are gods, with a small *g*. This is one of the neters—Anubis [Fig. 5-6]. They are mythical human beings with animal heads, and each one represents a different chromosome, a different aspect and characteristic of life. Neters represent the pathway of how to go from the first to the second level of consciousness. The ascended masters used Osiris' particular genetic coding to help other

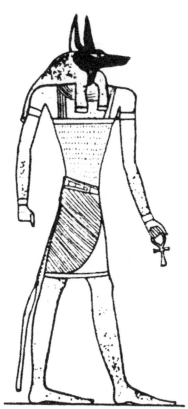

Fig. 5-6. The neter Anubis.

people learn how to ascend. In other words, Osiris had lived the experience of ascension, and now the pathway was in his DNA, specifically the chromosomes. The genetic keys were then opened to the initiate through the neters, who represented Osiris' chromosomes.

But a problem developed from this way of representing their religion, especially as Upper and Lower Egypt again became more separated. Both Lower *and* Upper Egypt had 42 + 2 gods, or neters, representing these stages. But Upper Egypt had images slightly different from those of Lower Egypt; the images had changed over time when the two countries were separate. When Menes put the two countries together as a single country called Egypt, in order to be politically correct he adopted all these images. So now they had 84 + 4 gods representing the same religious ideas. That was probably a big mistake, because it got very confusing. For instance, in one area they would take one of the neters like Anubis and say, "This is God," with a big G. Another area would say, "Isis is God," and another area would claim Sekhmet to be their God.

So then there were 88 different ideas of God in the country. They would say, "My God is *the* God, and your gods are wrong." It became very separated and occult, and after a while no one had any idea that there really was only one God. They didn't understand what the Tat Brotherhood was trying to tell them. From our American point of view, this would be like a chromosome breakage; it was a mutation, and it was not correct. Even with all the help from the Tat Brotherhood, they just couldn't get it right, and it got worse and worse.

All the evidence I've seen indicates that the Christian religion came directly out of the Egyptian religion. If you study both of them, they're parallel in every single way *except* for the Egyptians' understanding of God. The Christian religion came back later and totally discounted the Egyptian religion, even though Egypt is the probable source of the origins of Christianity. The Christians saw the Egyptians as being occult. And they were, but it was because their religious belief had become corrupted, with the clear exception of 17½ years during the Eighteenth Dynasty.

## The Rescue of Human Consciousness

### Akhenaten's Life: A Brilliant Flash of Light

For a very short period of 17½ years, a brilliant flash of light appeared, then disappeared again. And that brilliant flash of white light is what saved our spiritual lives. It began in approximately 1500 B.C., when the worshiping and arguing over so many gods was prevalent. The ascended masters finally decided that something must be done. Finally they chose a plan. Thoth told me the following story.

As the first step, they decided to bring in an actual Christ-conscious being in an actual Christ-conscious body so we could put back into the akashic records the memory of what Christ consciousness was all about. It had been lost in the Fall. This Christ-conscious body would be much taller than those on the planet at the time. This would be an example for the Earth people to see. That was the first part of the plan. It was a very bold step, and they did it.

The ascended masters had decided that the Christ-conscious person should become king of Egypt. In order to do this, they had to break all the rules, and I mean all of them. What they did was approach the king of that period, Amenhotep II, and ask him for a favor. Thoth simply walked into the room physically, went right up to him and said, "Look, I'm Thoth," which I'm sure was difficult for the king to believe. By that time the Egyptians probably thought that all those neters in their stories were mythical. Yet here's a real person standing there who was one of the neters. Thoth said, "We have a serious problem here in Egypt, and I need your help."

Thoth somehow got Amenhotep II to do something that no Egyptian king would ever do. Amenhotep's son was about to become king, and Thoth said, "I want your son to *not* become king; I want to put an outside lineage onto the Egyptian throne." Amenhotep II agreed to it. It must have been a pretty profound experience. I don't know what Thoth did—he probably came in glowing or levitating or something like that. But he did something to convince the king that it was necessary. Once they received the king's permission, they had to actually create the living body, which was not easy.

### Creating the Bodies of Akhenaten, then Nefertiti

So how did they do this? They went to Ay and Tiya—who were very, very old, no matter how you look at it—and said, "We would like you to have a baby." They had to go to someone who was immortal to get the immortal genes, because they have a different chromosome count—46 + 2 instead of 44 + 2. Ay and Tiya agreed, and they had a little baby. The baby was given to Amenhotep II to become the next king.

So the little baby grew up and became king. He became Amenhotep III, who then mated; I am not sure if it was physically or interdimensionally, and I don't know who it was, but he would almost have *had* to mate with someone who had the higher chromosome levels. Anyway, their baby boy became known as Amenhotep IV, and that baby was the one they had special plans for. That baby, Amenhotep IV, has a more popular name, which you know as Akhenaten.

Meanwhile Ay and Tiya waited a generation and then had another baby. That baby was a little girl whose name was Nefertiti. Nefertiti grew up with Akhenaten, and then they married. They were really brother and sister because they had the same bloodline. The Osiris story is similar—brother and sister marrying and becoming a new possibility in life. So these two people grew up and became the king and queen of Egypt.

## The New Rulership and the One God

For a while Amenhotep III and his son Akhenaten ruled the country together—two kings at the same time, again breaking the rules. Meanwhile they built a brand new city called Tel el Amarna in the exact center of Egypt. We still don't know how they got it in the exact center. Akhenaten put a stone there that says, "This is the center of the country." Today we could not have done it better from a satellite. It makes you wonder who these people were who could locate right down to the square inch the center of a country hundreds of miles long. It's pretty amazing. They built an entire city out of white stones. It was beautiful—it was space-age.

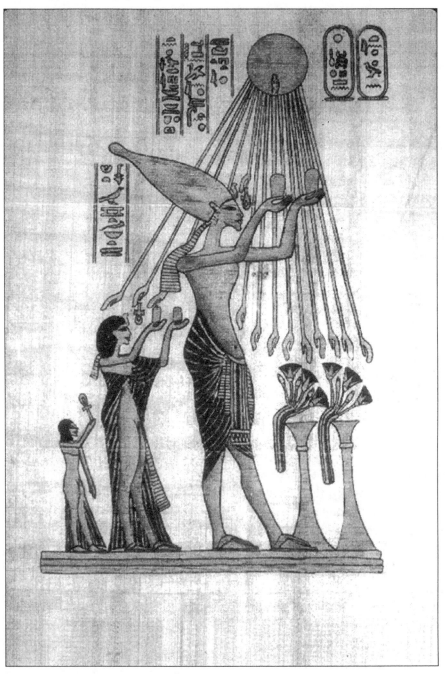

Fig. 5-7. Akhenaten teaching about God, a copy of the carving in Fig. 5-8.

Akhenaten and his father ruled the country simultaneously from two places for a while—from Thebes and from Tel el Amarna. The father resigned the throne while he was still alive—which again breaks the rules—and gave the country to Akhenaten, who then became the first pharaoh of Egypt. There were no pharaohs before Akhenaten, only kings. Pharaoh means *that which you will become*. In other words, they were showing the people what they would literally become in the future. Akhenaten, Nefertiti and their children were not exactly human.

This tall figure [Fig. 5-7] is Akhenaten. I'm going to talk about this picture for a moment. Akhenaten's main purpose was to break up all the occult religions and bring the country back to a single religion where they believed that there was simply one God. At that time all the people were worshiping statues, so they were used to believing in things. Akhenaten had to give them something to see to believe in, so he gave them the image of the Sun as God, because this image was something they couldn't stick on their altars again.

There was another reason he gave them the image of the Sun. He told them that the breath of life, the prana field, came from the Sun. This is true in terms of third-dimensional thinking, though prana is really anywhere and everywhere—there are infinite amounts of it at any point. Since prana also comes from the Sun, this image shows the Sun's rays coming down; and on two of the rays are little ankhs, which the rays are holding up to the nose, to the breath, showing that eternal life is through the breath.

In this same picture you also see the lotus, the national flower of Atlantis. It was the Naacals who brought the lotus to India. The Naacals are written about in Indian Sanskrit writings and are talked about even in modern times. They came long before Buddha and were there during Buddhist times. In Egypt the lotus flower represented Atlantis, and in this picture you see them out of the vases. Everyone knew that Atlantis was dead, but they were still paying homage to it by having the lotuses out of the vase. Figure 5-8 is the original wall carving.

Notice that Akhenaten, the main figure, has a long, skinny neck, skinny hands, a high waist, wide thighs and skinny legs. The usual Egyptian explanation is that he had a disease and was deformed—of course, so was Nefertiti and all their daughters. (Evidently they all had the same disease.) I believe something very different.

### The Reign of Truth, Which Depicts a Different Genetics

Besides making the religions monotheistic again, Akhenaten also said, "In this new religion we're not going to have any more lying, no more untruthfulness. And we're going to change our art so that it reflects the total truth." So during the Eighteenth Dynasty—never before nor after—there was a totally unique art form. The artists were instructed to sculpt or paint things just as their eyes saw it, like a photograph. So began an art that looked realistic instead of stylized, as it had been before. You see ducks that look like ducks [Fig. 5-9], just like we see in modern art. This is important to remember when you're looking at art of the Eighteenth Dynasty, because that means that whatever you see is exactly what the artist saw. They were not allowed to lie.

Fig. 5-8. Akhenaten teaching about God, original carving.

Fig. 5-9. Truth in ducks.

Fig. 5-10. Maat, the neter of truthfulness.

This issue about truth was taken to such an extreme that they were not even allowed to wear clothes, because wearing clothes was hiding, and that was a form of lying. No one was allowed to wear clothes during the Eighteenth Dynasty except for ceremonial and other special purposes.

This neter's name is Maat [Fig. 5-10]. That's a feather on top of her head. She became one of the most important neters in this new religion because of her name, which translates as *truth* or *truthfulness*. She was the important issue in everything. Everything was to be absolutely truthful, and there were to be no distortions, no lies, so that everything could get back into focus. This was an important part of Akhenaten's teachings.

This is a statue of Akhenaten in the Cairo Museum [Fig. 5-11]. Akhenaten was 14½ feet tall, not counting his headdress. When I stood next to this, the top of my head came up to the widest part of his hips. Nefertiti was ten feet-something. She was actually small for her race. The daughters were also very tall. This is according to Thoth. Hard evidence of this has recently come into official hands, and they don't know what to think about it. They found two caskets in Tel el Amarna, Akhenaten's city.

Fig. 5-11. Statue of Akhenaten in the Egyptian Museum, Cairo.

One of the caskets had the Flower of Life etched directly over the head of the mummy inside, and the second casket held the bones of a seven-year-old boy—but he was eight feet tall! That casket is sitting in the basement of the Cairo Museum at this moment—at least it probably is. It's the only real proof so far of what these bodies looked like. From Thoth's teachings, this statue of Akhenaten is exactly what he looked like, just as if you took a photograph of him.

This is a bust of Nefertiti [Fig. 5-12] that was found in Tel el Amarna. There is almost nothing left of that city. At one point the city was dismantled brick by brick and spread all over the world. The Egyptians did not want you to know that Akhenaten and Nefertiti had ever lived. The only reason we do know is because they had buried some things in rooms deep underneath the ground that earlier people didn't find. This bust was found there. Many people think of Nefertiti as a very beautiful woman, but they don't realize that she was extremely tall and that her body was very unusual in certain ways.

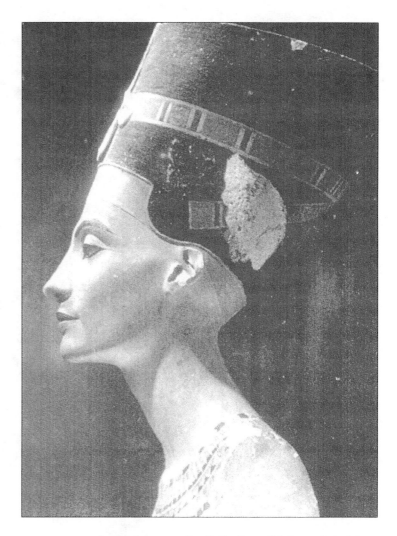

Fig. 5-12. Bust of Nefertiti, State Museum, Berlin.

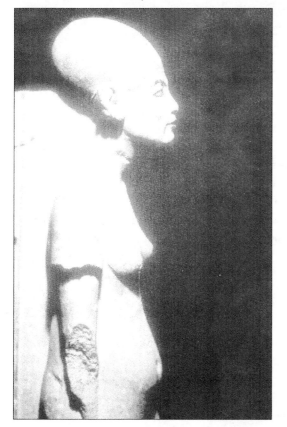

Figure 5-13 is a little-known statue of Nefertiti found in the same room as the bust. She's not wearing clothes because they didn't believe in that at the time. She had a huge head, large ears, a long, skinny neck and a high waist. She also has a kind of bulging tummy. And if you could see the rest of her, she has skinny legs and wide thighs.

Fig. 5-13. Nefertiti in the nude.

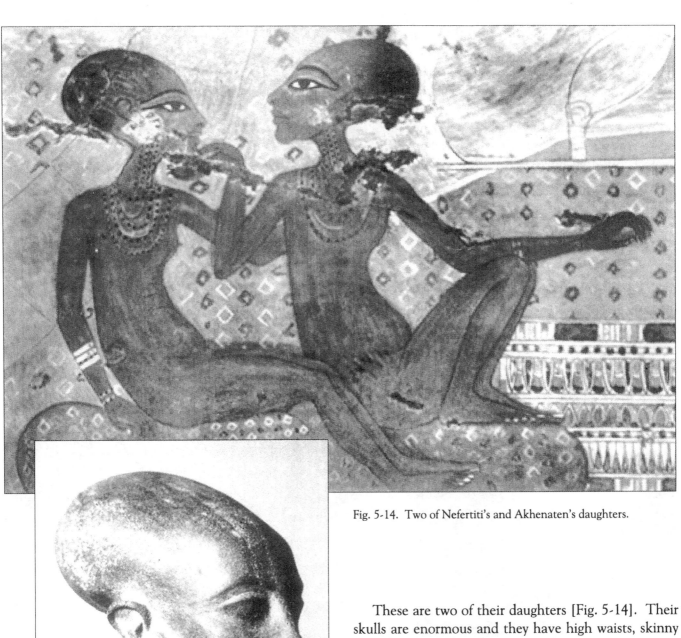

Fig. 5-14. Two of Nefertiti's and Akhenaten's daughters.

These are two of their daughters [Fig. 5-14]. Their skulls are enormous and they have high waists, skinny calves and huge ears.

This is another one of the daughters [Fig. 5-15]. I feel certain that it is exactly what she looked like. If you could see that head from the back, you would see its size. It was big. It's hard to see the size of these ears until you actually get right next to it.

Fig. 5-15. Another daughter.

Fig. 5-16. A younger daughter.

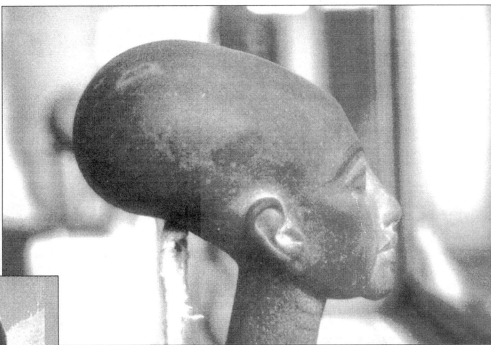

[Fig. 5-17].

Fig. 5-17. Teenager of one of the daughters.

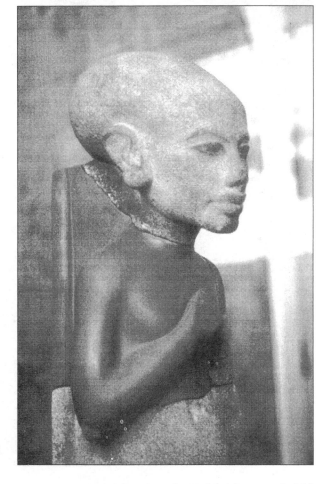

Figure 5-16 is another daughter, younger than the last one—little neck, huge skull extending back.

This is an image of one of the daughters as a teenager [Fig. 5-17].

This is another [Fig. 5-18]. You can see how big the head is relative to the body.

Fig. 5-18. Another young daughter.

This is a baby [Fig. 5-19]. Again, the skull goes way up and around. The ears are about half the size of the head.

Physiologically these bodies are vastly different from human bodies. There are all kinds of differences—brain differences and other unusual things. For example, they have two hearts. The only reason we have one heart is because we have one sun. But these are Sirian beings—actually,

Fig. 5-19. A baby in Akhenaten's family.

they were members of the 32 beings who were sitting around the original flame—and their bodies are from the star Sirius. The Sirian star system has two stars, Sirius A and Sirius B. It's a binary system, as are a vast majority of the star systems. And in those systems life forms have two hearts. If there's only one sun, life forms have one heart. (If there are more stars than two in the system, there will still be two hearts.)

### King Tut—and Other Elongated Skulls

This is King Tut [Fig. 5-20], who took over directly after Akhenaten was disposed of. King Tut was only eighteen years old when he became king. Nobody knows for certain where he came from. The slide says he was a son-in-law of Nefertiti and Akhenaten, married to their daughter. He was obviously part of this lineage, though his skull doesn't appear as big. But he does have the big ears. According to Thoth, King Tut was allowed to take over for only one year. He ruled during the transition between Akhenaten and the next phase. King Tut was in telepathic communication with Nefertiti while she ran the country through him for that one year. She was in hiding.

Fig. 5-20. Bust of King Tut.

Fig. 5-21. Museum in Lima.

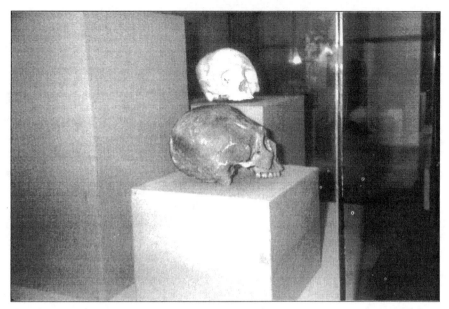

Fig. 5-22. Skulls found in Peru.

This is the museum at Lima, Peru [Fig. 5-21]. I just want to note that they also have some pretty amazing skulls there. Peru is another of the places Thoth went to. They found these skulls [Fig. 5-22] in Peru, just like those in Egypt. These large skulls are found in three areas of the world: in and around Egypt, Peru and Tibet—nowhere else, at least that I know of. Remember, these are the primary areas where these beings went.

Fig. 5-23. Kalu Rinpoche.

This was one of my teachers, who is now dead. His name was Kalu Rinpoche, a Tibetan lama. I've had many teachers, but I feel especially close to this one; I really love him a lot. Notice the shape of his skull.

## Memory: The Key to Immortality

You might wonder, If Akhenaten and others were immortal, then why are they dead? I'll give you the definition of immortality from a Melchizedek point of view, which hopefully will help. Somebody else may have a different definition, but this is what we feel. Immortality has nothing to do with living in the same body forever. You're going to live forever anyway; you have always been alive and you always will be, but you might not be conscious during all that time. The definition from our point of view has to do with memory. When you become immortal, you reach the point where your memory remains intact from then on. In other words, you're conscious from then on, with no unconsciousness coming in. It means you stay in the body as long as you want to, and when you

want to leave it, you leave. To have to stay in a single body forever would be a jail or a trap, because it means you couldn't leave. There might be a reason for leaving that body, and you will eventually find that you want to go beyond wherever you are. This is the definition of eternal life: Simply put, you have continuous, unbroken memory.

Back now to what happened after Akhenaten was dethroned. In order to let things get back to the old ways, which they wanted to do, the country went into a transitional state. The people who became king and queen directly after him are almost comical—they let Ay and Tiya take over the country. We have a long time lag here, then they became king and queen. It's written right in the records. They took over for around thirty years, and then they gave it to Seti I, who became the first king of the Nineteenth Dynasty. He immediately changed everything back to the old way, erased everything and called Akhenaten the same name they called Jesus—"the criminal." He called him the worst king who ever lived because of his teaching that there was only one God.

## What Really Happened to Akhenaten?

Most of Egypt hated Akhenaten, except for a small group. The priesthood hated him most of all because Egyptian religious beliefs were centered on the priests. They controlled the people, their way of life and the economy. They became rich and were more powerful than anybody else. Then Akhenaten came along and said, "You don't need priests; God is within you. There is only one God, and you can access God from within your own self." The priests reacted to protect themselves and their vested interests. Also, Egypt had the most powerful military in the world, and when Akhenaten became pharaoh, they were chomping at the bit, ready to go out and take over the world. Akhenaten said no. He was a complete pacifist and said, "Come back onto our soil. Do not attack anyone unless you're attacked." He made the military come back and sit by idly, and they didn't like that.

So he had not only the priesthood, but the military against him. On top of that, the people themselves were into their little religions, and they loved worshiping their little gods. This wouldn't ultimately do them any good—it wouldn't get them where they needed to go according to the DNA plan of the universe—which was back home to God, to the one God—but nevertheless they were really into what they were doing.

When the people were forcefully told that they could no longer do certain religious acts, this caused great animosity toward Akhenaten. It would be like our president saying, "Okay, there are no more religions in the United States; there's just the president's religion." And if the president brought all the military back onto American soil with an isolationist point of view, he wouldn't be very popular. Neither was Akhenaten. But he knew that he had to do it no matter what, even if it meant his own death. He had to do it to correct the pathway that our collective DNA had encoded into the Reality. In addition, he needed to put into the akashic records the memory of the sacred purpose that Christ consciousness held.

So what happened then? According to the accepted history, the priest-hood and the military got together and gave Akhenaten a poison that killed him. According to Thoth, that is not exactly what happened, because they *couldn't* kill him. He could drink the poison, but it wouldn't hurt him. They did something much more exotic. Thoth says that the priesthood hired three black Nubian sorcerers, who made a concoction similar to what is used in Haiti today to make someone *look* dead. It was given to Akhenaten at a public meeting called by the priesthood and the military. After Akhenaten drank the liquid, all life signs appeared to stop. As soon as the royal doctor pronounced him dead, they rushed him off to a special room where they had a sarcophagus waiting. They placed him in the sarcopha-gus, put on the lid with a magical seal and buried it in a hidden place. Thoth said that Akhenaten had to wait inside the sarcophagus for almost 2000 years before a piece of the seal broke away and the magic was broken. He then returned to the Halls of Amenti. This was not a problem for Akhenaten. Thoth said that to an immortal being like Akhenaten, it was more like a nap. My question is, did he really allow this to happen to him?

### Akhenaten's Mystery School

What's important here is one fact: Akhenaten developed a mystery school. The school was called the Egyptian Mystery School of Akhenaten, the Law of One. As it turned out, he had only 17½ years to produce results. He brought students from the Left Eye of Horus (the feminine side) Mys-tery School, which I'll talk about later—graduates who were at least 45 years old—into the Right Eye of Horus Mystery School. This right-eye in-formation had never been taught before in Egypt. He taught them for twelve years, after which he had only five and a half years to see if he could get them to live immortality. And he did it! He got about 300 people into immortality. I believe they were all, or almost all, women.

Someone once asked, "Why didn't Akhenaten work with the popula-tion in a different way so as to not get himself into such a dangerous situa-tion?" But can you think of a way to change a whole population in such a short time without causing strife? Could you do that in the United States right now—in one year bring all religions into one? I don't think there is a way except to just do it, even if it means getting "killed." Besides, the only thing he really needed to do was simply live his life. It would get into the akashic records and be a memory that we all have in our DNA. One day alone would get it encoded, then afterward they could do whatever they wanted with him. He wasn't really concerned about it. He knew that the country, the society and the customs would all go back to the old way. But he did have these 300 immortal people who would go on beyond him and Egypt.

### The Essene Brotherhood and Jesus, Mary and Joseph

After Akhenaten was gone, the 300 immortal Egyptians joined the Tat Brotherhood and waited from roughly 1350 B.C. to about 500 B.C.—about 850 years or so. Then they migrated to a place called Masada, Israel, and formed the Essene Brotherhood. Even today Masada is known as a capital of the Essene Brotherhood. These 300 people became the inner circle, and mostly ordinary people formed an outer circle, which became very large.

Mary, the mother of Jesus, was one of the members of the inner circle of the Essene Brotherhood. She was immortal even before Jesus became immortal. Joseph came from the outer circle. This is according to Thoth; it's not written in the records. It was part of the Egyptian plan that the next step would be to bring in someone who would demonstrate *exactly how* to become immortal when starting as an ordinary human, put the experience into the akashic records and make it real. Somebody had to do it. According to Thoth, Mary and Joseph came together and mated interdimensionally (which we'll talk about later) to create the body for Jesus, which would allow his consciousness to come in from a very, very high level. When Jesus first came in, he began life on Earth as human as any of us. He was totally human. And through his own work he transformed himself to the immortal state through resurrection, not through ascension, and put into the akashic records the process of exactly how to do it. This is according to Thoth, and it was planned a long, long time before it ever took place.

### The Two Mystery Schools and the 48 Chromosomal Images

We're now changing direction again and beginning a new system of knowledge that will continue for a while until you see this symbol again a long way down the line. This was the symbol for the Egyptian Mystery School of Akhenaten, the Law of One [Fig. 5-24]. It's the Right Eye of Horus. The right eye is controlled by the left brain; it's male knowledge. Although the right eye "sees" directly to the right brain, this is not what the Egyptians were communicating. It is not the "seeing" but rather the *interrupting* of the "seeing" information that was important here. It is the left brain that makes this interruption of what is seen; it controls the right side of the body, and vice versa. In the same manner, the Left Eye of Horus, controlled by the right brain, is female knowledge, which was taught in the twelve primary Egyptian temples along the Nile. The thirteenth temple was the Great Pyramid itself. It took twelve years of initiation, spending a year, one cycle, in each of these temples learning all the feminine components of consciousness.

But the male component, the Right Eye of Horus, was taught only once, and it was not written down anywhere. It was purely an oral tradition, though its primary components are etched on a single wall under the Great Pyramid that leads into the Hall of Records. As you go down that hall, you get almost to the bottom, and just before it makes a 90-degree turn, high up on the wall you see an image about four feet in diameter, which is the

Fig. 5-24. Symbol for the Right Eye of Horus Mystery School.

Flower of Life. Beside it you would see 47 other images, one after another, which are the images of the chromosomes of Christ consciousness, the level of consciousness we're moving into now. After these two volumes are published, we may publish a book of these images.

These images will be given throughout this book, mixed up and in slightly different form. This is what the Great Pyramid is all about. Its primary purpose, beyond anything else, is to take someone from our level of consciousness into the next level. There are lots of other reasons why it's in existence, but ascension and resurrection are the absolute purpose.

## Genesis, the Creation Story

### Egyptian and Christian Versions

We're going to begin with a realization that the Christian and the Egyptian understandings of Reality are almost identical. The Christian understanding is derived from the Egyptian. Here are the first three sentences of the Christian Bible: "In the beginning God created the heaven and the earth. And the earth was without form and void, and darkness was upon the face of the deep, and the spirit of God moved upon the face of the waters. And God said, 'Let there be light,' and there was light."

To begin with, this statement that the Earth was without form until it came out of the Void, out of nothing, is exactly what the Egyptians believed. It's also what many other religions believe. Both Egyptian and Christian religions believe that all that's needed to start the process of creation is *nothing* and *spirit*, and when those two concepts are brought together, then all things can be created. They believe that creation begins by the *movement* of spirit. In the second sentence it says, "The earth was without form and void" and that the spirit of God *moved* upon the face of the waters. Then in the very next sentence, God says, "Let there be light." The movement happened first, then the light happened immediately after.

According to the Egyptian belief, one tiny detail was left out of the current Christian Bibles. It isn't necessarily wrong in the older Bibles, though. There are 900 versions of the Bible in the world, and in many of the older ones the first sentence says, "In the beginning there were six." It starts out in other ways too; it's been changed many times over the years.

The ancient Egyptians would say that the way our modern Bibles begin creation is impossible, especially if you think about it from a physics point of view. Imagine a dark, infinite space that goes on forever and ever in all directions. There's nothing in it—just infinite space with nothing in it. Imagine yourself—not your body, but your consciousness—being in the middle of that. You're just floating there with nothing. You can't really fall, because where would you fall to? You wouldn't know if you're falling down or going up or off to the side; in fact, there's no way to experience any motion at all.

From a purely physics or mathematical point of view, motion itself, or kinetic energy, is absolutely impossible in a void. You can't even rotate, because motion cannot become real until there's at least one other object in the space around you. There has to be something to move *relative* to. If you don't have something relative to move to, how would you know you're moving? I mean, if you went up thirty feet, how would you know that? There's no change. With no change, there's no movement. So the ancient Egyptians would say that before God "moved upon the face of the waters," He/She had to first create something to move relative to.

## How God and the Mystery Schools Did It

Now, think of yourself standing in a dark room, near the door to a second room. You are ready to go into the second room, which is very, very dark. You can barely see the door leading into it. You go into the second room, close the door behind you, and it's pitch black.

When you're faced with that situation, you have the ability to project a sensing beam from your third-eye area, and you can also sense from your hands. (You can actually sense from any chakra, but people usually do it from their third eye or their hands.) You can project a beam of consciousness into that dark room for a certain distance. It might go only an inch, or maybe you can feel outward a foot or two, and you just know that nothing (or something) is in that space. Your consciousness goes out this distance and then it stops. Your knowingness quits, and you don't know what's beyond that. You probably all know what I'm talking about, though a lot of us have allowed that sense to retreat because we rely on our eyes so much.

But some people, especially the ancient Egyptians, were really good at this. They could go into a dark room and feel all around and know if anything was there even though they couldn't see a thing with their eyes. There are blind people who can also demonstrate this ability.

We actually have six of these sensing rays—not just one, but six. They all come from the center of our heads, the pineal gland. One ray comes out the front of our head at the third eye and another goes out the back; one goes out of the left and another out of the right side of our brain; and another goes straight up through the crown chakra and the sixth straight down through our neck—the six directions. These are the same directions of the x-y-z axes of geometry. The Egyptians believed that this innate aspect of consciousness is what allows creation to begin. They believed that if we didn't have this ability, creation would never have happened.

In order to understand this process of creation on the deepest level, Egyptian students were told to imagine and enact the process we are about to go through. The following description is how they explained and practiced it in their mystery schools. The way they learned isn't the only way it could have been done, but this is how they were trained.

The dark background in this picture represents the Great Void, and the little eye represents the spirit of God [Fig. 5-25]. So here's the spirit of God

Fig. 5-25. Spirit of God in the Great Void.

existing in the Void, out in nothing. Imagine that you're that little spirit in the middle of the Void. (When you're in the Great Void, by the way, you will realize that you and God are one, that there is no difference at all.) After hanging out in the Void for a long time, you probably would get bored or curious or lonely, and you would want to try something new, to have some new adventure in your life.

### First Create a Space

So spirit, the single Eye, shoots a beam of consciousness out into the Void. It shoots this beam first to the front, then to the back, then to the left, then the right, then straight up and straight down [Fig. 5-26]. Realize that whatever distance you project out front, you project the same distance out back, also to the left, the right and up and down. The consciousness beam projects the same distance in all six directions for any one individual. Even though each one of us is different in how far we can project this beam (one of us might project an inch, another two feet and another fifty feet), there is equality in all six directions. So spirit projects those beams outward in those six directions, defining space: north, south, east, west, up and down.

This might be why the American Indians and native people all around the world find the six directions so important. Have you ever noticed this in their ceremonies, how important it is that they define the directions? It's also important in the Kabala, in some of the meditations they do.

### Next, Enclose the Space

In the mystery schools, after they've projected these six beams in the six directions, the next thing they do is connect the ends of these projections. This forms a diamond, or square, around them [Fig. 5-27]. Of course, when it's at the angle shown in this diagram, it looks like a rectangle, but you can see that it would actually be a square. So they make a little square around their point of consciousness. Then from the square they send a beam up to the top, forming a pyramid around the base of the square [Fig. 5-28].

After they create the pyramid on top, they then send a beam down to the bottom point, forming a pyramid below [Fig. 5-29]. If you look at this in actual 3D space, the two back-to-back pyramids form an octahedron. Here's another rendition of the octahedron [Fig. 5-30].

Remember that this is just spirit. You don't have a body in the Great Void; you're just spirit. So you're in the Great Void, and you've created this field around you. Now, once you've defined the space by mapping out the octahedron with two back-to-back

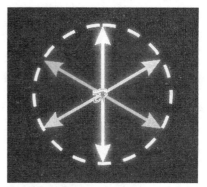

Fig. 5-26. Spirit projecting consciousness into the six directions.

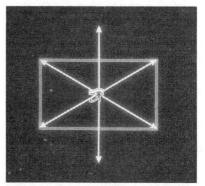

Fig. 5-27. Spirit in its first created diamond.

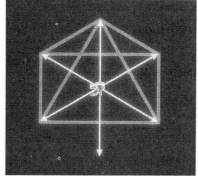

Fig. 5-28. Projecting a pyramid above.

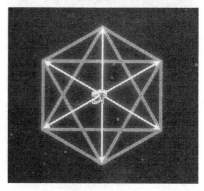

Fig. 5-29. Projecting a pyramid below.

Fig. 5-30. Octahedron around spirit.

pyramids, you have an object. Kinetic energy or movement is now possible; something is now possible that was not possible before. Spirit can move outside the shape and move around it. It can go in any direction for miles and miles, then come back and have a center place for everything. The other thing spirit can do is remain stationary in the middle of the shape, letting the shape move instead. The shape can rotate or wobble or move in all possible ways. So relative movements are now possible.

## Then Spin the Shape to Create a Sphere

The octahedron the students created this way had three axes—front to back, left to right, and up and down. They were told to spin the shape around one of the axes—it didn't matter which, and it didn't matter which direction. They would spin it one way or the other, then they would spin the shape once around another axis, and once around the third axis. With just one spin around each of the three axes, they traced the parameters of a perfect sphere. Before the students were allowed to move their own point of consciousness, they were taught to spin this octahedral form and create a sphere around themselves.

It has been agreed upon by everyone involved in sacred geometry that I know of, that a straight line is male and any curved line is female. Thus one of the most male forms is a square or a cube, and one of the most female forms is a circle or a sphere. Since the octahedron that spirit projected is made up of only straight lines, it's a male shape; and since the sphere is made of only curved lines, it's a female shape. What the Egyptians did was to create a male form and then convert it to a female form. They went from maleness to femaleness.

This same story is related through the Bible where Adam was created first, and then from Adam, or out of Adam's rib, was created the female. Of course, the image of spirit inside the sphere is also the image of the school.

Sacred geometry started when spirit made its first projection into the Void and created the first octahedron around itself. The Void is infinite—nothing in it—and these forms being created are also nothing. They're just imaginary lines created out of consciousness. This gives you an indication of what Reality is—nothing. The Hindus call Reality *maya*, which means illusion.

Spirit can sit in the middle of its first creation for a long time [Fig. 5-31], but eventually it'll make a decision to do something. To re-create this process, mystery school students were given instructions to reenact the same motions that spirit took. *Two simple instructions* are all that's required to create and complete everything in the entire universe.

## The First Motion in Genesis

Remember that spirit is now sitting in a sphere. The instructions are to move to that which is *newly created*, then *project another sphere exactly like the first*. That does something very special and unique. This is an absolutely

Fig. 5-31. Spirit in the middle of its first creation.

foolproof system for creating Reality. You cannot make a mistake no matter what you do. All you do is move to what is newly created and project another sphere the same size as the first one. In this system, since nothing exists except this bubble in the Void, and the inside of the bubble is the same as the outside, the only thing that's new or different is the membrane itself, the *surface* of the sphere.

So consciousness decides to go to the surface. It makes no difference where it goes on the surface; it can go anywhere. It doesn't make any difference *how* it gets there either, whether it goes in a straight line or curves or spirals out or explores every speck of space in between. It can be really creative; it doesn't make any difference. But somehow or another it will end up somewhere on the surface of the sphere.

For purposes of this example we'll say spirit went up to the top (just to be symmetrical and easier to deal with). Anyway, spirit, this little single eye, lands on the surface [Fig. 5-32]. It has just made the first motion in Genesis: "And the spirit of God moved upon the face of the waters." And the very next thing was: "God said, 'Let there be light,' and there was light."

At this point spirit knows how to do only one thing—actually, it knows how to do two things, but the end result is one. It knows (1) how to project the little octahedron and create a sphere and (2) how to move to what's newly created. That's it, a very simple Reality. So once it arrives on the surface, it makes another octahedron, spins it through the three axes and forms another sphere identical in size to the first one. It's identical in size because its ability to project into the Void is the same. Nothing has changed in that respect. So it creates a second sphere exactly the same size as the first.

Fig. 5-32. Spirit's first motion.

### The Vesica Piscis, through Which Light Is Created

When it does that, it has done something that, in terms of sacred geometry, is very special. It has formed a vesica piscis at the intersection of the two spheres [Fig. 5-33]. Have you ever seen two soap bubbles together? When two soap bubbles intersect, a line or a circle goes around their linkage. If you were looking at the two bubbles from the side, the newly formed section would look like a line, but if you were looking down at the two bubbles from the top, you would see the newly created form's circumference *inside* the larger spheres.

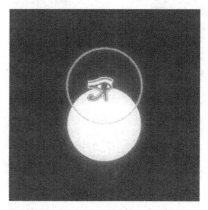

Fig. 5-33. First motion/day; the first two spheres of creation make a vesica piscis.

The vesica piscis circumference is symmetrical to, and smaller than, the circumference of the larger spheres. In other words, it would appear from the side like a straight line [Fig. 5-34, center], and from the top like a circle [right]. Even though the vesica piscis is usually two-dimensional like a coin, its

Fig. 5-34. First motion/day. The first two spheres of creation (left); section view (center); and plan or overhead view (right).

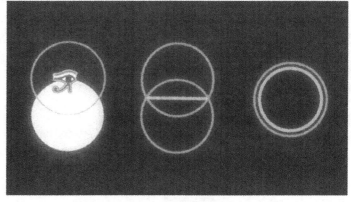

Fig. 5-35. A 3D vesica piscis, a three-dimensional solid shape taken out from the two spheres that made it.

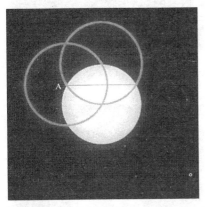

Fig. 5-36. Third sphere, second motion/day of Genesis. When sitting in the center of the uppermost circle/sphere and looking down, the horizontal line is seen as a circle.

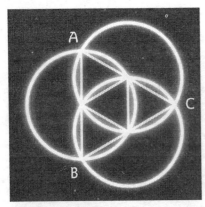

Fig. 5-37. Small and large tetrahedrons in three spheres.

three-dimensional aspect is just as valid. If you were to take it out of the middle of the two spheres, it would look similar to a football, like Figure 5-35.

I cannot prove this to you now, but later in this book I'll be able to prove that this image is light. It's the geometric image through which light was created. It's also the geometric image through which your eyes were created, which receive light. Besides light, it's also the image of the patterns that are connected to your emotions and many, many other aspects of life. This is the basic geometry of the electromagnetic field. It's too simple to understand here. I have to wait until things get more complex; then I can explain it. I'll show you that the first motion of Genesis creates the pattern that is life. That's the reason why God said, "Let there be light." He couldn't say that until He had projected the second sphere and made the vesica piscis.

### The Second Motion Creates the Star Tetrahedron

When spirit is in the center of its second sphere and looking down at the vesica piscis, it's looking upon a newly formed circle, the circle of the vesica piscis. This circle is the only thing that's new, and spirit's instructions are to go to what's newly created. It doesn't make any difference where it goes on the new circle. It cannot make a mistake; it just moves to somewhere on that circle and projects a new sphere as in Figure 5-36.

No matter where spirit lands, we can rotate the spheres to look like this drawing. So I'm going to say that it moved on the circle to point A, on the left. At that moment a *huge* amount of information was created (in every motion of Genesis, vast amounts of knowledge come out). The first *creation* produced the sphere. The first *motion/day* produced the vesica piscis, which is the basis of light. The second motion/day produced, in the interpenetrating relationship between the three spheres, the basic geometries of the star tetrahedron [Fig. 5-37], which you will soon see is one of the most important shapes for life.

We're not going to get into all the information that was formed at this time, but each time a new sphere is formed, more and more information unfolds and more and more creative patterns become visible. After the first and second motions have taken place—from anywhere on the sphere to anywhere on the circle (no matter how spirit moved, no matter where it went on the circle/sphere, it will always be perfect)—it will begin to move exactly on the equator of the original sphere. There are an infinite number of equators on that sphere, but it will choose a perfect one.

### "Move to That Which is Newly Created" until Completion

After that pattern is created, there's only one instruction left to follow—forever. The only other action to be taken until the end of time is always to *move to the innermost circle point(s) and project another sphere.*

For the sake of clarity, let's define what we mean by "innermost circle point." Look at Figure 5-36. In this case there are three innermost circle points. If your eye were to trace the outside perimeter of this pattern, it would come to three places that are the closest places to center. It is these "closest places to center" that we are calling the innermost circle points. In the case of the Genesis pattern that this movement of spirit is creating, there are six innermost circle points.

So with this in mind, spirit starts moving exactly around the equator of the original or central sphere. When it has traversed the full 360 degrees and reaches the point at which it started (which will be six points or movements), it begins to follow its second impulse (or instruction, for the mystery school students): *Move to the innermost circle points*, which are now located on the circumference of the original sphere where two vesica pisces intersect. Simply put, they are the points as close as possible to the outside of the pattern. That continual movement begins to form a vortex. This vortex motion creates different types of three-dimensional forms, one after another, which are the building blocks or blueprints of the entire Reality.

Once spirit has created the third sphere, it now moves to the innermost circle point and projects another sphere [Fig. 5-38]. There is information here, but it is too complex to discuss at this time.

This is very interesting; it is the fourth motion/day [Fig. 5-39]. It says in many Bibles in the world that on the fourth day of Genesis exactly one half of creation was completed. Starting from the first motion, exactly one half of the circle was formed [Fig. 5-39a]. We have moved exactly 180 degrees from the point of the first motion.

Figure 5-40 is the fifth day of Genesis—more information.

And then on the sixth day [Fig. 5-41] a geometric miracle takes place: the last circle forms a complete six-petaled flower. This is what many of the earlier Bibles meant when they said, "In the beginning there were six." Our Bible *now* says that creation was formed in six days, and this fits exactly. This is the pattern of Genesis, so we refer to it as the Genesis pattern. It's the beginning of the creation of this universe we live in.

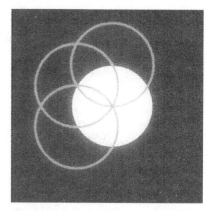

Fig. 5-38. Fourth sphere, third day of Genesis.

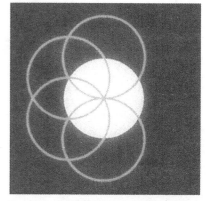

Fig. 5-39. Fifth sphere, fourth day of Genesis.

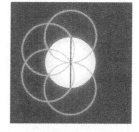

Fig. 5-39a. Half of creation.

Fig. 5-41. Sixth sphere, fifth day of Genesis.

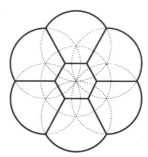

Fig. 5-41a. Showing a 3D view of this.

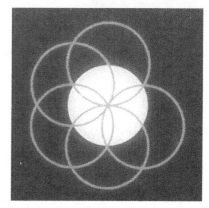

Fig. 5-40. Sixth sphere, fifth day of Genesis.

These original movements of spirit are really important. This is why I spend so much time going through this near the beginning of this course. Later on we'll get more complex, but for now this is just the beginning of how the manifestation of Reality is created.

We'll pull these 3D shapes off the page in a minute, one by one. If they could be made solid, you could look at them and hold them in your hands. We will begin to ground this abstract information into Reality for you. Then we're going to take them further to show you how they actually create the Reality we live in. If you study this on your own, you'll be seeing some extremely elaborate aspects of creation come from this explanation of the Reality. If you were constructing these geometries yourself, you would draw a line somewhere in the sacred geometry that spirit makes as it moves through the Void, and it'll mean something amazing; then another line will mean something else even more amazing. Life began simply, then created the complex world we live in.

This is not just mathematics, and it's not just circles or geometries. *This is the living map of the creation of all Reality.* You must understand this or you'll get lost and won't understand what this book is leading to. The reason we're doing all this is so that your left brain can understand the unity of all creation so that polarity consciousness can be transcended.

# The Significance of Shape and Structure

## Developing the Genesis Pattern

### The Torus, the First Shape

Let's look at the first object that comes off the page—the Genesis pattern itself (see Fig. 5-41). If you look at a math book, this Genesis pattern has the minimal amount of lines that can be drawn on a flat surface to delineate the three-dimensional form called a torus. A torus is formed when you rotate the Genesis pattern around its central axis, creating a shape that looks like a doughnut, but the hole in the middle is infinitely small.

A torus, here called a tube torus because this particular one is shaped like an inner tube [Fig. 6-1], is unique in that it's able to fold in on itself, turning either inward or outward. No other shape in existence can do this or anything similar. A torus is the first shape that comes out of the completed Genesis pattern and is absolutely unique among all forms in existence.

It was Arthur Young who discovered that there are seven regions on this shape, which are collectively called *the seven-color map*. You can pick up almost any mathematics book, and if you go to the torus, it'll talk about the seven-color map. There are seven regions, all the same size, that will exactly fit in the tube torus with nothing left over. Just like on the Genesis pattern, six circles going around the seventh, central one take up the entire surface. It's perfect, flawless.

In sacred geometry there's something called ratcheting. You take a circle or a line and ratchet it, like when you take a ratchet tool in car mechanics and use it to rotate something a certain distance. For instance, imagine two Genesis patterns superimposed on each other. One pattern is fixed; if you rotate the other pattern 30 degrees,

Fig. 6-1. The colorful tube torus.

you would have twelve spheres around the central one. It would look like this [Fig. 6-2] in two dimensions. In three dimensions it would look like a tube torus. Then if you connect all possible lines in the middle, you get this pattern [Fig. 6-3].

Ratcheting the twelve spheres once more, this time 15 degrees, so that there are 24 spheres, you would get this pattern [Fig. 6-4]. This pattern has what is called a transcendental pattern associated with it. What is a transcendental pattern? A transcendental number in mathematics, from my way of looking at it, is a number that comes from another dimension. In that dimension it is probably whole, but when it gets here it does not completely translate into this world. We have a lot of those. One of them, for example, is the *phi ratio*, which I'm going to talk about later. It's a mathematical proportion that starts out with 1.6180339 and continues forever, meaning you never know what the next digit is going to be, and it never ends: people have let computers run for months without coming to an end. As a simple explanation, that's what a transcendental number is.

Fig. 6-2. Genesis pattern ratcheted once.

The shape of the torus is what governs many aspects of our lives. For example, the human heart has seven muscles that form a torus, and it pumps in the seven regions shown in the map of the torus. We have embodied all knowledge. The torus is literally around *all* life forms, all atoms, and all cosmic bodies such as planets, stars, galaxies and so on. It is the primary shape in existence.

Fig. 6-3. Ratcheted Genesis pattern with all possible connected lines.

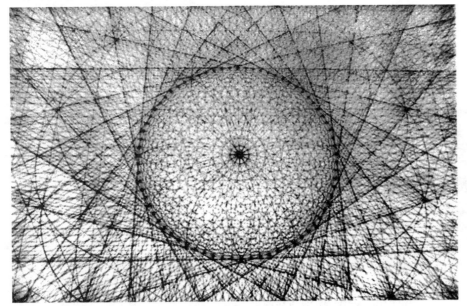

"In the beginning was the Word." I believe that time will reveal that language/conscious sound/the word will all be revealed in the torus. There are those who believe this to be true now, but only time will tell.

### The Labyrinth As a Movement of Life-Force Energy

Figure 6-5 is a sevenfold labyrinth. This is found all over the world—everywhere from China to Tibet to England to Ireland to Peru to the American Indians.

One was just found in Egypt. You'll find this labyrinth on the floors of many of the churches in Europe. The same form is on stone walls everywhere. It must have been of great importance to ancient mankind. There are seven regions in it, which relates to the torus and to the beating of the human heart. Later on I'll be talking about the ancient Druid mystery school on the Island of Avalon in England. To get to the top of the hill there, you have to walk through this same labyrinth, going back and forth through this motion.

While I was in England, I spoke to Richard Feather Anderson, who is an author and an expert on labyrinths, and I learned something. As part of his research, he has people walk through the labyrinth. He's discovered that when you walk through it, you are forced to move through different states of consciousness, giving you a very specific experience. It causes the life-force energy to move through the chakras in the following pattern: three, two, one, four, seven, six, five. The energy starts in the third chakra, then goes to the second, then to the first; then it jumps up to the heart (fourth), then into the center of the head to the pineal gland (seventh), then to the front of the head to the pituitary gland (sixth), and then down into the throat (fifth).

When you walk this labyrinth, unless you block the experience, you will automatically move through these changes. Even if you don't know about these things, you will go through the experiences anyway. People all over the world have found this to be true. Mr. Anderson believes that if you draw lines (the number of lines indicating which of the seven paths it is) in the order you walk the path—three, two, one, four, seven, six, five—it forms what looks like a cup [Fig. 6-6]. He feels that this particular labyrinth is related to the shape of the Holy Grail and to its secret knowledge. From my experience, this feels right, but I am keeping an open mind. I don't know about this yet; it may be true.

I experimented with this labyrinth on myself, and it is true that those changes did happen for me. However, I was also able to experience these same changes in a different way. I was able to walk a straight line toward the center of the labyrinth and simply make the changes within myself as I reached each place where the turn would be in the labyrinth. I was able to reach the same state without walking through the whole pattern. Remember the labyrinth; I'll come back to it after a while.

Fig. 6-4. Twice-ratcheted Genesis pattern with all possible connected lines.

Fig. 6-5. A sevenfold labyrinth.

**Update: I have just seen a picture from Europe [1998, see below] of the biblical Melchizedek, in which he is holding the key to the labyrinth inside a bowl.**

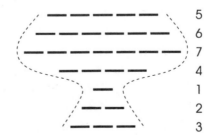

Fig. 6-6. The labyrinth sequence creates a cup.

```
5
6
7
4
1
2
3
```

PATRI ARCH          MELCHI SEDEC

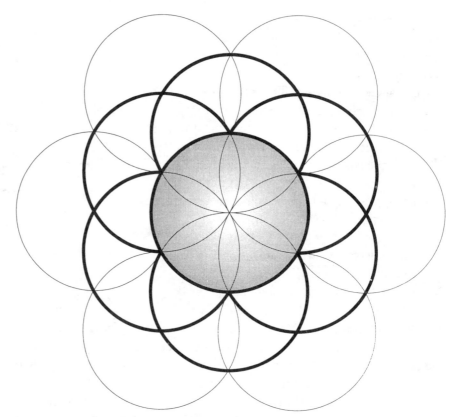

Fig. 6-7. Vortex beyond the Genesis pattern.

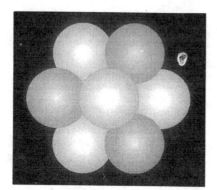

Fig. 6-8. 3D spheres/balls.

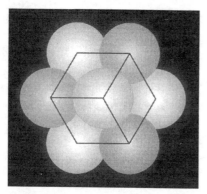

Fig. 6-8a. Connecting centers to form a cube.

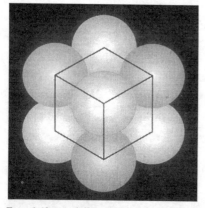

Fig. 6-8b. A different view.

## The Egg of Life, the Second Shape beyond Genesis

The dark innermost circles show the six days of Genesis [Fig. 6-7]. Once the consciousness projects the first seven spheres and completes this Genesis pattern, it then continues moving in a rotational pattern from each consecutive innermost place until it completes its second vortex motion as seen by the light outermost circles. That motion in turn completes a three-dimensional shape you can hold in your hand, which looks like Figure 6-8. If you were to take Figure 6-7 and erase all the lines in the middle and certain other lines, you would see this pattern. The pattern of spheres is like what spirit would have seen had it moved outside its creation and said, "Aha, I see this thing! It looks like that" [Fig. 6-8].

The eighth sphere is actually behind these visible spheres. If you were to connect their centers, you would see a cube [Figs. 6-8a and 6-8b].

So what? Who cares? Well, the ancients did, because they were concerned with creation, life and death. They called this cluster of spheres the Egg of Life. I'll soon show you how the Egg of Life is the morphogenetic structure that created your body. Your entire physical existence is dependent on the Egg of Life structure. Everything about you was created through the Egg of Life form, right down to the color of your eyes, the shape of your nose, how long your fingers are and everything else. It's all based on this *one form*.

### The Third Rotation/Shape: The Fruit of Life

The next vortex is the third rotation [Fig. 6-9]. The spheres in this vortex are centered at the innermost places in the perimeter of the previous round, as shown by the six arrows here. So when spirit rotates in this third vortex, you get the gray rings shown here. Then you notice a new relationship where the six circles touch the center one and each other. If you took seven pennies and pushed them together on a table, they would look like that. This third rotation is an extremely important relationship in the creation of our Reality. When you look carefully at the Flower of Life, you see these seven circles that touch each other.

There are nineteen circles in the Flower of Life [Fig. 6-10], and they're surrounded by two concentric circles. For some reason, that image is found all over the world. The question is, why did they do that all over the world and stop at nineteen circles? It's an infinite grid and could have been stopped anywhere. The only place on the whole planet where I've seen them go out beyond those nineteen circles was in China, where they made room-divider screens [Fig. 6-11]. One of the most famous patterns they used on those screens was the Flower of Life. They made it in a rectangular shape, carrying it all the way out to the edge.

But in all others that were found, you would usually see just the Flower of Life pattern. This is because when the ancient beings realized what the other component was and how important it was, they decided to make it secret. They didn't want people to see this relationship I'm about to show you. It was so sacred and important that they just could not allow it to become common knowledge. It was appropriate at that time; however, now we either use the information or fall further into the darkness.

Notice that in the Flower of Life pattern you see many incomplete circles, which, of course, can also be spheres. Look all around the outer edge of Figure 6-10. If all you did was complete all of these circles, then the secret would unfold. This was the ancient's way of coding the information.

Fig. 6-9. The third rotation.

Fig. 6-10. Flower of Life.

Fig. 6-11. Chinese screen, stylized Flower of Life.

Fig. 6-12. Completing the incomplete circles.

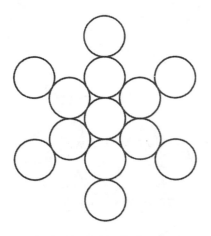

Fig. 6-13. The Fruit of Life.

The additional circles/spheres that extend beyond the original Flower of Life pattern inside the large gray ring in Figure 6-12 complete all the incomplete circles at the edge of that pattern.

As soon as you complete these spheres, with one more step you'll have the secret: Go to the innermost places of the perimeter, shown by the arrows, and rotate the next vortex. When you do, you get the pattern of thirteen circles, shown here by the smaller gray circles, including the center. When it's extracted from the rest of the pattern, it looks like Figure 6-13.

This pattern of thirteen circles is one of the holiest, most sacred forms in existence. On Earth it's called the Fruit of Life. It is called the fruit because it is the result, the fruit, from which the fabric of the details of the Reality were created.

### Combining Male and Female to Create Metatron's Cube, the First Informational System

Now, all the circles in this pattern are female. And there are thirteen ways, with these thirteen circles, that you can superimpose male energy—in other words, straight lines. If you superimpose straight lines over this in all thirteen ways, you'll come up with thirteen patterns that, along with the Egg of Life and the torus, create everything in existence. The Egg of Life, the torus, and this Fruit of Life, a total of three patterns, create everything in existence without exception—at least I have not been able to find an exception. I'll give you what I've learned; obviously I cannot show you everything, but I'll show you enough to convince you this is true. I'm going to call these *informational systems*. There are thirteen informational systems associated with the Fruit of Life pattern. Each system produces a vast and diversified amount of knowledge. I'm going to show you only four of those. I think that's enough.

The simplest system comes forth by simply connecting all the centers of the circles with straight lines. If you decided to put straight lines on this pattern, probably about 90 percent of you would think first of connecting all the centers. If you do that, you end up with this pattern [Fig. 6-14], which is known throughout the universe—everywhere —as Metatron's Cube. It is one of the most important informational systems in the universe, one of the basic creation patterns of existence.

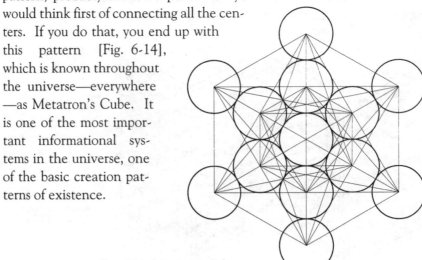

Fig. 6-14. Metatron's Cube.

# The Platonic Solids

Anyone who has studied sacred geometry or even regular geometry knows that there are five unique shapes, and they are crucial to understanding both sacred and regular geometry. They're called the *Platonic solids* [Fig. 6-15].

A Platonic solid has certain characteristics by definition. First of all, its faces are all the same size. For instance, a cube, the most well-known of the Platonic solids, has a square on every face, so all its faces are the same size. Second, the edges of a Platonic solid are all the same length; all edges of a cube are the same length. Third, it has only one size of interior angles between faces. In the case of a cube, this angle is 90 degrees. And fourth, if a Platonic solid is put inside a sphere (of the right size), all the points will touch the surface of the sphere. With that definition, there are only four shapes besides the cube (A) that have all of those characteristics. Second (B) is the *tetrahedron* (tetra means four), a polyhedron that has four faces, all equilateral triangles, one edge length and one angle, and all points touch the surface of a sphere. The other simple one is (C) an *octahedron* (octa means eight), whose eight faces are equilateral triangles of the same size, edge length and angle, and all points touch the surface of a sphere.

The other two Platonic solids are a little more complicated. One (D) is called an *icosahedron*, which means it has 20 faces, made of equilateral triangles with the same edge length and angle, and all points touch the surface of a sphere. The last one (E) is called a *pentagonal dodecahedron* (dodeca is 12), whose faces are 12 pentagons (five sides), with the same edge length and angle, and whose points all touch the surface of a sphere.

If you're an engineer or an architect, you have studied these five shapes in college, at least cursorily, because they're the basis of structures.

## Their Source: Metatron's Cube

If you study sacred geometry, no matter what book you pick up, it shows the five Platonic solids, because they are the ABCs of sacred geometry. *But when you read all these books—and I've read almost all of them—and ask the experts, "Where do the Platonic solids come from? What is their source?" almost everyone says they don't know.* Well, the five Platonic solids come from the first informational system of the Fruit of Life. Hidden within the lines of Metatron's Cube [see Fig. 6-14] are all five of these shapes. When you look at Metatron's Cube, you're looking at all five Platonic solids at once. In order to see each one better, you have to do that trick again where you erase some of the lines. If you erase all the lines except certain ones, you get this cube [Fig. 6-16].

Can you see the cube? It's actually a cube within a cube. Some of the lines are dotted because they would be behind the front faces. They are invisible when the cube becomes solid. Here's the solid form of the larger cube [Fig. 6-16a]. (Make sure you see this one, because they get harder and harder to see as we go.)

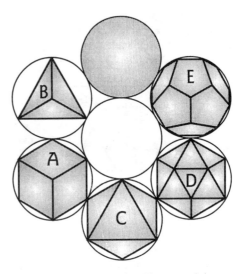

Fig. 6-15. The five Platonic solids.

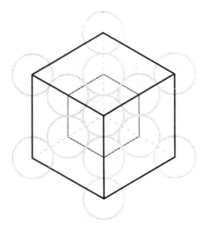

Fig. 6-16. Here are the two cubes extracted from Metatron's Cube.

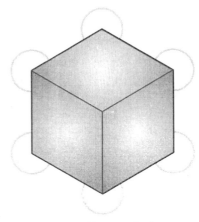

Fig. 6-16a. Solid larger cube from previous figure.

Fig. 6-17. The star tetrahedrons extracted from Metatron's Cube.

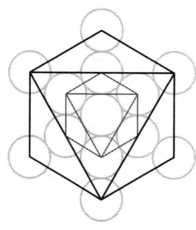

Fig. 6-18. Two octahedrons extracted from Metatron's Cube.

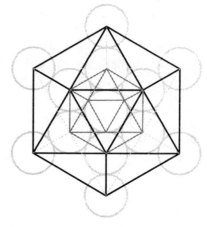

Fig. 6-19. Two icosahedrons extracted from Metatron's Cube.

Fig. 6-17a. Solid larger star tetrahedron in Fig. 6-17.

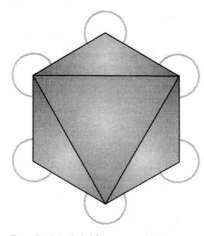

Fig. 6-18a. Solid larger octahedron.

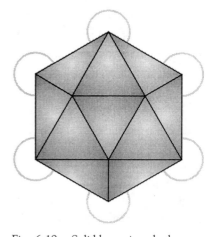

Fig. 6-19a. Solid larger icosahedron.

By erasing certain lines and connecting other centers [Fig. 6-17], you get two superimposed tetrahedrons, which form a star tetrahedron. Like the cube, you actually get two star tetrahedrons, one inside the other. Here's the solid form of the larger star tetrahedron [Fig. 6-17a].

Figure 6-18 is an octahedron inside another octahedron, though you're looking at them from a special angle. Figure 6-18a is the solid version of the larger octahedron.

Figure 6-19 is one icosahedron inside another, and Figure 6-19a is the solid version of the larger one. It somehow becomes easier if you see it this way.

These are three-dimensional objects coming out of the thirteen circles of the Fruit of Life.

Fig. 6-20. Sulamith Wulfing's painting of the Christ Child.

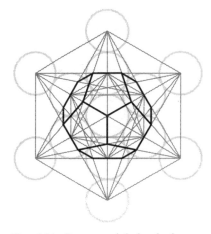

Fig. 6-21. Pentagonal dodecahedron in Metatron's Cube.

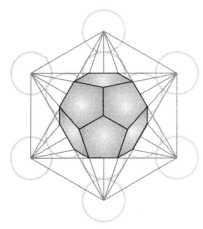

Fig. 6-21a. Solid dodecahedron.

This is Sulamith Wulfing's painting of the Christ Child inside an icosahedron [Fig. 6-20], which is very appropriate, because the icosahedron represents water, as you will see in a moment, and the Christ was baptized in water, the beginning of the new consciousness.

This is the fifth and last shape—two pentagonal dodecahedrons, one inside the other [Fig. 6-21] (here showing only the inner dodecahedron for simplicity).

Figure 21a is the solid version.

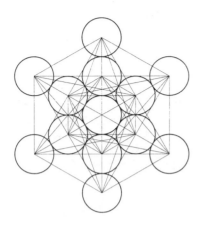

Fig. 6-22. Metatron's Cube.

As we have seen, all five of the Platonic solids can be found in Metatron's Cube [Fig. 6-22].

## The Missing Lines

When I was looking for the final Platonic solid in Metatron's Cube, the dodecahedron, it took me over twenty years. After the angels had said, "They're all in there," I started to look, but I could never find the dodecahedron. Finally one day a student said, "Hey, Drunvalo, you forgot some of the lines in Metatron's Cube." When he pointed them out, I looked and said, "You're right, I did!" I thought I had connected all the centers together, but I had forgotten some of them. No wonder I couldn't find that dodecahedron, because those missing lines defined it! For over twenty years I'd assumed that I had all the lines when I hadn't.

This is one of the great problems in science, believing you have solved a problem, then moving on and using that information to build on. Science is now having to deal with the same kind of problem around falling bodies in a vacuum, for example. It has always been assumed that they fell at the same rate, and much of our higher science is based on this fundamental "law." It has been proven wrong, yet science continues using it. A spinning ball falls much faster than a nonspinning one. Someday there will be a scientific day of reckoning.

When I was married to Macki, she was also deeply involved in sacred geometry. Her work is very interesting to me because it's female—right-brained pentagonal energies. She shows how emotions and colors and shapes are all interrelated. Actually, she found the dodecahedron in Metatron's Cube before I did. She took it and did something I never would have thought of doing. Metatron's cube, you know, is usually drawn on a flat surface, but it's really a three-dimensional shape. So one day I was holding the three-dimensional shape and trying to find the dodecahedron in there, and Macki said, "Let me look at that thing." She took the three-dimensional shape and rotated it by the phi ratio. (Something we've not talked about yet is that the Golden Mean ratio, also called the phi ratio, is approximately 1.618.) Rotating the shape like that was something I would never have thought of doing. After she did that, she cast a shadow through it and got this image [Fig. 6-23].

Macki originally created this, then gave it to me. It has a center at pentagon A. Then if you take the five pentagons coming off of A (pentagons B) and one more pentagon coming off of each of *those* five (pentagons C), you have an *unfolded* dodecahedron. I thought, Wow, this is the first time I've ever found *any* kind of dodecahedron in there. She did that in three days. I'd never found it in twenty years.

We once spent almost a whole day looking at this drawing. It was exciting, because *every single line* in this drawing is in a Golden Mean ratio. And there are three-dimensional Golden Mean rectangles all over. There's one at point E, where the two diamonds above and below are the top and bot-

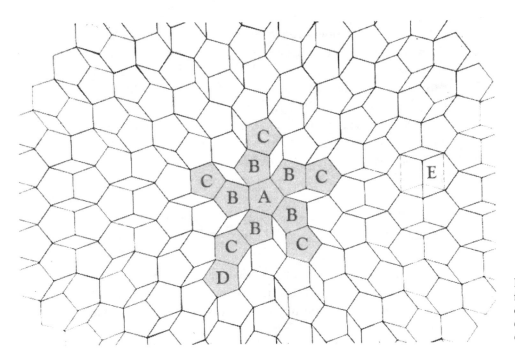

Fig. 6-23. Macki's pentagon design from Metatron's Cube. When cut out and folded, it makes a three-dimensional pentagonal dodecahedron.

tom of a three-dimensional Golden Mean rectangle, and the dotted lines are the sides. It's amazing stuff. I said, "I don't know what this is, but it's probably important." So we put it aside to consider at another time.

### Quasi Crystals

Later I found out about a brand-new science. This new science is going to change the technological world dramatically. Using this new technology, metallurgists believe they will be able to make metal ten times harder than diamonds, if you can imagine that. That would be incredibly hard.

For a long time when they looked into metals, they were using what's called x-ray diffraction to see where the atoms were. I'll show an x-ray diffraction photograph of this shortly. Certain specific patterns came up that revealed there were only certain kinds of atomic structures. They thought it was all there was to learn because that was all they could find. This limited their ability to make metals.

Then there was a game going on in *Scientific American* which was based on Penrose patterns. Roger Penrose was a British mathematician and relativist who wanted to figure out how to lay pentagon-shaped tiles and fully cover a flat surface. You cannot lay only pentagon-shaped tiles on a flat surface—there's no way to make it work. So he came up with two diamond shapes that are derivatives of a pentagon, and with those two shapes he was able to form lots of different patterns that would fit on a flat surface. It became a game in *Scientific American* back in the eighties to put these patterns together in new forms, which then led some metallurgical scientists who were watching this game to suspect something new in physics.

**Update: According to David Adair, NASA has just made a metal in space that is 500 times stronger than titanium, as light as foam and as clear as glass. Is it based on these principles?**

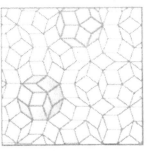

UPDATE: In 1998 we are beginning to open up another new science: *nanotechnology.* We have created microscopic "machines" that can go into a metal or crystal matrix and rearrange the atoms. In 1996 or 1997 in Europe a diamond was created out of graphite using nanotechnology. This diamond was about three feet across, and it is real. As the science of quasi crystals and nanotechnology merge, our experience of life will also change. Look at the late 1800s compared to now.

Ultimately they discovered a new kind of atomic grid pattern. It was always there; they merely discovered it. These grid patterns are now called quasi crystals; it's a new thing (1991). They're unraveling what shapes and patterns are possible through metals. Scientists are finding ways to use these shapes and patterns to produce new metal products. And I'll bet that the pattern Macki got out of Metatron's Cube is the grand master of all, and that any Penrose pattern in existence is derived from it. Why? Because it's all Golden Mean, it's basic—it came straight out of the basic pattern in Metatron's Cube. Though it's not my business, at one point I will probably determine if it's really true. I see that instead of using the two Penrose patterns and the pentagon, it uses only one of them and a pentagon. (I just thought I'd offer that.) What's happening in this new science right now is interesting.

As this book begins to unfold, you'll discover that sacred geometry can describe in detail any subject whatsoever. There is not one thing you can pronounce with your mouth that cannot be *completely, utterly and totally described, with all possible knowledge,* by sacred geometry. (And we are making the distinction between knowledge and wisdom: Wisdom needs experience.) Yet a more important purpose of this work is to remind you that *you* have the potential of a living Mer-Ka-Ba field around your body and to teach you how to use it. I'll continually come to places where I digress into all kinds of roots and branches and talk about every subject you can think of. But I'm going to keep coming back on track, because I'm heading in one particular direction, toward the Mer-Ka-Ba, the human lightbody.

I've spent many years studying sacred geometry, and I believe you can know everything there is to be known about any subject whatsoever just by focusing on the geometries behind it. All you need is a compass and a ruler—you don't even need a computer, though it does help. You have all knowledge in you already, and all you have to do is unfold it. You simply learn the map of how spirit moves in the Great Void, and that's it. You can unravel the mystery of any subject.

To summarize, the first informational system comes out of the Fruit of Life through Metatron's Cube. By connecting the centers of all the spheres, you have five shapes—really six, because you have the central sphere, which started the whole thing. So you have six primal shapes—the tetrahedron, the cube, octahedron, icosahedron, dodecahedron and the sphere.

## The Platonic Solids and the Elements

These six shapes were considered by the ancient alchemists and great souls like Pythagoras, the father of Greece, to have had an *element* aspect to them [Fig. 6-24].

The tetrahedron was considered fire, the cube was earth, the octahedron was air, the icosahedron was water and the dodecahedron was ether. (Ether, prana and tachyon energy are the same thing; they extend everywhere and are accessible at any point in space/time/dimension. This is the great secret of zero-point technology.) And the sphere is voidness. These six elements are the building blocks of the universe. They create the qualities of the universe.

In alchemy, they usually talk only about fire, earth, air and water; they seldom discuss ether or prana because it's so sacred. In the Pythagorean school, if you even uttered the word "dodecahedron" outside the school, they would kill you on the spot. That was how sacred the shape was. They wouldn't even discuss it. Two hundred years later when Plato was alive, he would discuss it, but only very carefully.

Why? Because the dodecahedron is near the outer edge in your energy field and is the highest form of consciousness. When you get to the 55-foot limit of your energy field, it's a sphere. But the very next shape inside the sphere is the dodecahedron (actually, the dodecahedron/icosahedral relationship). In addition, we live in a big dodecahedron that contains the universe. When your mind reaches out to the end of space—and there *is* an end—there's a dodecahedron enclosed in a sphere. I can say this because the human body is a hologram of the universe and contains the same principles. The twelve constellations of the zodiac fit inside it. The dodecahedron is the terminating point of the geometries, and it's very important. On a microscopic level, the dodecahedron and the icosahedron are the relational parameters of the DNA, the blueprint of all life.

You can relate the three columns in this figure to the Tree of Life and to the three primary energies of the universe: male (on the left), female (right) and child (center). Or if you go right down to the fabric of the universe, you have the proton on the left, electron on the right and neutron in the center. This central column, which is the creating one, is the child. Remember, we went from an octahedron to a sphere to begin the process out of the Void. It is the beginning process of creation, and it is found in the child, or central column.

The left column, holding the tetrahedron and the cube, is the male component of consciousness, the left side of the brain. The faces of these polygons are triangles or squares. The center column is the corpus callosum, which links the left and the right sides. The right column, holding the dodecahedron and the icosahedron, is the female component of consciousness, the right side of the brain, and the polygon faces are made up

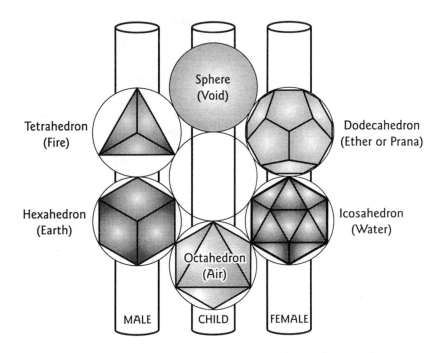

Fig. 6-24. Relating the six elements to the six primal shapes, shown in three columns that depict the trinity of polarity. The left (male) column represents the left brain and the proton and includes 3- and 4-sided faces; the center (child) column represents the corpus callosum and the neutron. The right (female) column represents the right brain and the electron and includes 3- and 5-sided faces. The ether is the basic form of the Christ consciousness grid.

of triangles and pentagons. Thus the polygons on the left have three- and four-sided faces and the shapes on the right have three- and five-sided faces.

In terms of the Earth's consciousness, the right column is the missing component. We have created the male (left) side of Earth's consciousness, and what we are doing now is completing the female component for wholeness and balance. The right side is also associated with Christ or unity consciousness. The dodecahedron is the basic form of the Christ consciousness grid around the Earth. The two shapes in the right column are what are called duals of each other, meaning if you connect the centers of the faces of a dodecahedron with straight lines, you get an icosahedron; and if you connect the centers of an icosahedron, you again get a dodecahedron. Many polyhedrons have duals.

### The Sacred 72

In Dan Winter's book, *Heartmath*, the DNA molecule is shown to be constructed by the dual relationship of dodecahedrons and icosahedrons. One can also see the DNA molecule as a rotating cube. When you rotate a cube through 72 degrees in a particular pattern, it makes an icosahedron, which is in turn a dual with the dodecahedron. So there's a reciprocal pattern going up the DNA strands: the icosahedron, then the dodecahedron, the icosahedron, continuing back and forth. This rotation through the cube creates the DNA molecule. It has been determined that this is the exact sacred geometry behind the DNA, although there may be further hidden relationships.

This 72-degree angle rotating in our DNA connects with the blueprint/purpose of the Great White Brotherhood. As you may know, 72 orders are associated with the Great White Brotherhood. Many people speak of the 72 orders of angels and the Hebrews speak of the 72 names of God. The reason for 72 has to do with the way the Platonic solids are constructed, which is also related to the Christ consciousness grid around the Earth.

If you take two tetrahedrons and superimpose them (though in different positions), you get a star tetrahedron, which, from a different view, is nothing but a cube [Fig. 6-25]. You can see how they're interrelated. In a similar manner, you can also put five tetrahedrons together and make an icosahedral cap [Fig. 6-26].

If you make twelve icosahedral caps and put one on each face of the dodecahedron (it would require 5 x 12, or 60 tetrahedrons to create a dodecahedron), it would be a *stellated* dodecahedron because a point comes out of the center of each face. Its dual is the 12 points in the center of each face of the dodecahedron, which forms an icosahedron. The 60 tetrahedrons plus the 12 points of the centers equal 72—again, the number of orders associated with the Great White Brotherhood. The Brotherhood actually functions through the physical relationships of this stellated dodecahedron/icosahedron form, which is the basis of the Christ consciousness grid around

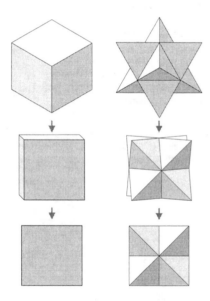

Fig. 6-25. Cube and star tetrahedron sitting next to each other so you can see the squareness of the star tetrahedron.

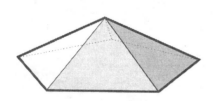

Fig. 6-26 An icosahedral cap.

the world. In other words, the Brotherhood is attempting to bring out the consciousness of the planet's right brain.

The original order was the Alpha and Omega Order of Melchizedek, which was formed by Machiventa Melchizedek about 200,200 years ago. Since then 71 other orders have been created. The youngest one is the Brotherhood of the Seven Rays in Peru/Bolivia, the seventy-second order.

Each of the 72 orders has a life pattern like a sine-wave curve, where some of them come into existence for a certain length of time and then disappear for a while. They have biorhythms just as a human body does. The Rosicrucians, for example, are on a hundred-year cycle. They come out for a hundred years and then disappear totally for a hundred years—they literally disappear off the face of the Earth. Then a hundred years later they're back in the world and functioning for another hundred years.

They're all on different cycles, and they're all functioning together for one purpose—to return Christ consciousness back to this planet, to set up this lost feminine aspect of consciousness and bring balance between the left and the right side of the planet's brain. There's another way to look at this that is really extraordinary. When we talk about England, I will get to it.

### Using Bombs, and Understanding the Basic Pattern of Creation

*Question: When they detonate an atomic bomb, what happens to the elements?*

As far as the elements are concerned, they are converted into energy and other elements. But there is more to the picture. You have two kinds of bombs: fission and fusion. Fission is splitting matter apart and fusion is putting it together. It's okay to put it together—nobody complains about that. All the known suns in the universe are fusion reactors. I realize what I am about to say is not accepted by science yet, but when you rip matter apart through fission, there's a corresponding outer-space location associated with it that is affected—as above, so below. In other words, inner space (the microcosm) and outer space (the macrocosm) are connected. This is the reason that fission is illegal throughout the universe.

Detonating atomic bombs also creates an enormous imbalance on Earth. For example, when you consider that creation balances earth, air, fire, water and ether, an atomic bomb causes a massive amount of fire in one place. That's an out-of-balance sequence and the Earth must respond.

If you dumped 80 zillion tons of water on a city, that would also be an out-of-balance situation. Anywhere you have too much air, too much water, too much of anything, it's out of balance. Alchemy is the knowledge of how to keep all these things in balance. If you understand these geometries and know what their relationships are, you can create what you want. The whole idea is to understand the *map* underneath it all. Remember, the map is the way spirit moves in the Void. If you know the underlying map, then you have the knowledge and understanding to cocreate with God.

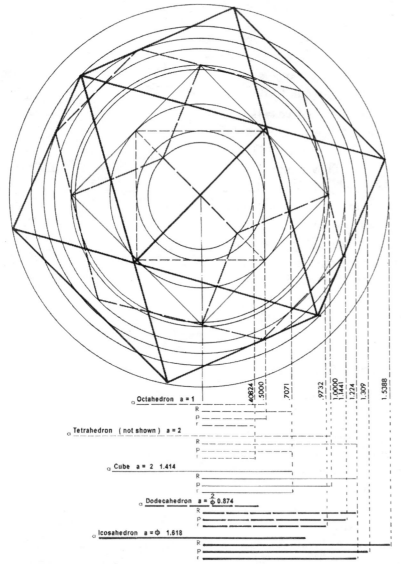

Fig. 6-27. Interrelated shapes.

Octahedron a = 1

Tetrahedron ( not shown ) a = 2

Cube  a = 2  1.414

Dodecahedron  a = $\frac{2}{\phi}$ 0.874

Icosahedron  a = $\phi$ 1.618

.0824  .5000  .7071  .9732  1.0000  1.1441  1.224  1.309  1.5388

R
p
r

Figure 6-27 shows the interrelationship of all these shapes. Each point connects to the next one, and they all have certain mathematical relationships related to phi ratios. The more you study this, the more these five shapes become one. We've only recently begun to remember this ancient science, though they fully understood everything in Egypt, Tibet and India a long time ago. They understood it in Greece, then they forgot for a long time. They remembered it again during the Italian Renaissance, then forgot again. The modern world has almost completely forgotten what shape really means, and we are just now remembering.

## Crystals

### Grounding Our Learning

Now we're going to take this abstract information that doesn't really seem to apply to us in our everyday lives, and we're going to tie it to our everyday experience. Some of this is not in everyday experience, but we can more or less understand and connect with the subjects.

First I'm going to ground this information to crystals. There are lots of other areas of nature I could use, but it's so obvious in crystals that anybody can see it. I could use viruses or diatomaceous earth. I could show it in a lot of things, but crystals are good because people like them.

To begin looking at these crystals, let's first examine this x-ray diffraction pattern [Fig. 6-28]. When you shoot x-rays down the C axis of the atomic matrix of a crystal or metal, you'll get these little dots showing you exactly where the atoms are located. In this case, this is a beryl crystal that actually displays the Flower of Life pattern. The beryl crystal uses the pattern to arrange its atoms and form this specific crystal. It's really amazing that these little atoms simply line themselves up in space, often with enormous distances between them. These microscopic spaces are relatively vast, like between the stars in the night sky. The atoms perfectly align themselves in cubes and tetrahedrons and all kinds of geometric shapes. Why?

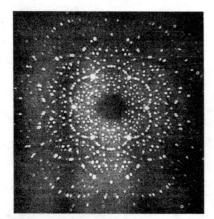

Fig. 6-28. Atomic pattern of a beryl crystal.

This is an x-ray diffraction pattern of a crystal [Fig. 6-29]. You can see how the atoms have arranged themselves in a cubical design. It's interesting that in all the various forms manifested in the Reality, the atoms themselves are spheres. This simple fact has been overlooked by most researchers, but the sphere is the main form that everything came from in the beginning. It is important in understanding creation.

The entire fabric of everything in our existence is made up of "marbles" —all different sizes of spheres. We're sitting on a sphere, the Earth, and spheres are rotating around us. The Moon, Sun and stars are all spheres. The whole universe, from macrocosm to microcosm, is made up of little spheres in one way or the other. The light waves moving through space are all spheres. We think of a light wave as making waves through space, but it's much more complex. An electrical field spins one way around it and a magnetic field rotates at 90 degrees to the electrical field, and they expand in spherical patterns.

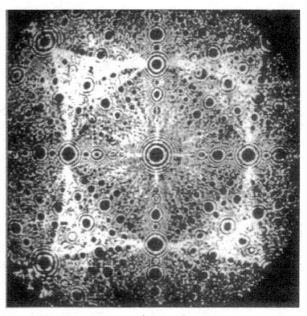

Fig. 6-29. Atomic pattern of a crystal matrix.

Imagine a cube in deep space, and see a bright light flashing from it, going out in all directions, 360 degrees. What do you have? Do you have a cubical light-wave energy field moving away from it? At first thought you might say it would be an expanding cube, getting bigger and bigger and bigger. But that's not what happens. Light waves move radially away from their source at 186,200 miles a second, so when a light wave moves from the surface of a cube I hold in my hand, in one second the light from the face of the cube is already 186,200 miles away. And the wave that moved off a *corner* of the cube, which is a little farther away from the center than the face, is, in one second, 186,200 miles away from the center plus maybe a fraction of an inch. If you could see a fraction of an inch at 186,200 miles, you'd have super vision. And that's only in one second; two seconds later the form has expanded twice that far, and a minute later it's enormous.

So you have a *sphere* moving away from something that originated as a *cube*. If the object happens to be really big, then the light wave first tends to take the shape of the object, but it slowly turns into a sphere as it moves away and the object becomes smaller and smaller relative to that light field. So what you have out there is a bunch of light spheres, moving away in all directions and interconnecting with each other.

When you see light coming directly toward you, it's white. But if it's *not* moving directly toward you, it's black. In fact, the entire night sky is filled with brilliant white light, but we see the light only when it's coming toward us. We don't see the light waves that move sideways from us; we just see black. If we could see it all, it would be blinding. Light is everywhere, and there is noplace in space where it is not, as far as I know. The sphere is literally everywhere.

## Electron Clouds and Molecules

Atoms are also made up of spheres. If you look at the hydrogen atom, the proton is compacted in the center and the electron is way out there orbiting the proton. If the proton were the size of a golf ball, the electron would be about a football field away—and that electron is moving *real fast!* I remember that when I was studying physics, I could not believe that the little electron, *which is a pinpoint you cannot even see,* is moving around and around in some microscopic space *at nine-tenths the speed of light.* This means that the electron travels around the proton about *170,000 miles every second, around something you can't even see!* My mind was totally boggled! I went home and lay on the bed and stared at the ceiling for a long time. That was just inconceivable to me.

The little electron moves around so fast that it appears as a cloud. In fact, they call it an electron cloud. There's only one electron, but it's moving so fast that it appears to make a sphere around the central proton. It's like a television screen, where there's only one electron beam moving across that screen at any one moment, moving carefully and intentionally down the screen, zigzagging back and forth until it gets all the way down to the bottom, then starts all over again. It's doing this so fast that you see a very believable image.

So spheres are the primary component of the Reality we're experiencing. Although an electron orbit describes a sphere, it can also describe other patterns, such as a figure eight. Physicists have been able to calculate this only for hydrogen, and so far they're just guessing about the rest. An atom is called an ion if it has too many or too few electrons and has either a positive or a negative charge. So the primary characteristics of an atom are how big it is and what its charge is [Fig. 6-30]. These two main factors determine whether or not different atoms will fit together into molecules. There are other subtle factors involved, but size and charge are primary.

Figure 6-31 shows how atoms combine. These were the primary patterns known for a long time, until they figured out about quasi crystals. The atoms on this chart have several varieties. A shows a linear pattern with a smaller atom in the middle. B shows a triangular

Fig. 6-30. Sizes and charges of ions.

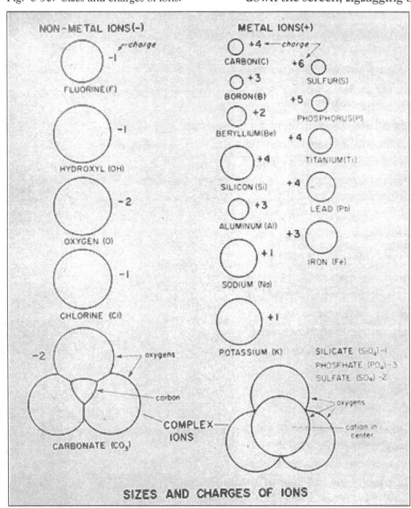

NON-METAL IONS(-)  METAL IONS(+)

charge

FLUORINE (F)  -1

+4 — charge
CARBON(C)   +6
SULFUR(S)

+3
BORON(B)   +5
PHOSPHORUS(P)

+2
BERYLLIUM(Be)   +4
TITANIUM(Ti)

+4
SILICON (Si)   +4
LEAD (Pb)

+3
ALUMINUM (Al)   +3
IRON (Fe)

+1
SODIUM (Na)

+1
POTASSIUM (K)

HYDROXYL (OH)  -1

OXYGEN (O)  -2

CHLORINE (Cl)  -1

-2  oxygens

carbon

CARBONATE (CO₃)

COMPLEX
IONS

SILICATE (SiO₄) -4
PHOSPHATE (PO₄) -3
SULFATE (SO₄) -2

oxygens

cation in
center

SIZES AND CHARGES OF IONS

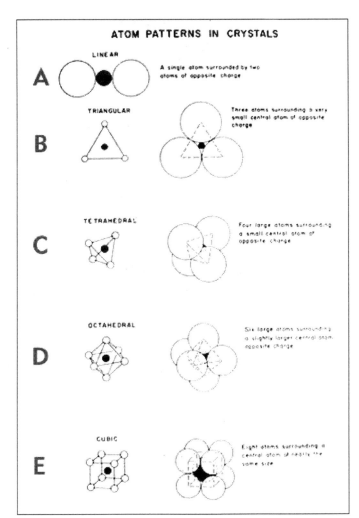

## ATOM PATTERNS IN CRYSTALS

**LINEAR**

A

A single atom surrounded by two atoms of opposite charge

**TRIANGULAR**

B

Three atoms surrounding a very small central atom of opposite charge

**TETRAHEDRAL**

C

Four large atoms surrounding a small central atom of opposite charge

**OCTAHEDRAL**

D

Six large atoms surrounding a slightly larger central atom opposite charge

**CUBIC**

E

Eight atoms surrounding a central atom of nearly the same size

Fig. 6-31.
Atom patterns
in crystals.

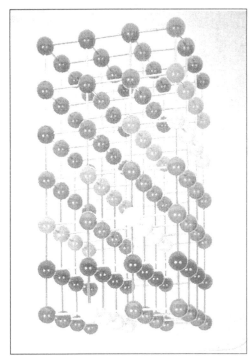

Fig. 6-32. Simple lattice formation of atoms.

pattern of three with a little atom in the middle. The little atom can literally either be there or not be there. *C* shows a tetrahedral pattern, with one atom in the middle, or not. *D* shows an octahedral pattern, and *E* shows a cubical pattern. Now, because of new scientific information, we can add icosahedral and dodecahedral patterns.

Atoms always line up in specific ways when they crystallize [Fig. 6-32]. They form into, say, a cube, and then that cube puts another cube next to itself and another cube next to it, and soon you get one cube connected to another, connected in turn to another cube and so on, forming what is called a lattice. There are all kinds of ways that atoms can join. The resulting molecules are always associated with sacred geometry and the five Platonic solids. It makes you wonder how those little atoms know to go only into those certain places, especially when they get very, very complex!

Even when you get into this complicated molecule [Fig. 6-33] and break it down, you see the shapes in it, and they *always* revert to one of the five Platonic solids—it doesn't matter what the structure is. No matter what you call it—metal, crystal, anything else—it will always come down to one of these original five shapes. I'll show you more examples as we get further into this.

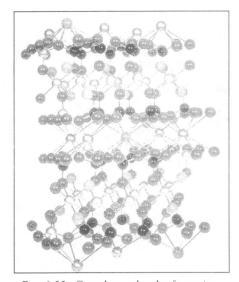

Fig. 6-33. Complex molecular formation.

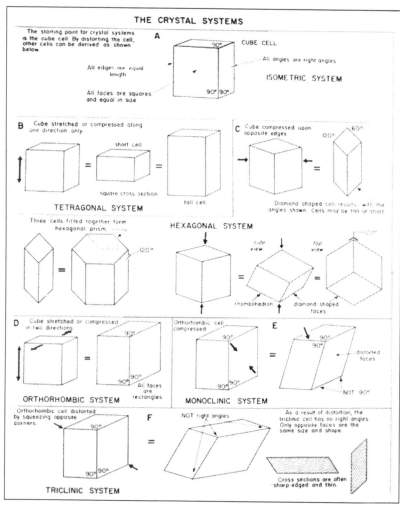

THE CRYSTAL SYSTEMS

A — CUBE CELL

The starting point for crystal systems is the cube cell. By distorting the cell, other cells can be derived as shown below.

All angles are right angles

All edges are equal length

All faces are squares and equal in size

ISOMETRIC SYSTEM

90° 90° 90°

B — Cube stretched or compressed along one direction only.

short cell

square cross section

tall cell

TETRAGONAL SYSTEM

C — Cube compressed upon opposite edges.

120° 60°

Diamond shaped cell results, with the angles shown. Cells may be tall or short.

HEXAGONAL SYSTEM

Three cells fitted together form hexagonal prism

120°

side view

top view

120°

rhombohedron

diamond shaped faces

D — Cube stretched or compressed in two directions.

90° 90° 90°

All faces are rectangles

ORTHORHOMBIC SYSTEM

E — Orthorhombic cell compressed

90° 90° 90° 90°

distorted faces

NOT 90°

MONOCLINIC SYSTEM

F — Orthorhombic cell distorted by squeezing opposite corners.

90° 90°

NOT right angles

As a result of distortion, the triclinic cell has no right angles. Only opposite faces are the same size and shape.

Cross sections are often sharp-edged and thin.

TRICLINIC SYSTEM

Fig. 6-34. Crystal systems.

## The Six Categories of Crystals

Now we'll get into crystals. There are at least a hundred thousand different kinds of crystals. If you've ever been to the Tucson Gem and Mineral Show, you know exactly what I'm talking about. This show takes over eight or ten hotels, with every room in the multistory hotels filled with crystals. In the auditorium you'll see all the gems. There are lots and lots *and lots* of different kinds of crystals. And more are being found; almost every year there are eight, nine, ten brand-new crystals never known before. But no matter how many crystals there are, they can all be put into six categories: isometric, tetragonal, hexagonal, orthorhombic, monoclinic and triclinic [Fig. 6-34]. And all six of those systems used for organizing all known crystals are derived from the cube, one of the Platonic solids. It's a matter of which angle you are viewing the cube from—the square, hexagonal or rectangular view as opposed to the normal 90° cubic angle. Now, this is where it starts to get interesting, at least for me—hopefully, for you, too.

These are fluorite crystals [Fig. 6-35a and b]. Fluorite is found in just about any conceivable color you can think of, including clear. There are two primary fluorite mines in the world: one is in the United States and the other in

Fig. 6-35a. Fluorite crystal with a cubical structure.

Fig. 6-35b. Fluorite crystal with an octahedral structure.

China. Fluorite is found with two totally different atomic structures: one is octahedral and the other cubical. This purple fluorite crystal is made up of tiny cubes all clumped together. They were not cut that way, they grew that way. The clear fluorite crystal is an actual octahedron. It was not cut that way, but in this case it didn't grow that way, either. It usually comes in sheets, and if you drop it or strike it, it breaks along the weakest bonds, which happen to be octahedral, because the atoms are in an octahedral lattice. If I were to drop it onto a hard surface, it would break into a whole bunch of baby octahedrons.

But what's especially interesting is that it's been discovered that fluorite will grow from one shape to the other—from cubical to octahedral and back again. In its natural state, given enough time, a cubical crystal will someday become octahedral. And given enough time, an octahedral fluorite crystal will become cubical. They oscillate over time, first becoming one, then the other, back and forth over very long periods of time. Geologists have found some fluorite crystals in the process of change, but they could not understand how they oscillated like that.

### Truncating Polyhedrons

One geology book tried to explain how fluorite changes like this [Fig. 6-36]. At the bottom right you see a cube. If you were to cut off its corners by the same amount, it's called truncating. You can truncate any polyhedron, meaning any of these many-sided shapes. When you do that (in this case a cube), you can cut off either the *corners,* the *edges* or the *faces,* as long as you cut them all the same.

If you truncate this cube by cutting the corners at 45 degrees all the way around, you get the next shape to its left. If you truncate it again in exactly the same way, you come up with the next shape to the left. If you do it once more, you get an octahedron (on the far left). You can go back the other way, truncating the corners of the octahedron, and come back through the whole procedure until it turns back into a cube. This was the geology book's attempt to explain how in the heck fluorite changes shapes like that. The book actually explains only how this change *could* take place geometrically. But in truth, something far more amazing takes place when fluorite changes. The ions actually *rotate and expand or contract* to become a different lattice! It's much more complex than the book shows.

This is another fluorite crystal [Fig. 6-37], one of my own. It's very big, about four inches on a side. You don't often see them this big anymore. In case you can't quite see it, it comes up to a point in the center.

Fig. 6-36. A fluorite crystal.

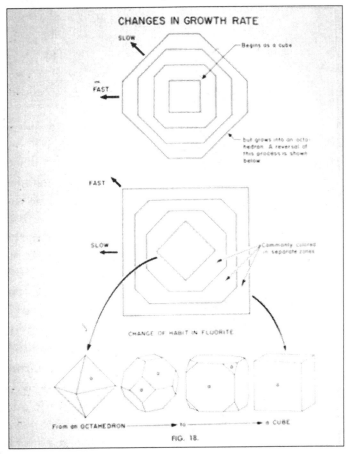

Fig. 6-37. My own fluorite crystal.

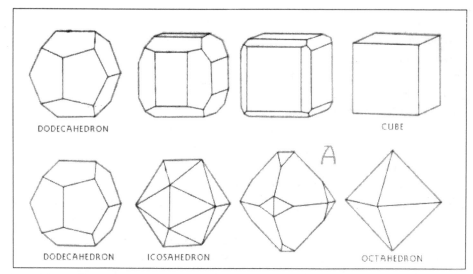

DODECAHEDRON                                                    CUBE

DODECAHEDRON          ICOSAHEDRON                           OCTAHEDRON

Fig. 6-38. Different truncating possibilities. Top line: truncating edges; bottom line: truncating points.

Fig. 6-39. Pyrites: a cube (top) and a cluster of pentagonal dodecahedrons (bottom).

Somebody put this in a window where the sunlight hit it, and because the bonds in fluorite are so weak, when the sunlight struck it, it cracked along the octahedral atomic lines, of course.

In the upper right corner of Figure 6-38 is a cube. The cube to its left is truncated along its edges. Truncated twice more, the darn thing turned into a dodecahedron. This is an example of the cube/dodecahedron in crystals.

In Figure 6-39 the upper crystal is a pyrite cube. It grew that way, no one cut it. There's a huge one like this in Silverado, Colorado, about six feet square, I believe. They simply took it out of the earth as a perfect cube. This little pyrite is square on two ends, rectangular on the sides. The lower crystal is a tiny pyrite dodecahedron cluster. Some of them are almost perfect—and it grew this way in Peru. If this little slab had been left in the earth long enough, those little dodecahedrons would turn into cubes; and over enough time after that, they would turn back into dodecahedrons. If you take the dodecahedron [bottom left in Fig. 6-38] and truncate its points, it turns into an icosahedron [next to it on the right]. If you keep truncating the points, it turns into an octahedron. I could go on with this truncating business for a long time. There are thousands of ways to do it. Each pattern and crystal, no matter how complex it gets, will turn into one of the five Platonic solids if you truncate it just right, showing the innate nature of the five Platonic solids in crystal structure.

A little side note: If you look inside a point-truncated tetrahedron made of glass or crystal or even mirrors, it will reflect the light. The mirrored reflection inside it is a perfect icosahedron. Check it out.

You can go on and on with this. You'll see some that look really strange, like they couldn't possibly be based on anything logical, but all you have to do is a little geometry, and *every time* you will find out that it's derived from one of the five Platonic solids. There are no known exceptions. No matter what the crystal pattern is, it's always based on a Platonic solid. Crystal structures are a function of the five Platonic solids that came out of the Fruit of Life, out of Metatron's Cube. If you want to see more of these crystals, you can find plenty in the *Rocks and Minerals* book by Charles A. Sorrell.

There's one more set I want to talk about that refers back to Figure 6-38, "Different truncating possibilities." When you truncate an octahedron by cutting off all the corners so that they are 90° to each other (shown at A on the figure), it makes the shape on its left. If you were to draw it on a flat surface, it would be a square with a diamond in the middle [Fig. 6-40]. This pattern happens to be related to our consciousness, to the very nature of who we are.

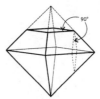

Fig. 6-40. Looking at the face (right) created by truncating all 6 points of an octahedron (left, shown with only one point truncated and another at 90°).

### Buckminster Fuller's Cube Equilibrium

This is what that shape looks like three-dimensionally [Fig. 6-41]. It's called a cuboctahedron or vector equilibrium. You can see that it's originally a cube, but if the angle at point A were continued upward, it would form an octahedron. It's both at once, an octahedron and a cube. It doesn't know which one it is; it's somewhere in the middle. When Buckminster Fuller found this polyhedron, he became almost preoccupied with it. He thought that the cuboctahedron was paramount, the greatest shape that ever was in creation, because it does something that no other known shape does. It was so important to him that he gave it a brand-new name: the vector equilibrium. He discovered that this shape, through different rotational patterns, turns into *all five* of the Platonic solids! This one shape seems to have them all contained within itself [Fig. 6-42].

If you find this interesting, buy this toy [see the reference section] and play with it. It will answer all your questions if you let it.

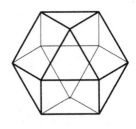

Fig. 6-41. Views of a vector equilibrium (cuboctahedron).

### Deep inside a Sesame Seed

Other people have also studied the cuboctahedron. Is anybody familiar with a man named Derald Langham? Not too many people know of him. He has been pretty quiet during his life. His work is called Genesa, if you want to study it. I really respect him. First of all, he was a botanist who single-handedly saved South America during World War II. They were starving to death, and he created a corn that grew like a weed. You just threw it on the ground, and it grew almost without water. It was a great service to the South American continent. Later he studied the sesame seed, and when he explored deep inside it, he found a cube. In fact, when you get inside any seed, you'll find little geometrical shapes that are associated with the Platonic solids, primarily the cube.

Derald Langham found thirteen rays that came out of the sesame seed's cube. Carrying those studies further, he discovered that the same energy fields that are in plant seeds also exist around the human body—which is what we will eventually talk about. But he focused on the cuboctahedron,

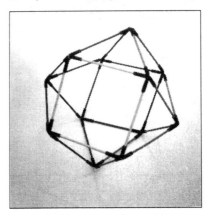

Fig 6-42. Vector or cube equilibrium toy called a Vector Flexor.

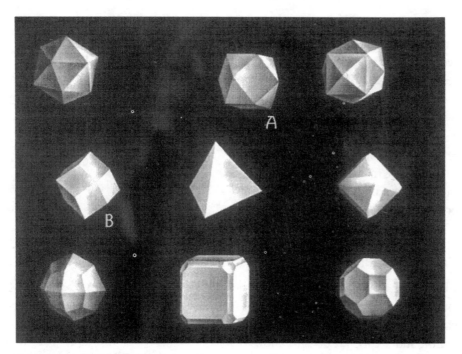

Fig. 6-43. A variety of polyhedrons. A is a cuboctahedron and B is a rhombic dodecahedron.

Fig. 6-44. Comparing atoms and crystals, hexagonal (beryl) and orthorhombic (topaz) systems.

which is interconnected with the fields around the body. We will be discussing that, though my instructions are to focus on another shape: the star tetrahedron. We have a star tetrahedral field around our bodies, which is also around seeds, but which makes a series of geometrical progressions that are different from the cuboctahedron/vector equilibrium. Langham made a series of what you might call sacred dances (in Sufi talk) in which you move and connect with all the points in your field in such a way that you become aware of them. It's really good information.

Figure 6-43 shows some of the three-dimensional forms of the polyhedrons we have been talking about. The one at A is the cuboctahedron we just discussed; the one at B is the rhombic dodecahedron. The latter is important because it's the dual of the cuboctahedron. If you connect the centers of the cuboctahedron, you get the rhombic dodecahedron, and vice versa. Figure 6-44 shows how the internal geometries of the atoms are reflected in the angles of these crystals. We've seen that already, in terms of the crystals being cubes, octahedrons and other forms.

## The 26 Shapes

From my way of thinking, the first five Platonic solids are the first five notes of the pentatonic scale. The octave has seven notes, the last two corresponding to the cuboctahedron (A) and the rhombic dodecahedron (B) shown in Figure 6-43. Five additional shapes form the chromatic scale, and there's a thirteenth one, the return. Thus there are 13 polyhedrons that form the chromatic scale of music. From those 13, 13 more are formed that are the same, only stellated, to total 26 shapes—two octaves within each other. In terms of form, those 26 shapes are the key to all the harmonics of the Reality. We don't need to get into such complexity here, but it just goes on and on and on.

Some of you may know of Royal Rife, the man who was trying to cure cancer through electromagnetic fields (EMF) such as light, which I believe is absolutely possible and has been done. Rife knew of 7 of the 13 (or possibly 26) frequencies. The ones he published were incorrect, but he purposely did that. Those he published cause cancer, though if they're shifted slightly in a certain mathematical way, they return to the original frequencies, and each frequency destroys most or all of a specific virus or bacterium.

However, Rife only knew part of the equation. If he had known the sacred geometry we now know, he could have come up with all 26 forms and eliminated any virus in existence. It doesn't matter how many AIDS viruses there are, there's nothing to finding a solution. There are a maximum of 26 templates, and the right frequencies will eliminate every single virus (or bacterium). Because every virus is a polyhedron—structurally, they look just like the polyhedrons in Figure 6-43—there are various ways you can deal with them. You can either blow them up through certain harmonics of EMF, or you can match them [Fig. 6-45]. If you can match them, you can couple with them, much like an antivirus does. Or you can simply make them nonexistent by creating a waveform that's a mirror image of what they are. There are lots of ways to work with AIDS, but one primary key is understanding that there are a maximum of 26 geometries associated with it.

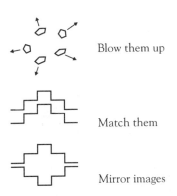

Blow them up

Match them

Mirror images

Fig. 6-45. Possible uses of the 26 templates.

Crystallized water—ice crystals—form these hexagonal patterns we call snowflakes [Fig. 6-46]. You can see the relationship to the Flower of Life. Over and over and over again you will find this relationship of 3D patterns to the geometries that come out of this one central Flower of Life pattern.

### The Periodic Table

This is an interesting version of the Periodic Table of the Elements [Fig. 6-47], because it shows that every element, with a few exceptions that cannot be determined because they will not crystallize, is related to the cube. One of these few exceptions is fluorine, because fluorine reacts with almost nothing. It's one of the most inert gases. But on almost all the other elements we find this cubical relationship, except the fourth-dimensional atoms that fall outside the natural Table of Elements and those that are synthetic or man-made. They don't happen naturally in nature.

Each atomic element has an associated crystalline structure. In every single case scientists have found

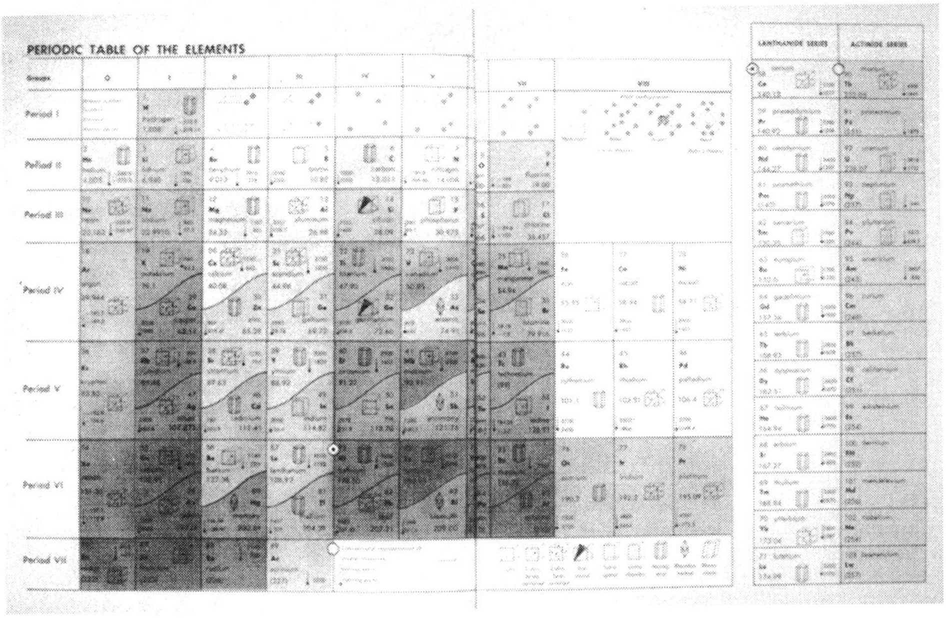

Fig. 6-46. Ice crystals, or snowflakes.

Fig. 6-47. A periodic table showing that all elements known to crystallize are a function of the cube.

that the different crystalline structures associated with atoms can be reduced to the structure of a cube. You might have noticed that the cube seems to be more important than the other polygons. For example, crystals are divided into six different categories, but the cube is the basis of all of them. In the Bible it says that the throne of God is so many cubits in different directions. When you make one, it's a cube. The pharaohs in Egypt sat on a cube. What the heck *is* it about the cube?

### The Key: The Cube and the Sphere

Well, the cube is different from the other Platonic solids because it has one characteristic the others do not—except for the sphere, which also has the same characteristic. Both the sphere and the cube can perfectly contain the other four Platonic solids and each other symmetrically, by their surface, assuming you have the right sizes. The cube is the only Platonic solid with this special characteristic: You can take a sphere, slip it inside a cube, and it will touch the six faces perfectly and symmetrically. And a tetrahedron will slide right down one of the axes and become the diagonals of the cube, fitting perfectly and symmetrically. A star tetrahedron will also fit perfectly inside a cube. The octahedron is actually the dual of the cube; if you connect the centers of the adjacent cube faces, you get an octahedron. That one is easy.

When you get to the last two Platonic solids, it doesn't look like they could fit symmetrically into the cube and the sphere, but they do. It is a little difficult to show here, but you can see for yourself. Using a real model, just find where both the icosahedron and the dodecahedron have six edges in the planes of the cube, and you have it. You will see how they slide into the faces of the cube [Fig. 6-48].

You can see how the other four Platonic solids fit symmetrically into the cube and the sphere. What is important here is that only the sphere and the cube have this capability. The cube is the father, the most important male form. The sphere is the mother, the most important female form. So in the entire Reality, the sphere and the cube are the two most important forms and will almost always dominate when it comes to primary relationships in creation.

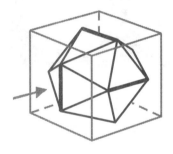
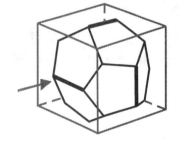

Fig. 6-48. Icosahedron and dodecahedron fitting exactly into a cube.

It was for this reason that a man named Walter Russell did some work long ago that was absolutely phenomenal. I don't believe he knew anything about sacred geometry—he was sacred-geometry illiterate, to my knowledge. Yet he intuitively grasped it in his mind. And when the images were happening in his mind, he chose the cube and the sphere as the main geometries to talk about what he understood. And *because* he chose those two forms and not others, he was able to go far. If he had selected any others, he would have made a big mistake and would have been unable to do the work he did.

## Crystals Are Alive!

This amplifies my thoughts about crystals being alive. Before I taught this course I used to give courses on crystals, back in the early or mid '80s, I guess. And I discovered—not through giving the courses, but through my actual interaction with the crystals themselves—that *these crystals are alive.* They are living and conscious. I was able to communicate with them, and they communicated with me. Through these interchanges I found out all kinds of things. The more I lived with them and learned how to connect with them, the more I discovered just how conscious they were. It was one of the most interesting awakenings in my life.

One time I was in San Francisco giving a course to about thirty people, and I was saying this very thing, "These guys are alive." Everybody was listening and saying, "Yeah, yeah, yeah." Then one person said, "Prove it." I said, "Okay," then I quickly thought up something to do. I gave everybody a piece of paper and a pencil, and said, "We're going to grab a crystal at random." I selected a crystal that nobody had seen—actually took one and kept it hidden. We didn't let anybody see it. Then I said, "Now, nobody gets to examine this crystal or even see what it is. You're just going to put it on your forehead, and you have one second—that's it. You're going to ask the question, Where are you from? The very first word that comes in, write it on a piece of paper and fold it up so no one sees it. Just take the crystal, ask the question, hand it to the next person, then write down what you get." That was the only way I could think of to prove it.

We passed that crystal around to thirty people, and everybody wrote down an answer. Then we looked to see what we received. And *every single person* had "Brazil" written down! What are the odds of that?

Crystals have phenomenal abilities. They affect people in all kinds of ways. Katrina Raphaell has written a lot about this in her books, but many other people have also learned about the abilities of crystals over the years. Many ancient beings and civilizations were also well aware of this. Crystals don't just happen as the result of a chemical reaction either; they *grow.* When you study how crystals are formed, they grow very much like people in lots of ways.

An aerial view of your energy field (shown back in Fig. 2-32) is in part simply the Flower of Life pattern, which is hexagonal in nature. Our fields grow hexagonally, just as crystals do. Though the silicon molecule is a tetrahedron, when it forms quartz it links with another silicon tetrahedron to form a cube. Then it throws out a long line of little star tetrahedrons or cubes to form a row. Then the row begins to spin, changing direction exactly at 60 degrees to form a hexagon, the same structure seen around the human body from above.

Crystals have genders. They're either male or female or both. If you know what to look for, you can look at a crystal and see which way it's rotating. Find the lowest window or face and look to see where the next face is. If it is on the left, then it is rotating clockwise, and that crystal is female. If it

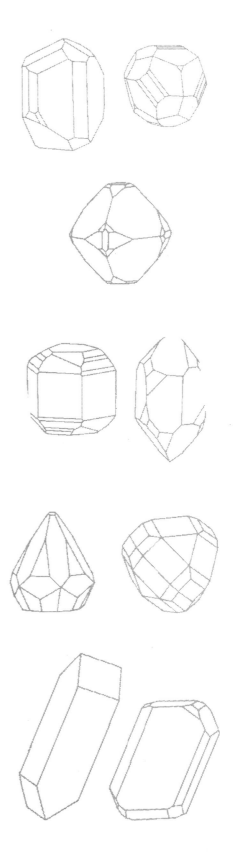

is on the right, then it is rotating counterclockwise, and it is male. If there are faces on both sides at just about the same height, you should see two spirals moving around this crystal in opposite directions, and that crystal would be bisexual.

Often two crystals are joined at the base and wrap somewhat around each other. These are called twinned crystals, and these are almost always male and female. It's rare for them to do it differently.

## The Future Silicon/Carbon Evolutionary Leap

Here's an image I love to talk about. The sixth element on the Periodic Table is carbon. It is the most important element as far as we're concerned, because it's us. It makes up organic chemistry; it is the element that makes our bodies possible. We have been told that carbon is the only living atom on the Periodic Table, that only organic chemistry produces life, nothing else. But that's definitely not true. They suspected this as far back as the '50s when scientists began to study these things.

Fig. 6-49. Silicon makes forms and relationships.

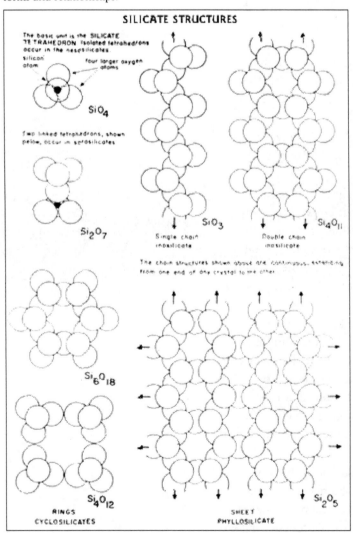

They realized that silicon, which is directly below carbon on the chart (one octave apart) also exhibits the principles of life. There appears to be no difference. Figure 6-49 shows how silicon forms certain chains and patterns. These are only a few. Silicon makes endless patterns, and it will react chemically with almost anything that comes near and form something with it. Carbon has the same ability, making endless forms and chains and patterns and reacting chemically with almost anything nearby. This is the primary characteristic that makes carbon a living atom.

On a chemical level, it appears that there should also be silicon life forms. After this was discovered, several science fiction movies were made in the '50s based on the belief that there might be silicon life forms on other planets. There were a bunch of scary movies about living crystalline structures. They didn't know when they were making those movies that there really are silicon life forms right here on this planet. Some of these were recently found several miles deep in crevices in the ocean. Silicon sponges were found—live sponges that grow and reproduce, demonstrating all the principles of life, and with not a single carbon atom in their bodies!

Here we are, sitting on Earth, which is over 7000 miles in diameter. Its crust, 30 to 50 miles thick, is, like an eggshell, made up of 25 percent silicon, but because silicon reacts with just about anything, the crust is actually 87 percent silicon compounds. That means that the Earth's crust is almost pure crystal, 30 to 50 miles deep. So we're on this huge crystal ball floating through space at seventeen miles a second, totally oblivious of the connectedness of carbon life with silicon life. It would seem that silicon and carbon must have a very special relationship. We carbon-based beings are living on a crystal ball made of silicon, our crystal planet, looking for life outside ourselves in outer space. Perhaps we should look toward our feet.

Now, think about computers and the modern world. We're making computers that are performing all kinds of incredible things. The computer is rapidly moving humankind into a new experience of life on Earth. What are computers made of? Silicon. And what is the computer industry trying to do as fast as it can? Make self-aware computers. We're very close to accomplishing this, if we haven't already. I feel sure that very soon we will have self-aware computers. So here we are, carbon-based life forms creating silicon-based life forms, and we're interacting with each other.

When we have self-aware silicon-based computers, nothing will ever be the same again. We're going to have two different life forms/components of the Earth connecting with each other, and the speed with which we will evolve at that point, aside from everything else, is going to be very, very fast—faster than anything we would normally expect. I believe that this will come true in this lifetime.

# The Measuring Stick of the Universe:
# The Human Body and Its Geometries

## Geometry within the Human Body

It's easy to see how the five Platonic solids influence the structural patterns of crystals and metals. Metals also have atomic lattices. It's simple to see the geometrical relationship of these types of molecules, but when you look at yourself or at a baby being formed, it's much more difficult to see how this kind of geometry could have anything to do with us at all. *Yet it does.* In the beginning of your life in the womb, you were nothing but geometrical forms [Fig. 7-1]. In fact, all life forms—trees, plants, dogs, cats, everything—have the same geometrical and structural patterns running through them that ran through you when you were microscopic. Their very life and structural support depend on the forms. In fact, all life forms *are*

Fig. 7-1. The human fetus.

these geometrical patterns, but it is not apparent to the casual eye. These geometrical relationships are important to perceive, not only so the left brain can realize the unity of all life, but for another reason: *so that we can understand these electromagnetic structural patterns around our body and begin to re-create the living Mer-Ka-Ba around us.*

## In the Beginning Is the Sphere, the Ovum

Figure 7-2 is a sea urchin egg with sperm swarming around it. I'm going to be talking primarily about human beings and human conception, but I'm actually discussing *all* life forms known on Earth, because the procedure illustrated in the next few figures is identical for every life form known—not just humans, but everything.

Every known life form begins as a sphere. It's the most female form there is, so it makes perfect sense that the female would choose that shape to form the ovum [Fig. 7-3]. The ovum is a perfectly round ball. Another example of a round ovum is inside a chicken egg. When you remove the yolk from a hard-boiled egg, you can see how perfectly round it is. All of us begin as a sphere.

I would like you to notice some simple things about this ovum. First, there's a membrane around it called the *zona pellucida.* Remember this, because I will refer to it over and over again; it has to do with why the ancients put two circles around the Flower of Life instead of just one or none.

Inside the membrane is a liquid, and inside that, just like the chicken egg, there's another perfectly round sphere called the female pronucleus, which contains 22 + 1 chromosomes—half the chromosomes necessary to create a human body. The number of chromosomes changes, depending on the life form, and those particular chromosomes are different in every life form. Inside the zona pellucida are two polar bodies. I'll explain those in a moment.

## The Number Twelve

When you were first learning about human biology, you were probably told that it takes one sperm for conception to occur. That isn't true, according to *Time* magazine, even though most textbooks still state this. It is now known that the ovum must be absolutely saturated with hundreds of sperm, or conception is not even possible. Second, out of those hundreds, ten, eleven or twelve must come together in some kind of pattern on the surface—a pattern they're still trying to figure out—that allows the eleventh, twelfth or thirteenth sperm to enter the ovum [Fig. 7-4]. One sperm cannot get through the membrane without the other ten, eleven or twelve. It's not possible except under unnatural conditions, where a human manipulates the conception.

This image brings up what was possibly hidden in the life of Jesus. Jesus came here to a round ball called Earth, which was saturated

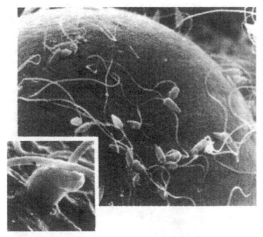

Fig. 7-2. Sea urchin sperm swarm around egg; one penetrates (inset).

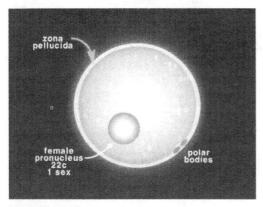

Fig. 7-3. The human ovum.

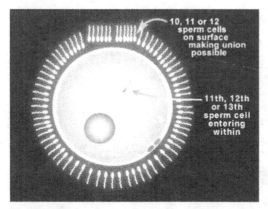

Fig. 7-4. Twelve sperm allowing the thirteenth to penetrate the ovum.

with people. The first thing he did was gather twelve males together, no females. Jesus—from my point of view and from his, I'm sure, because he did it—could not have done what he did without the twelve disciples. Seldom does anyone wonder why he gathered those twelve disciples together. He absolutely *had* to have them. If we are right, he could have done it with ten or eleven, but he chose twelve. I believe that the *number* of sperm that join to allow the one sperm to enter the egg determines the sex—and Jesus chose twelve. Prior to Jesus' time, in Greece, near the area of his ministry, people saw the Earth as a sphere. Right after that they began to see the Earth as a cube and flat. Then 400 years ago, Copernicus came along and changed it back to a sphere. So people's perception of the Earth went from a sphere to a cube and back to a sphere. Exactly the same thing (sphere to cube to sphere) goes on during conception, only at a much faster rate. I don't know if this analogy is true or not, but it sure does look like it.

### The Sperm Becomes a Sphere

Anyway, the little sperm gets in through the zona pellucida with the help of the other sperm and then starts swimming toward the female pronucleus [Fig. 7-5].

The first thing that happens is that the sperm's tail breaks off and disappears—it's just gone. Next, the tiny sperm head expands and becomes a perfect sphere, which is the male pronucleus. It becomes *exactly* the same size as the female pronucleus, and it contains the other half of the necessary information. The words "exactly the same size," I believe, are very important when you look at the next figure.

Next, they pass through each other and form a geometrical relationship called the vesica piscis [Fig. 7-6]. It's not possible for two spheres to pass through each other and perfectly coincide without forming a vesica piscis. This means that at that exact moment, the male and female pronuclei form the image of the first motion of the first day of Genesis, and literally all the information of the Reality (and light) is contained in that geometry. It's so simple. That image could not be formed *unless these two pronuclei were the same size.* It's for that reason I believe that the female determines which sperm will enter. Science proved around 1992 that the determining factor for which sperm will enter is the female. She selects the one to allow in.

Just as everybody in this room has a different projection length into a dark space or into the Void, each little sperm also has a different-size sphere around it. She's not going to let him in unless his size is identical to hers. If it's a matching key, okay; if it's not, forget it. This could explain why many people who have tried to have babies cannot have them; there's no explanation that anybody can see. This might be at least one explanation.

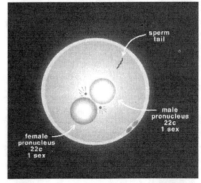

Fig. 7-5. The sperm's breakthrough.

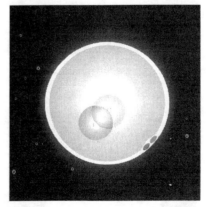

Fig. 7-6. Union of male and female pronuclei.

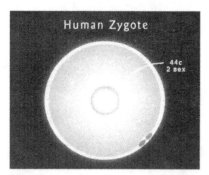

Fig. 7-7. Oneness in the human zygote.

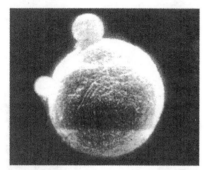

Fig. 7-8. First cell of a mouse egg.

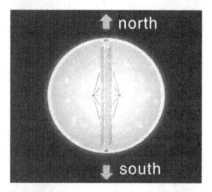

Fig. 7-9. Migration of polar bodies to form a central tube.

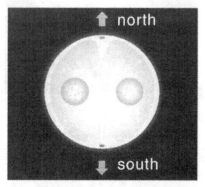

Fig. 7-10. Chromosomes forming the first two cells.

## The First Human Cell

After the two pronuclei make a vesica piscis, the male pronucleus continues to permeate the female pronucleus until they are one [Fig. 7-7]. At this time it's called a human zygote, the first cell of the human body. So you began as a sphere before you created your familiar human body. Actually, you were a sphere within a sphere.

The next thing you need to know is that the human zygote will not change size during the first nine cell divisions. It's fixed, as is the size of the outer membrane. The human zygote is about 200 times bigger than the average cell in the human body, so big you can actually see it with your naked eye. When it divides into two, each of those two cells are half the original size; and when those two cells divide into four, each cell is a quarter of the original size. The cells keep dividing like this, getting littler and littler, until they've divided eight times and number 512. At that point the average cell size of the human body is reached. When that happens, mitosis continues, and the dividing cells expand beyond the boundaries of the original zona pellucida.

So, first the growth goes into itself, then out beyond itself. When the first growth goes inward, it's as if it's trying to figure out how to do it. Once it figures that out, it goes beyond itself. All life uses this process. I use that same understanding to figure out some of the geometries, which you'll see later.

Figure 7-8 is an electron microscope photograph of the first cell of a mouse egg.

## Forming a Central Tube

The next thing that happens in the conception process is that those little polar bodies begin to migrate through the zona pellucida. One goes down and becomes the south pole and the other becomes the north pole. Then out of nowhere a tube appears, running right down through the center of the cell. Then the chromosomes break in half, and half of them line up along one side of the tube and half along the other [Fig. 7-9].

This is a familiar image in human energy fields—it's very much like the energetics of an adult human being. As you study this further, you'll see that you have a similar sphere of energy around you. You have a north pole and a south pole, and you have a tube running right down through your body. Half of you is on one side of that tube and half is on the other. So this picture is very much like the energy field of an adult human being, though the human energy field is much, much more defined than that. But we've got to wait until we get further along to see how true this is.

After the chromosomes have lined up along the two sides of the tube, they form into two cells, one on each side of the tube, and each cell contains 44 + 2 chromosomes [Fig. 7-10].

Here are the first two cells in a mouse egg [Fig. 7-11]. The zona pellucida has been taken away so you can see the inner part.

An important piece of information came up around 1992. Many books said that the female gave 22 + 1 chromosomes and the male gave 22 + 1. That was flat-out true, according to them; it wasn't even considered that it could be anything else. But that has now been found to be untrue. The female can give *any number whatsoever*. She can give 22 + 1 or all 44 + 2 or any number in between. This new information has completely changed the field of genetics. They've thrown almost everything they knew out the window and started over.

Scientists used to depend on electron microscopes for photographs. Now they have laser microscopes that can take movies, so they can watch these things happening. They're gaining information very rapidly. I'm sure they're a lot further now than we are showing you. Science is in the midst of mapping every one of the 100,000 chromosomes in the DNA of the human body. Within just a few more years we'll know what every single chromosome is and what it does, which means that we'll be able to engineer any kind of human being you can imagine, create any appearance or intelligence or emotional body—anything we want. We'll be able to do it and know exactly what we will get. Are we God? This is a question that must be answered.

### The First Four Cells Form a Tetrahedron

The next step is that the cells divide again, going from two to four—a binary sequence—1, 2, 4, 8, 16 etc. Most textbooks show the first four cells forming a little square, but that's not what happens. They actually form a tetrahedron—one of the Platonic solids—and the apex of the first tetrahedron points either to the north pole or the south pole [Fig. 7-12]. (The tetrahedron is formed by linking the centers of the spheres together.) I believe that whether it points north or south probably determines which sex it is. They haven't discovered that yet, but they'll probably figure it out, based on the polarities of the tetrahedron. If the tetrahedron forms with an apex pointing to the south pole, toward the feet of the newly forming fetus, it should be female; if it forms with an apex pointing to the north pole, toward the head, it should be male. If this is true, they'll be able to determine immediately what the sex is. Since they'd have to do that within about an hour or so after conception, it would be fairly inconvenient.

These are the geometries of the first tetrahedron [Fig. 7-13]. The side view is on the right and the top view is on the left.

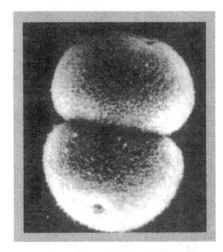

Fig. 7-11. First two cells in a mouse egg.

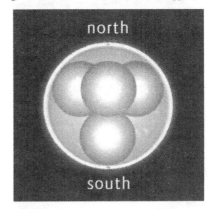

Fig. 7-12. The first four cells form a tetrahedron.

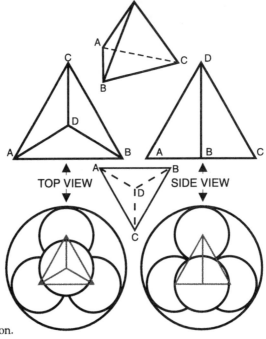

Fig. 7-13. Geometries of the first tetrahedron.

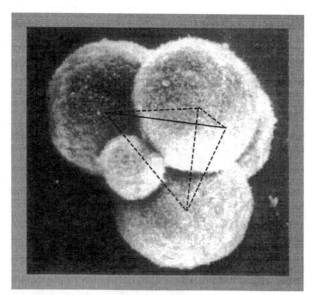

Fig. 7-14. The four-cell tetrahedron in a mouse egg.

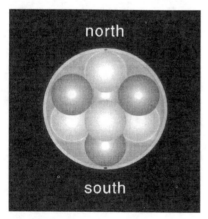

north

south

Fig. 7-15. Egg of Life in first eight cells.

Figure 7-14 is an electron microscope view of a mouse egg. In this picture it's growing really fast, but it's still aligned through the north-south pole. That tiny cell is beginning to form beyond the original tetrahedron. The fourth point of the tetrahedron is in the center of the large cell in the background.

Next, the cells divide into eight; they form one tetrahedron facing up and one tetrahedron facing down, and you get the star tetrahedron. Here it is—the Egg of Life [Fig. 7-15]. This form came out of Genesis, remember? It came out of spirit's second rotation. Every single life known—on Earth anyway, and probably everywhere—must pass through the Egg of Life. According to the angels, this point where the original eight cells form a star tetrahedron—or a cube, depending on how you look at it—is one of the most important points in the creation of the body. Science has also recognized that this particular stage of development is different from any other, and it has many unique qualities that don't occur at any other time in its development.

The most important quality of these original eight cells is that they appear to be identical—there appears to be nothing different about them at all. Usually it's easy to see the difference between one cell and another, but here they all appear to be the same. Researchers have tried to find differences, but they couldn't. It would be as though there were eight identical twins in this room, dressed exactly alike, with their hair combed exactly the same way. Scientists have found that they can split the egg in two at this point, through the middle of the cube, with four cells in one part and four in the other, and two identical people—or rabbits or dogs or anything else—will be created. They've also been able to sever it once more, making four identical life forms. I don't know if anybody has been able to go further than that and make eight life forms, but they've definitely gone as far as four.

## Our True Nature Is in Our Original Eight Cells

According to the angels, these original eight cells are closer to who you really are than your physical body is, closer to your true nature. That sounds odd, I know, because we're used to identifying with our human bodies. But these eight cells are closer to who we *really* are. The angels say these eight cells are immortal relative to your body. You get a brand-new body every five to seven years; every single cell in your body dies within a five- to seven-year period and is replaced with a new one, except for the original eight cells. They remain alive from the time you're conceived until the time you die and leave the body. All the rest go through their life cycles, but not these eight.

These cells are centered in the precise geometric center of your body, which is slightly above the perineum. For the female the perineum is located between the anus and the vagina. For the male it's between the anus and the scrotum. There's a little piece of skin there, and even though there's not a physical opening, there is actually an energetic opening. That's where the central tube runs through your body, coming out the top through the crown chakra at the top of your head. If you look at a newborn baby during the first few weeks, you'll see the top of its head pulsing. If you were to look at the bottom of the baby, at its perineum, you'd see the same pulsing. That's because the baby is breathing in the proper way. Both ends are pulsing because the energy is flowing from the two poles—coming not only from the top down, but from the bottom up—and meeting. This is the basic understanding of the Mer-Ka-Ba. From the point where the original eight cells are located, it's the same distance to the top of your head as it is to the bottom of your feet. And the cells are arranged just as they were when they first came into existence—in the Egg of Life pattern—north up, south down.

If you notice in the previous illustration, when the Egg of Life is oriented to the north and south, you can actually see through the middle to the light-colored sphere on the back side. That's very different than when you look at it as a hexagon—you can't see through a hexagonal pattern. I want you to notice this difference for later, when we talk about doing the meditation to activate the Mer-Ka-Ba.

Figure 7-16 and the next are two views of the first eight cells. These original eight cells are the key, because according to the angels, we don't grow like a string bean, getting longer and longer. We actually grow radially in 360 degrees, from the original eight cells.

This picture of the mouse egg was taken just as the eight cells started to divide again [Fig. 7-17]. It's not a great photograph, as these pictures are difficult to get; the cells are dividing very quickly. They have to strip off the zona pellucida, have the cells stop at the right place, then take the photograph.

### The Star Tetrahedron/Cube of 16 Cells Becomes a Hollow Sphere/Torus

After the eight-cell division, it divides into 16 cells, whereupon it forms another cube or star tetrahedron on the end. This is the last time it will be symmetrical. When it divides into 32, 16 cells are in the middle and 16 on the outside. If you take the 16 on the outside and try to fill in the empty spaces to keep it symmetrical, you will find it is not possible. (I've actually done this. You end up with two open spaces no matter how you

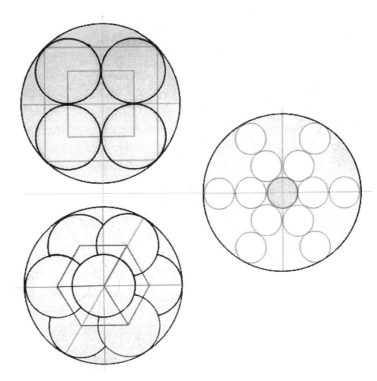

Fig. 7-16. Geometries of the first eight cells, 2 views.

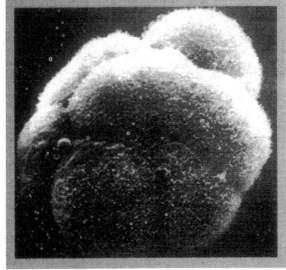

Fig. 7-17. Mouse egg starting to divide beyond the first eight cells.

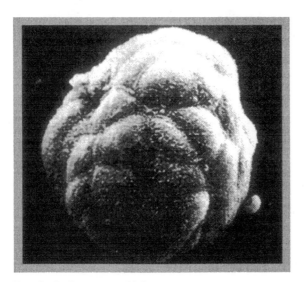

Fig. 7-18. Becoming a blob.

do it.) It needs 18 cells to be symmetrical. You wonder why. At the next division there are 32 more cells, but it gets worse [Fig. 7-18]. You wonder, What's going on here? It's getting weird. Where did all the symmetry go?

Well, it was meant to do that. It starts turning into a blob. We become a blob for a while. But the blob has consciousness in its blobness. Then it stretches and the inside starts turning out, becoming a hollow ball like this photo [Fig. 7-19].

Once it gets to this stage, it becomes a perfect hollow sphere. Then the north pole starts dropping through the space inside, going down toward the south pole, and the south pole comes up through the space to meet the north pole. The embryo in this photo has been broken apart so the center could be photographed. If you could see this in its completeness, it looks just like an apple cored through the middle. The hollow sphere then becomes a torus—a spherical torus like the photo on the right.

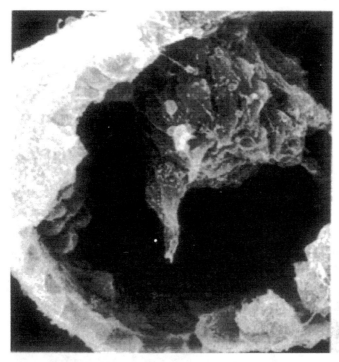

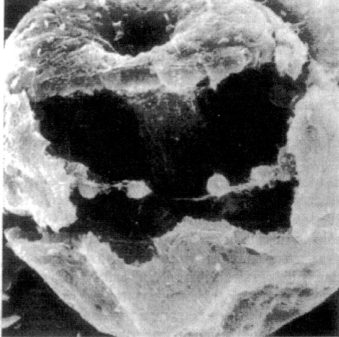

Fig. 7-19. Original cells forming into a torus (see the photo at right). A sea-urchin embryo, magnified 2000 times, begins as a hollow ball of cells. It forms a gut by folding inward (left) until its cells reach the opposite side.

Every single known life form goes through this torus stage. This formation in the apple/torus shape is called the *morula*.

After this the expansion goes beyond the zona pellucida and the cells begin to differentiate. The hollow space inside the torus becomes the lungs, the north pole becomes the mouth, the south pole becomes the anus, and all the internal organs form inside the tube that runs through the middle. If it's a frog it begins to get little legs, or if it's a horse a little tail grows. For a fly, little wings develop, and a human starts to look like a human. But before this differentiation, we all look like a torus.   I suspect this is why, though I don't have any proof, biblical tradition says that the tree of knowledge of good and evil is an apple tree. We really *do* turn into something that looks very much like an apple at one stage.

## Progression of Life Forms through the Platonic Solids

To summarize, we start out as a sphere, the ovum. We then move to a tetrahedron at four cells, then on to two interlocked tetrahedrons (a star tetrahedron or a cube) at eight cells.  From two cubes at sixteen cells we turn back into a sphere beginning at 32 cells, and from the sphere we become a torus at 512 cells.  Planet Earth and its magnetic field is also a torus. All of these forms are sacred shapes that come out of the first informational system of the Fruit of Life, which is based on Metatron's Cube.

We could go on for probably another seven or eight months talking about this subject, showing how more and more and more things are connected to these five shapes—the Platonic solids.  But I think you can see exactly what I mean.  By the way, modern mathematicians say that the Platonic solids have been known only since civilization began about 6000 years ago, but this is not true.  Some put their discovery during the time of Greece.  Archaeologists have recently found some perfect models in the earth—perfectly cut in stone—that were found to be 20,000 years old. Those hairy barbarians obviously knew more that we give them credit for.

## Underwater Birthing and Dolphin Midwives

I would like to take a quick digression from the geometries of birth to something slightly different.  A Russian named Igor Charkovsky has been involved in underwater birthing for a long time.  He has probably assisted with at least 20,000 underwater births.  His daughter, one of the first to be born underwater, was in her twenties, I think, when the following incident took place.  Charkovsky and his team had taken a woman to the Black Sea for an underwater birth.  They were sitting there prepared for the birth, with the woman lying in water about two feet deep.

As I remember, three dolphins approached, pushed everybody away and took over.  The dolphins did something that looked like scanning up and down her body—something I have experienced, and which does something to the human system.  The woman gave birth with almost no pain or fear.  It was a phenomenal experience.  That experience with underwater birthing began a new practice of using dolphins as midwives, which has now spread all over the world.  There's something about the sonar that dolphins project at the time of birth that seems to really relax the mother.

Dolphins have preferences with humans.  This is not an absolute rule, but is usually true.  If you go swimming with dolphins and there are children around, the dolphins go to the children first.  If there are no children, they go to the women.  If there are no women, they go to the men.  And if there's a woman who's pregnant, everyone else can forget it—she gets their total attention. That little incoming baby is the greatest thing of all. The dolphins become very excited when they see a human giving birth. They just love it.

Dolphins can do things that are really amazing. Babies who were born with midwifing dolphins, at least as it's going in Russia, are extraordinary children. From everything I've read so far, not one of those babies has an IQ under 150, and they all have extremely stable emotional bodies and extremely strong physical bodies. They seem to be superior in one way or another.

France has also had underwater births—over 20,000. They give birth in big tanks. When they first started doing this, they had all the instruments laid out on tables and all the emergency supplies ready, with a doctor standing by in case there was a problem. But they didn't have a problem for a long time; a year went by and they still hadn't had a problem. Still another year went by, and finally 20,000 births went by without *one single complication!* Now they just have the instruments and equipment stuck in a corner somewhere because there simply aren't any problems. I don't know if they know why, but for some reason, when a woman is floating in water, it seems like most complications solve themselves.

I got to spend some time with a woman who was an assistant with Charkovsky in Russia. She had brought back many films that were taken during the births. I watched two movies of two different women giving birth who not only were not in pain, but they were having orgasms while having their babies—long, extended orgasms lasting about twenty minutes. It was total pleasure. I know that's the way it's supposed to be. It simply makes sense, and these women were proving it.

I've also seen some Russian movies where babies and children two or three years and older sleep on the bottom of swimming pools. They literally sleep underwater on the bottom of the pool, and about every ten minutes they come up while they're asleep, roll their faces over the surface, take a breath, go back down and settle on the bottom again. These kids live in water—that's their home. They're being given a name, almost like they're a different species. People are calling them *homodolphinus.* They seem to be a blend between humans and dolphins. Water is becoming their natural medium, and they're extremely intelligent.

So I have a great deal of respect for underwater birthing. And the possibility of having dolphins there at the same time is truly a gift. I think it's a healthy trend the way many countries are allowing this new way to birth, though in the United States there's a lot of pressure against it. Lately in the U.S., the pressure seems to have subsided, and I think you can do this legally now in Florida and California. Around the world, in New Zealand, Australia and other places, there are lots of centers. And, of course, the more women see other women not in pain, obviously they're going to want to do it, too.

## Geometries That Surround the Body

Here we go with the next adventure. We've now seen how the geometries unfold in conception. We saw how we started with a little cube of eight cells, which became the center of our bodies. Now I want to look at the geometries outside the body. The way the angels explained it to me is the way I'm going to give it to you.

This began when I was in Boulder, Colorado, sometime between 1976 and 1978; I can't pinpoint it for sure. I was living in a communal home with a bunch of friends and had my own bedroom. One night the angels came in with a new teaching for me. They showed me the geometries by projecting glowing forms in space. It would be like holographic images that would appear maybe seven or eight feet away from me, and I'd work with them from there. In my room the angels showed me this image of a circle and a square [Fig. 7-20]. They said they wanted me to find this image in Metatron's Cube [Fig. 7-21]. Then they said good-bye and left, leaving me with no real instructions on how to proceed.

After they left, I figured this wouldn't be too hard, because they were always giving me little things to do. I'd do them, wait for them to come back, then they'd give me something else to do. I figured it wouldn't take long. But as I found out, it wasn't that easy. At least four months went by and I still couldn't figure it out. The way I see it, the angels intervened directly to help me with this.

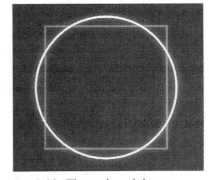

Fig. 7-20. The circle and the square.

I was sitting there in my room one night around nine, the floor covered with drawings. (I used my floor as a table because I had so many drawings.) My door was closed, and I was sitting there studying my drawings, trying to solve the problem the angels had given me. I had so many drawings you wouldn't believe it, trying to figure out where the circle and the square were in Metatron's Cube.

In those days I didn't tell anybody what I was doing; I didn't tell people for a long, long time because it was a very personal experience for me. And quite frankly, nobody was interested anyway. Nobody cared about geometry back then, because it had not emerged into most people's consciousness as it has now.

### The Masonic Key to Squaring the Circle

Someone knocked on the door. I opened my bedroom door, and here's this tall guy standing there. I had never seen him before in my life. He looked kind of sheepish, and he said, "I was supposed to come here to tell you some things." I asked his name and more about what he wanted.

"Well," he said, "I was sent here by the Masons to tell you about the circle and the square."

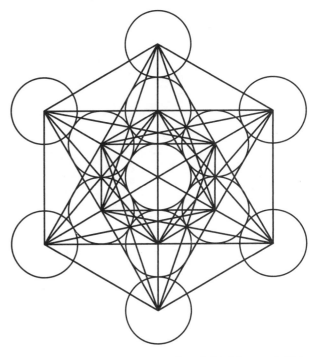

Fig. 7-21. Metatron's Cube.

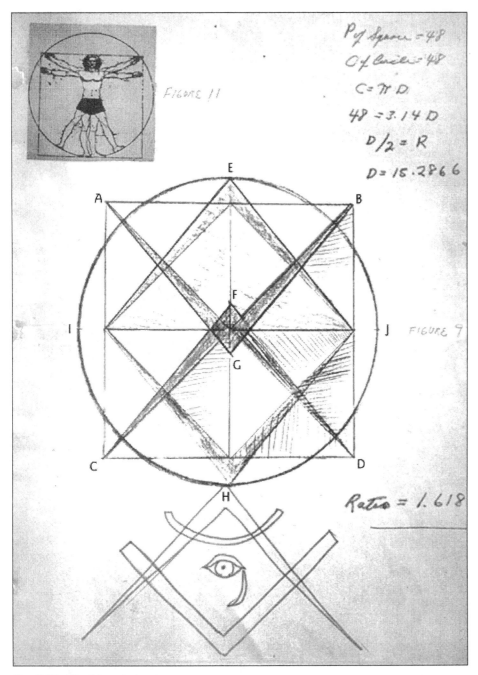

Fig. 7-22. The Mason's drawing.

This really jolted me. I sort of froze in my tracks and just looked at him for a moment, trying to understand how this was happening. Then I figured I didn't really care *how* it was happening, only that it was. I just grabbed him by the hand and said, "Get in here," pulling him in and closing the door. I said, "Anything you have to tell me, I want to know what it is." So he drew this drawing [Fig. 7-22].

First he drew the square, then he drew the circle around the square in a particular way—and there was the image I had seen glowing in the room! I thought, This is going to be good. He divided the square into four sections, then he drew diagonals from the corners through the middle to the opposite corners. Then he drew diagonals through the four smaller squares. Then he drew lines from I to E and E to J. Next he drew lines from I to H and H to J (E and H being the points on the circle's circumference where the vertical center line intersects it).

Up to this point I'd had no problem, but then he drew a line from A to nowhere (G) and back to B, and from D to nowhere (F) and back to C. I said, "Wait a minute, that isn't in the rules I was given. That doesn't fit—there's nothing there." And he said, "It's okay, because this line (A-G) is parallel with that line (I-H), and this line (D-F) is parallel to this line (J-E)."

"Well," I said, "that's a new rule. I didn't have that one before. I mean, there's nothing there. Parallel lines?—well, okay I'll listen."

Then he began to tell me all kinds of things. He said that the first key is that the circumference of the circle and the perimeter of the square are equal, which is what I told you before. This circle and square is the same image seen from the air as that of the Great Pyramid with the ship sitting on top.

## The Phi Ratio

He began to tell me about the phi ratio of 1.618 (rounded here to three decimal points). The phi ratio is a very simple relationship. If you had a rod and you were going to put a mark on it somewhere, only two places would mark the phi ratio, shown as points A and B in his illustration [Fig. 7-23].

There are only two places, depending on which end you're coming from. Shown on the lower drawing, it's a relationship such that if you divide D by C and E by D, the two answers will be the same—1.618 . . . . So you divide the longer portion by the shorter portion, and that gives you the ratio 1.618. When you divide the whole length of E by the next shorter portion, which is D, you'll get the same ratio. It's a magical place. Even though I was studying mathematics in college when this incident took place, the phi ratio somehow had gone over my head. I didn't get it. I had to go back and restudy all this stuff.

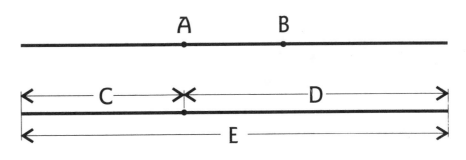

Fig. 7-23. Phi-ratio points.

This guy also brought up Leonardo's drawing with the circle and the square around it, giving me more information, which I'll tell you later. I asked him many questions, and about half the time he didn't know the answer. He'd just say, "That's the way it goes," or "I don't know; we don't know that." Though I can't say this for certain, I suspect the Masons have lost a great deal of their information. I think that they once had a brilliant knowledge that was very much like the Egyptians', and both of those disciplines have gone downhill.

Before he left, he drew the sketch at the bottom of his diagram [see Fig. 7-22], with a square and the right eye of somebody—I can't say Horus because I don't know who it is—and then left. I've never seen him since. I don't even remember his name.

Fig. 7-24. Three-dimensional Metatron's Cube, end view.

### Applying the Key to Metatron's Cube

This gentleman from the Masons didn't answer the question specifically—how the circle and the square fit into Metatron's Cube. In fact, I don't think he'd ever seen Metatron's Cube. But something he said triggered something in me so that I understood what it was. Right after he left I knew the answer. As you know, Metatron's Cube is really a three-dimensional object, not a flat object. Three-dimensionally, Metatron's Cube looks like this [Fig. 7-24]. It's a cube within a cube, three-dimensionally. Then if you rotate it to this view [Fig. 7-25], you have its square aspect.

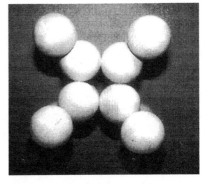

Fig. 7-25. Three-dimensional Metatron's Cube, squared view.

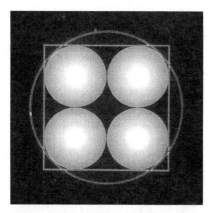

Fig. 7-26. The circle and the square in Metatron's Cube.

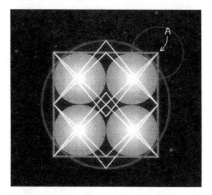

Fig. 7-27. The Mason's lines drawn over the Egg of Life.

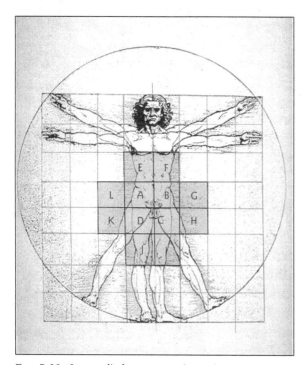

Fig. 7-28. Leonard's famous man (canon).

Once you do that, you have Figure 7-26. At this point you can drop the outer aspect; all you need are just the original eight cells. Around those eight cells there's already a sphere, the zona pellucida. The cells are in the shape of a cube, so if you draw both a circle and straight lines around it, you get the image of the circle and the square the angels showed me. I was happy!

### The Two Concentric Circles/Spheres

But then I calculated the perimeter of the square and the circumference of the circle—and they were *not* equal. I was bummed out for a long time because I figured I hadn't found it. About three years later I discovered that I *had* found it, but had just not understood. In sacred geometry, when you find something that appears incorrect or breaks the idea you're trying to form, you have to keep going deeper, because often you just don't have the whole picture yet.

What I discovered was that the zona pellucida has a thickness to it; there's an inner surface and an outer surface. Every membrane has an outer and an inner surface, and when you use the outer surface of the zona pellucida, the proportions go into a near-perfect phi ratio. The amount of imperfection is actually part of the equation. (You'll know what that means in a while.) This is why there are two lines around the Flower of Life—the inner and the outer circle of the zona pellucida. So from now on, whenever you see four circles in a square, we're talking about the Egg of Life, the original eight cells. Just take it for granted.

So in this drawing [Fig. 7-27] I drew in all the lines that the Mason drew just to see how they would line up and what would happen, comparing the Mason's drawing to the eight cells. Nothing appeared to be happening in the middle of the drawing that I could see, though I suspected something at this point, which had to do with a circle that would just fit in the middle of the four spheres. But I did discover that the corners of the square (a cube, actually) define the exact centers of the outer layer of cells in the 16-cell division, as at point A. This was an interesting observation. So I began to doodle and study further to see what they meant. Obviously, the angels wanted me to go down this road, but I had no idea where this road led.

### Studying da Vinci's Canon

I decided to look deeper at this drawing of Leonardo's [Fig. 7-28]. I had also majored in art, so I had studied much of Leonardo's work, but I didn't realize until later how much artwork he had done. This drawing has become probably one of his most famous works. It's perhaps even more important to us than the Mona Lisa or any other famous work of his. This kind of drawing, a standard for something (in this case, a standard for human beings), is called a canon, a human canon.

The first thing that struck me about this drawing is how amazingly we all attune to it. For instance, because there are 30 frames per second that come across on a video, you could flash this drawing of Leonardo's for just an instant, yet people would immediately recognize it. We know something there is important; perhaps we don't know exactly what it is, but we still retain the image. There is a tremendous amount of information about us in this drawing. But as it turns out, it's not really about us. It's about who we used to be, not about who we are now.

To begin this analysis, notice first that there are lines drawn over the arms and the trunk, across the chest and over the legs and neck. The head is divided into another series of lines. Notice that the feet are drawn at both 90 degrees and 45 degrees—subtle things. Also notice that if you were to stand with your arms straight out and your legs straight down, a square or cube forms around your body, as in Leonardo's drawing. The center of that square is located exactly where the original eight cells are, which is also a square or cube, in the center of your body. Notice the small cube around your original cells and the bigger cube around your adult body.

When you are standing with your arms outstretched like Leonardo's man, there is a difference between the height and the width of your square. Computers have shown by measuring a hundred people or more that there is one ten-thousandth of an inch difference between the width of your outstretched arms and your height. Though I couldn't understand for a long time why that difference was there, I think I know now. It has to do with the Fibonacci series, which life is based on. You will see this shortly.

If you put your legs out to the side, like the outer legs on Leonardo's drawing and stretch out your arms like the upper arms, a perfect circle or sphere fits around your body, and its center is located exactly at the navel. When you do that, the circle and the square exactly touch at the bottom. If you were to move the center of the circle down to the center of the square, the circle and the square would synchronize just like they do in the Mason's drawing and the drawing that shows the warship superimposed over the top of the Great Pyramid. It is a major secret of life.

When you measure almost all the copies of Leonardo's drawings, you find that the circle is really an oval and the square is really a rectangle. It's different in all of them because they've been copied and folded so many times. But in the original, accurate drawing, the hand length from the wrist line to the longest finger equals the distance from the top of the head to the top of the circle when the two centers are aligned; this same length shows up between the navel and the center of the square. So when you bring the two centers together, everything aligns.

### Phi Ratios in the Human Body

As I was discovering this, I thought, We have these geometrical forms that appear to be outside the body as well as inside it. One of the things the angels said, which really stuck with me, was that the human body is the

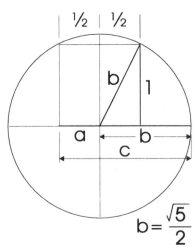

$$b = \frac{\sqrt{5}}{2}$$

Fig. 7-29. Phi-ratio diagram for the human body.

$$\frac{b}{a} = \frac{b+a}{b} = \frac{c}{b}$$

$$b^2 = a^2 + 1^2 = (\tfrac{1}{2})^2 + 1 = \tfrac{1}{4} + 1 = \frac{5}{4}$$

$$b = \frac{\sqrt{5}}{2}$$

$$c = a + b = \tfrac{1}{2} + \frac{\sqrt{5}}{2} = \Phi$$

$$\Phi = 1.6180339...$$

Fig. 7-30. Equation for the phi ratio.

measuring stick of the universe—that absolutely everything in the universe can be measured and determined from our bodies and from the energy fields around them. Since the phi ratio seemed to be such an important aspect to the Mason, and since he went on and on about it, I wanted to see where it was in the human body.

I discovered it—and of course other people have also discovered it. Realize that in Figure 7-29 the square shown is the square around the body as in Leonardo's drawing. And that the line dividing the square in half is the center line of the human body. Also notice that the line *b* is not only the diagonal of one-half of the square, but is also the radius of the circle.

Now, if you are interested in the math, see Figure 7-30, which proves that the phi ratio is found in the geometrical energy fields around the body in at least this one relationship. There are many, many other phi relationships in and around the body.

As you can see, the phi ratio $= \tfrac{1}{2} + \frac{\sqrt{5}}{2}$. If you put this into your computer, you will see the transcendental number of phi continue until your computer runs out of memory. I know most of you out there don't care, but I've presented this information for the few.

By the way, I'll just throw this out to you: When you're studying sacred geometry, you'll find that diagonals are one of the major keys for extracting information from your forms (in addition to shadows, expanding from two to three dimensions, comparing male to female and so on). It never fails.

I believe it was Buddha who asked his disciples to contemplate their navels. Whoever it was, I began to realize as I studied that there was more to the navel than meets the eye. Then I found a medical book, whose authors must have also listened to Buddha, because they did a tremendous amount of research on navels. What the geometries show is that in the ideal, the navel sits at the phi ratio between the top of the head and the bottom of the feet. This is what most books indicate.

The authors found out that when a baby is born, its navel is in the exact geometrical center of the body. Both male and female babies start out this way, and as they grow, the navel starts to move toward the head. It moves up to the phi ratio, then continues upward. Then it comes back down to below the phi ratio, oscillating during the formative years. I don't know what the ages are, but these movements and locations happen at specific ages. It never actually stops at the perfect phi ratio in either males or females, but if I remember correctly, the male navel ends up slightly above the phi ratio and the female navel just below it. If you average the male and female points, you get the perfect phi ratio. So even though Leonardo's drawing is of a male, it assumes that it is at the phi ratio, but of course in nature it would not be.

Da Vinci figured out that if you draw a square around the body, then a diagonal from foot to extended fingertip, then draw a parallel line (another one of those parallel lines) from the navel horizontally over to the side of the square, that horizontal line intercepts the diagonal line exactly at its phi ratio [Fig. 7-31] as well as that of the vertical line from head to feet. Assuming it's at that perfect point, not slightly above for females or slightly below for males, this means that the human body is divided into phi ratios from top to bottom, which we stated earlier. If these lines were the only places in the human body where the phi ratio is located, it would probably be just an interesting fact. But the truth is, the phi ratio is located in thousands of places throughout the body, and it is not just a coincidence.

Here are some obvious phi-ratio locations in the human body [Fig. 7-32]. The length of each bone in the finger has a phi ratio to the next bone, as shown in the lower drawing. That same ratio occurs with all your fingers and toes. This is a somewhat unusual relationship because one finger is longer than the other in what appears to be an arbitrary fashion, but it's not arbitrary—nothing in the human body is. The distances on the fingers marked A to B to C to D to E are all in a phi ratio, as well as the lengths of the phalanges, F to G to H.

If you compare the length of the hand to the length of the lower arm bone, it has a phi ratio, just like the length of the lower arm bone compared to the upper arm bone. Or take the length of the foot to the lower leg bone, or that bone to the thigh bone and so on. This phi ratio is found throughout the entire bone structure in all kinds of places and ways. It's usually at places where something bends or changes direction. The body also does it through proportionate sizes of one part to another. If you study this, you will be continually amazed.

Figure 7-33 is another way of showing the phi ratio. You make a curve so that you can see how one curve is linked with another, and you can see all the cascading phi ratios of the human body. This is from *The Power of Limits* by Gyorgy Doczi. I highly recommend this book. Notice that on this male he drew the line for the navel slightly above where the actual phi ratio is located. He knew about that, and very few people I have read understand it.

I want to talk about this Greek statue. The Greeks were well aware of this understanding of phi ratios. So were the Egyptians and many, many other people in ancient times. When they created a piece of art like this, they were actually using both sides of the brain simultaneously. They were using their left brain to very carefully measure everything—I mean *really* carefully, not kind of or sort of. They were measuring to make sure that everything was exactly mathematically correct according to the phi proportion. To be as creative as they wanted, they were also using their right brain. They could put any expression on the face and have the statue hold anything or do anything they wanted. The Greeks combined the left and right brain.

When the Romans came in and took over Greece, the Romans knew absolutely nothing about sacred geometry. They saw the Greeks' incredible art and tried to duplicate it, but if you compare Greek art to Roman art after they

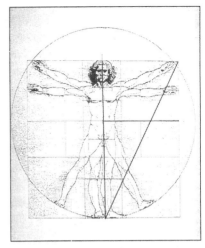

Fig. 7-31. Leonardo's drawing with more lines, one of which (the horizontal line) divides both the vertical and diagonal lines at a phi-ratio point.

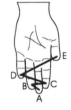

$$\frac{BC}{AB} = \frac{AB + BC}{BC} = \Phi$$

$$\frac{DC}{BC} = \frac{BC + DC}{DC} = \Phi$$

$$\frac{DE}{DC} = \frac{DC + DE}{DE} = \Phi$$

$$\frac{GH}{FG} = \frac{FG + GH}{GH} = \Phi$$

Fig. 7-32. Phi ratios in human body.

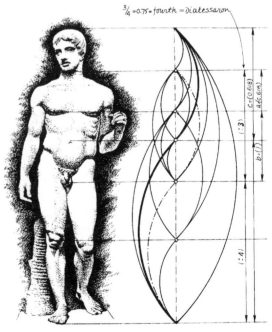

Fig. 7-33. Doryphoros the Spear-Bearer's phi ratios.

conquered Greece, Roman art looks like it was done by amateurs. Even though Roman artists were really good at what they did, they just didn't know they were supposed to measure everything—that there had to be this kind of perfection for the body to look real.

### The Phi Ratio in All Known Organic Structures

Phi-ratio mathematics goes not only through human life, but through the entire spectrum of all known organic structure. You can find this in butterflies [Fig. 7-34] or dragonflies [Fig. 7-35], where each little tail section is proportioned to the phi ratio. The lengths of the sections of the dragonfly form phi ratios. This illustrator was focusing on one thing, but you can also look where every little bend is in the legs, the length and width

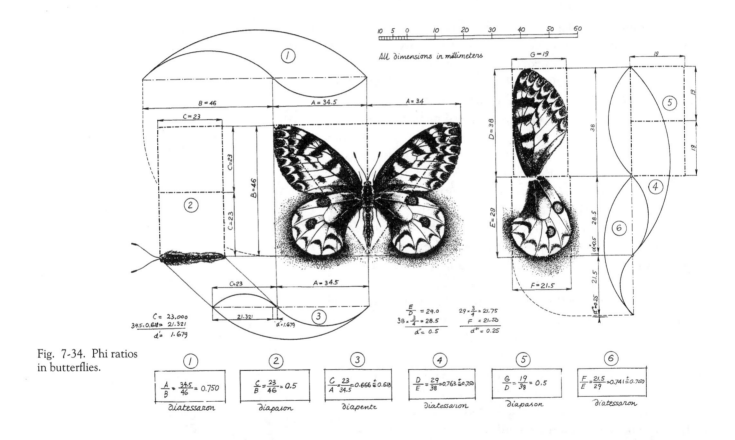

Fig. 7-34. Phi ratios in butterflies.

of the wings, the size of the head compared to its width and length—everything. You can go on and on and on, and you'll keep finding the phi ratio everywhere you look.

Look at this frog skeleton [Fig. 7-36] and see how every single bone is in phi-ratio patterns, just like in the human body.

Fish, I think, are really incredible, because fish don't look like they have any phi-ratio stuff going on—and there are so many different kinds. But when you analyze them, the phi ratio is there as well [Fig. 7-37].

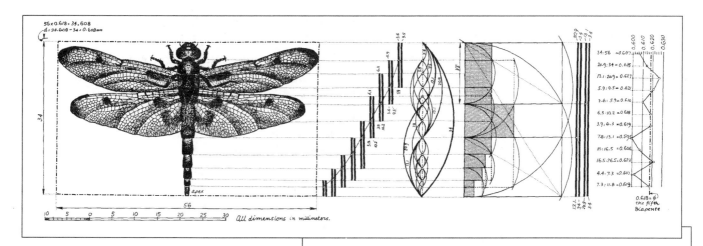

Fig. 7-35. Phi ratios in a dragonfly.

The other universal measurement you'll find, one I talked about before, is 7.23 centimeters, the wavelength of the universe. You'll find this wavelength scattered through the body, such as the distance between your eyes; but the phi ratio occurs more often than any other.

Once a measurement of any species has been determined, then every other measurement in that species follows in the phi-ratio proportion. To put it another way, there are only certain possibilities in human structure, and once the size of one part of the body is determined, that determines the size of the next, and on and on. Soon I'll show you the Egyptian building that Lucy Lamy reconstructed just by measuring one little piece of rubble. This is how she did it: Once she knew the size of the first

Fig. 7-36. Phi ratios in a frog skeleton.

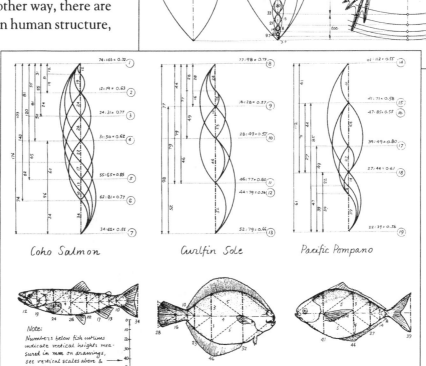

Coho Salmon    Curlfin Sole    Pacific Pompano

Note:
Numbers below fish outlines
indicate vertical heights measured in mm on drawings,
see vertical scales above &

Fig. 7-37. Phi ratios in fish.

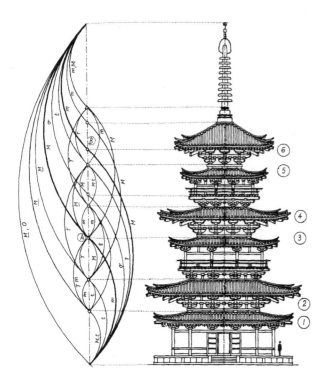

Fig. 7-38. Pagoda of Yakushiji Temple in Japan.

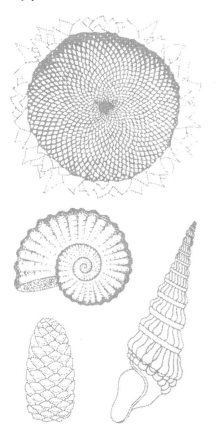

piece, she knew that every shape after that would relate to it in phi ratios.

The phi proportions are built into this Japanese pagoda architecture [Fig. 7-38]. This illustrates another point about creativity that I want to make. When they designed and built this structure, they carefully measured *every single distance* to match the various lines shown, and they carefully measured where to put each board—right down to that little ball on the very top, so that it could correspond with and form these relationships we have been studying. I'm sure if someone ever checks, they'll find that the size of the doors, the windows and probably every small detail are all based on phi proportions or other sacred geometry.

Other classical architecture around the world used the same principles. The Greek Parthenon looks really different from this Japanese structure, but the Parthenon embodies the same mathematics. And the Great Pyramid looks very different from either of those two buildings, but it also embodies the same mathematics—only a lot more. What I'm saying is, your left brain can understand and use these mathematics, and it doesn't hinder creativity at all. It can even enhance it.

## Golden Mean Rectangles and Spirals around the Body

Another sacred form we have in life is the spiral. You may wonder where it came from. We're living in a spiral—the galaxy, which has spiraling arms. You're using spirals to listen to the sounds around you because the little apparatus in your ears is in a spiral form. There are spirals all over nature. The more you look, the more you find. Spirals are found in pine cones, sunflowers, a few animal horns, deer antlers, seashells, daisies and lots of plants. If you put your open hand vertically in front of you, thumb toward your face, notice the movement as you roll your fingers into a fist, starting with your little finger. They trace out a Fibonacci spiral. This is a very special spiral, as you will see.

Where do spirals come from? They have to come from somewhere, and they have to be generated out of the dynamics of the original system, the Flower of Life, if what we believe is true. Well, all you have to do is go back to the human body—to the same pattern we came up with for the phi ratio [see Fig. 7-30]. If you simply take the diagonal line, lay it down flat, then complete the rectangle formed with that new extension—you have a Golden Mean rectangle, the source of the Golden Mean spiral.

The outer rectangle of this drawing [Fig. 7-39] is called a Golden Mean rectangle, the same as above. To get another Golden Mean rectangle, all you have to do is measure the rectangle's shorter edge (side A) and plot that distance along the longer side (side B), which makes a square (with equal sides; A = C). The area that's left over (D) is another Golden Mean rectangle. Then you can take the shorter edge again and plot that distance along the longer edge to make another square, and what's left over is still another Golden Mean rectangle. This can continue forever. Notice that each newly formed rectangle is turned 90 degrees. If you run diagonals across each rectangle, their crossing locates the exact center of the spiral they form. You can see how the diagonals become a key for more information: Line F has a Golden Mean ratio to line E, continuing inward. We can say that F is to E what G is to F and H is to G and I is to H and so on. There are other kinds of spirals, but the Golden Mean spiral is paramount in creation.

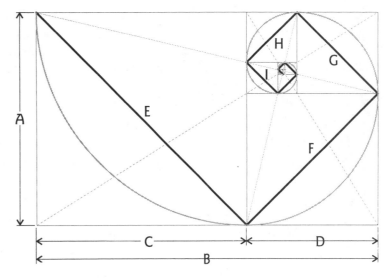

Fig. 7-39. The Golden Mean rectangle and male and female spirals.

### Male and Female Spirals

There are two kinds of energies that move through Golden Mean rectangles. One energy is the diagonals that cross the squares, moving at 90-degree turns, shown in black. That's the male energy. The female energy is the line that keeps curving in toward the center, shown in gray. So you have a female Golden Mean logarithmic spiral, along with a male spiral that uses straight lines with 90-degree turns at the phi ratio. In much of the work I will show you, we'll be looking only at the male aspect, but you must remember that the female aspect is always there.

Some books say that if you draw a horizontal line through the navel in da Vinci's man [Fig. 7-40], what's left over in the lower portion is a Golden Mean rectangle; and that if you draw a line from the top corner of the large square to the middle point at his feet (the center of the opposite side of the square), that semi-diagonal will pass through the exact center of a Golden Mean spiral as shown in the figure. You can create a spiral if you draw in the consecutively smaller Golden Mean rectangles like we did in Figure 7-39. I've read several books about this, and I believe it's *almost* true. But something else is actually happening that is important to understand if one really wants to know about Mother Nature.

In fact, I'm convinced that there are no Golden Mean rectangles or spirals in existence unless they're synthetically made. Nature does not use Golden Mean rectangles or spirals—it doesn't know how. The reason nature doesn't know how is because a Golden Mean spiral will literally go inward forever—maybe not with a pencil and

Fig. 7-40. Leonardo's canon and spiral.

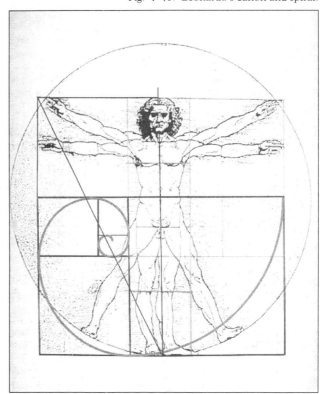

Fig. 7-41. Diagonal lines made by connecting each corner to the center of the opposite side of the square.

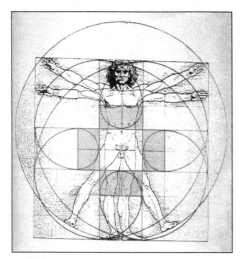

Fig. 7-42. Spirals and the original eight squares.

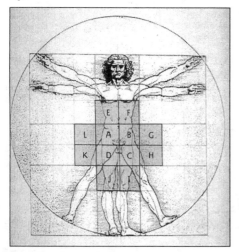

Fig. 7-43. Leonardo's surrounding grid.

paper, but technically it will go on forever and ever. It will also go outward forever too, because you can take the longest line of any Golden Mean rectangle, make a square to get a larger Golden Mean rectangle and continue to do this forever. So a Golden Mean rectangle has no beginning and no end. It will go inward and outward forever.

This is a problem for Mother Nature. Life doesn't know how to deal with something that has no beginning and no end. We can sort of deal with something that has no end, but if you think about it, it's difficult to think of something having no beginning. Just try to get that in your mind—something that has no beginning. This is hard for us because we are geometric beings, and geometry has centers, beginnings.

Since life doesn't know how to deal with this, it has found a way to cheat. It has found another spiral to create with. Life figured out a system of mathematics that approximates this so well that you can hardly tell the difference. The books say that this spiral on Leonardo's drawing in Figure 7-40 is a Golden Mean spiral, which I say can't be true. Also, there is not just one little spiral here; there are eight spirals rotating around the body— one for each Golden Mean rectangle, connected to the eight possible semi-diagonals around the human body [Fig. 7-41]. This drawing shows the eight that intersect the human body.

Figure 7-42 shows the eight spirals with their eight centers located around the center of the body, in the same pattern and with the same center as the original eight cells inside the body—right?

Leonardo drew these little lines that make a grid over and around the body [Fig. 7-43]: There are four squares in the center (A, B, C and D, clockwise) and eight squares surrounding them (E through L). Those outer eight squares happen to be where the eight semi-diagonals of Figure 7-41 intersect the body and where the eight spirals of Figure 7-42 begin. So we have eight places around the body and a central pattern of four squares in the middle, centered exactly around the original eight cells. Life is amazing, is it not?

When I noticed this about Leonardo's drawing, I figured there must be something important about this relationship. But when I realized that there's no such thing as a Golden Mean rectangle or spiral in nature, I began to suspect that these spirals were probably something slightly different. And that's what they turned out to be—slightly different.

It turns out that these spirals are Fibonacci in nature, which we will explore in the next chapter. Understanding the difference between the Golden Mean and Fibonacci spirals may seem simple and unimportant, until the bigger picture of nature unfolds to reveal something astonishing about this relationship. No one can ever understand why the 83,000 sacred sites on the Earth were built or what their purpose was without knowing this difference.

# Reconciling the Fibonacci-Binary Polarity

## The Fibonacci Sequence and Spiral

In order to understand why those eight spirals around da Vinci's canon are not Golden Mean spirals and to find out what they are, we have to go to another person—not Leonardo da Vinci, but Leonardo Fibonacci. Fibonacci preceded da Vinci by over 250 years. From what I've read about him, he was a monastic, often in a meditative state. He loved to walk through wooded forests and meditate as he was walking. But evidently his left brain was simultaneously active, because he started to notice that plants and flowers had number associations [Fig. 8-1].

Flower petals and leaf and seed patterns correspond to definite numbers, and the flowers on this list are the ones I think he saw, if I've got it right. He noticed that lilies and irises have three petals and that buttercups, larkspurs and columbines (the flower at the top right in Fig. 8-1) have five. Some delphiniums have 8 petals, corn marigolds have 13 and some asters have 21. Daisies almost always have either 34, 55 or 89 petals. He began to see these same numbers over and over again throughout nature.

This little plant [Fig. 8-2] doesn't actually exist; we created it with computer graphics, shuffling it around like a deck of cards. The original plant on which this illustration is based is called the sneezewort; we simply made the computer graphics fit that plant.

Fibonacci noticed that when the sneezewort plant first came out of the ground, it grew only one leaf, just one little leaf. As it grew taller, farther up on its stem it grew one more leaf; then a little bit farther it grew two leaves, then three, then five, then eight; then it had thirteen flowers. He probably said, "Gee, those are the same numbers I keep seeing in the petals of other flowers—3, 5, 8, 13."

Eventually this sequence of 1, 1, 2, 3, 5, 8, 13, 21, 34, 55, 89 and so on became known as the *Fibonacci sequence*. If you are given any three consecutive numbers in this sequence, you can recognize the pattern: you simply add two consecutive numbers to get the next number. See

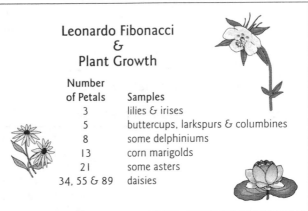

Fig. 8-1. Fibonacci sequence in plant growth.

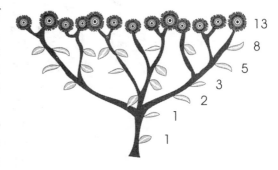

Fig. 8-2. The computerized sneezewort.

how it works? This is a very special sequence. It's crucial in life. Why is it important? This is perhaps my interpretation of why, but I'll do my best to show you.

Fig. 8-3. Hibiscus flower.

This is a hibiscus flower with five petals [Fig. 8-3]. The stamen inside has five terminating buds, and the direction of those two geometric forms are reversed to each other, one set pointing up and one pointing down. When most people look at this flower, they don't think, "Let's see, it has five petals." They simply look at it, notice it's beautiful, smell it and experience it from their right brain. They're not thinking about the geometry or mathematics going on in the other side of the brain.

### Life's Solution to the Infinite Golden Mean (Phi) Spiral

Remember that I said how the Golden Mean spiral has no beginning and no end, and that life has a hard time with that? It can cope with no end, but it has a difficult time grokking something that has no beginning. I have a really hard time doing it, and I think we all wrestle with that situation.

What nature did was create the Fibonacci sequence to get around the problem. It's like God said, "Okay, go out there and create with the Golden Mean spiral," and we said, "We don't know how." So we made up something that is not the Golden Mean spiral, but it rapidly comes so close that you can hardly tell the difference [Fig. 8-4].

$$\Phi = 1.6180339...$$
(Fibonacci Sequence)

| Current Term | Previous Term | Division | Ratio |
|---|---|---|---|
| 1 | 1 | 1 / 1 | 1.0 |
| 2 | 1 | 2 / 1 | 2.0 |
| 3 | 2 | 3 / 2 | 1.5 |
| 5 | 3 | 5 / 3 | 1.6666 |
| 8 | 5 | 8 / 5 | 1.600 |
| 13 | 8 | 13 / 8 | 1.625 |
| 21 | 13 | 21 / 13 | 1.615384 |
| 34 | 21 | 34 / 21 | 1.619048 |
| 55 | 34 | 55 / 34 | 1.617647 |
| 89 | 55 | 89 / 55 | 1.618182 |
| 144 | 89 | 144 / 89 | 1.617978 |
| 233 | 144 | 233 / 144 | 1.618056 |

Fig. 8-4. Fibonacci sequence.

For example, the phi ratio associated with the Golden Mean is approximated by 1.6180339. Look what happens when you divide each number in the Fibonacci sequence into the next higher number. Here's the sequence in the left column: 1, 2, 3, 5, 8, 13, 21, 34, 55, 89. In the second column I've shifted the sequence by one so we can divide the number in the first column by the number in the second column (see column 3). Notice what happens when you divide a column-two number into the one in column one. When we divide 1 into 1, we get 1.0. Now, 1.0 is a lot *less* than the phi ratio. But when we go to the next line and divide 1 into 2, we get 2, which is greater than phi, but closer than 1 is. When we divide 2 into 3 we get 1.5, which is a lot closer to phi than either of the previous two answers, but it's under.

Three into 5 is 1.6666, which is over, but a lot closer. Five into 8 is 1.60, and it's under. Eight into 13 is 1.625, which is over. Thirteen into 21 is 1.615, under. Twenty-one into 34 is 1.619, over. Thirty-four into 55, 1.617, under. Fifty-five into 89, 1.6181, over. The next one goes under, then over, each time getting closer and closer to the actual phi ratio. This is called asymptotically reaching a limit. It can never ever reach the actual number, but practically speaking, you wouldn't be able to tell the difference after a few divisions. You can see this graphically in Figure 8-5.

The light gray squares are the four central squares of the human body where the original eight cells are located. The eight dark gray squares around these central squares are where the spirals begin. Does everybody get that?

Rather than having them spiraling in forever and ever, we're going to do something different—because this is what life does, I believe. I'm going to use one of the outer squares as my starting point, and this will be true for all eight. I'm choosing one of them as an example.

Using a diagonal across just one of the tiny background squares as our measure, we'll call this diagonal line one unit. Then we move according to the Fibonacci numbers: 1, 1, 2, 3, 5, 8, 13, 21, 34, 89, with a 90-degree turn after each number. In our first step we go one length, then turn 90 degrees and go one again. Then we turn 90 degrees and go two lengths, turn another 90 degrees and go three lengths. Between each step we take a 90-degree turn. The next step is 5 units long, then 8. So we have 1, 1, 2, 3, 5, 8, 13.

Then we diagonally cross 21 squares, then 34 [Fig. 8-6]. Then 55, then 89 [Fig. 8-7]. As we do this, the spiral unfolds and gets closer and closer to phi, the Golden Mean spiral, until very rapidly there's no way to tell the difference in life, at least visually.

Comparing the two spirals must have been a very important feature if one studied life, because the ancient Egyptians displayed both the Fibonacci and the Golden Mean spirals at the Great Pyramid. Even though the spirals have two different origins, by the time they get out to steps 55 and 89, the two lines are practically identical. When people who studied Egypt saw the three pyramids lined up on the spiral, they thought it was the Golden Mean, not the Fibonacci spiral. Then they came back and found one of the holes (refer to page 109). Several years later they realized that just a little ways away, maybe a hundred yards or so, was another marker. They hadn't realized there were *two* spirals. I don't know whether the people working with this understand its significance even yet.

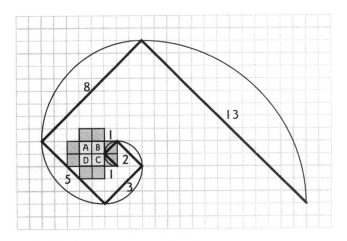

Fig. 8-5. Fibonacci female (curved) and male (angled) spirals on an expanded grid.

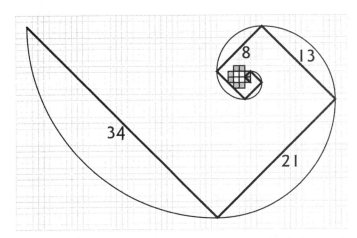

Fig. 8-6. A view of the Fibonacci spiral, both male (straight line) and female (curved).

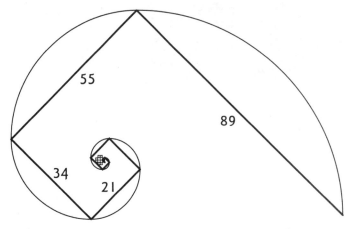

Fig. 8-7. A more distant view.

## Spirals in Nature

Here is sacred geometry in nature [Fig. 8-8], the real thing. It's a nautilus shell cut in half. It's an unwritten rule that every good sacred geometry book has to have a nautilus shell in it. Many books say this is a Golden Mean spiral, but it's not—it's a Fibonacci spiral.

You can see the perfection of the arms of the spiral, but if you look at the center or beginning, it doesn't look so perfect. You can't really see this detail here. I suggest that you look at a real one. This innermost end actually hits the other side and bends, because its value is 1.0, which is a long ways from phi. The second and third ones bend also, but not as much because they are coming closer to phi. Then they start fitting better and better, until you see this perfectly graceful form developing. You could think that the little nautilus made a mistake in the beginning; it looks like he didn't know what he was doing. But he's doing it perfectly, it's not a mistake. He's simply following exactly the mathematics of the Fibonacci sequence.

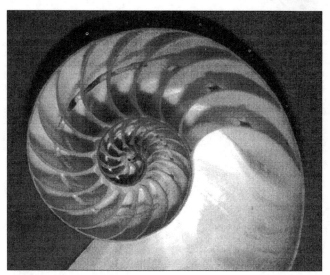

Fig. 8-8. Slice of a nautilus shell.

Fig. 8-9. Pine cone.

On this pine cone [Fig. 8-9] you see a double spiral, one going one way and one going the other. If you were to count the number of spirals rotating one direction and those going the other direction, you'd find that they're always two consecutive Fibonacci numbers. There are perhaps 8 going one way and 13 the other, or 13 going one way and 21 the other. The many other double-spiral patterns found throughout nature correspond to this in all cases that I know. For instance, the sunflower spirals are always related to the Fibonacci sequence.

Figure 8-10 shows the difference between the two. The Golden Mean spiral is the ideal. It's like God, the Source. As you can see, the top four squares on both drawings are the same size. The difference is in the areas where they originate (the bottom sections of the two diagrams). The bottom of the Fibonacci spiral has an area half the size (0.5) of the area above; the Golden Mean spiral has an area 0.618 the size of the area above. The Fibonacci spiral shown at near right is constructed using six equal squares, whereas the Golden Mean spiral

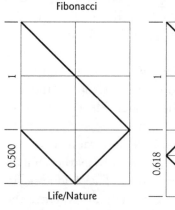
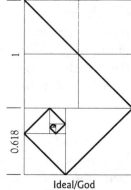

Fig. 8-10. Comparing Fibonacci and Golden Mean spirals.

starts deeper inside (actually, it never starts—it has been going on forever like God). Even though the originating point is different, they very quickly approximate each other.

Another example: Many books state that the King's Chamber is a Golden Mean rectangle, but it's not. It's also tied to Fibonacci.

### Fibonacci Spirals around Humans

When we draw a 64-square grid and incorporate this spiral pattern, we get Figure 8-11. Superimposing da Vinci's canon over this 8-by-8 grid [Fig. 8-12], the eight squares (shaded) seem to have a unique attribute. There are four possible ways to move a Fibonacci spiral out of one of the four double squares. Returning to Figure 8-11, let's use the upper double square as an example. One way to start is from the upper right corner, as shown by the darker line. It crosses one square (1), turns right to cross one more square (1), turns right again to cross two squares (2)—interestingly enough, it reaches the top of the grid at this point. Continuing to turn right, it crosses 3 (the next number in the sequence)—and, son-of-a-gun, it has now reached the right side of the grid! The next number is 5, which takes the line to the bottom of the grid. The following number, 8, takes the line across three squares before it leaves the grid. There's a perfect reflective quality as this spiral moves out from the beginning square.

Another way you could start in this double square is from the lower right corner, as shown by the lighter line (this forms a little pyramid in the top two squares. In this case your 90-degree turns will be to the left. So you cross one square (1), then one again (1), then 2—this time passing through the center four squares of the grid (where the original eight cells reside). After turning left again to cross 3 squares, the line touches the right side of the grid. The next number, 5, will leave the grid after crossing two squares. It's a perfect synchronicity of movement. Whenever you see this kind of perfection, you know you're almost surely hitting on really basic geometries.

All this is crucial to understand, if you care to know, how the Egyptians achieved resurrection. They were doing it scientifically, you might say. They were using science to create a synthetic state of awareness that would lead to immortality. We're not going to achieve our awareness synthetically; we're going to do it naturally, but you might find it useful to understand how an ancient civilization was attempting to achieve this.

### The Human Grid and Zero-Point Technology

This basic sacred geometry of a 64-square grid around humans is becoming understood in science. In fact, there's an entirely new science happening around it, though it's having a hard time getting out because of politics. This new science is called zero-point technology. This grid is, I believe, the geometry of

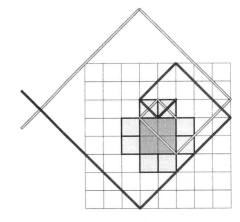

Fig. 8-11. Grid without canon, showing two mirroring Fibonacci spirals, male (dark line) and female (light line).

Fig. 8-12. Grid with da Vinci canon.

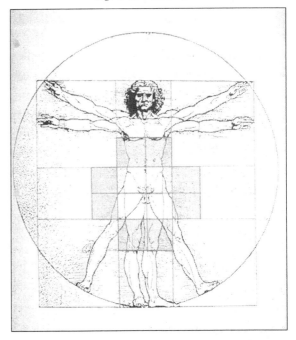

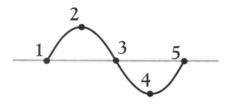

Fig. 8-13. Waveform showing 5 zero points.

**UPDATE: Since the time of Tesla, governments have not allowed the knowledge of zero point to come forth. Why? Tesla wanted to give free, unlimited energy to the world, which he knew would come from zero-point technology. But J.P. Morgan, who owned many copper mines, did not want electricity to be free. Instead, he wanted to force electricity to pass through copper wires so he could meter it, charge the public and make money. Tesla was stopped, and the world has been controlled ever since.**

**Since that time in the 1940s, any person who researched zero-point technology and talked publicly about it was killed or disappeared—until just recently. In 1997 a video company called Lightworks secretly brought together a few of these scientists and filmed their works.**

**They gave the history of what had happened since the 1940s and showed clear working models of the inventions. They showed machines that, once running, give off more electricity than it takes to run them. They showed batteries**

zero-point technology, though most scientists see it in a different way.

Most people involved in zero-point technology think of it in terms of waveforms or energy. They talk about the five places in a waveform, as shown here [Fig. 8-13]. Or they think of zero point as the amount of energy that matter has when (and if) it reaches zero degrees Kelvin, or absolute zero. To me, both of these ways are valid, but the way based on sacred geometry will eventually become the cornerstone of this new science because it is so fundamental.

These points associated with the waveform are also related to breathing. These points are where the zero point is accessed. They are like doorways into another world. Yogic pranayama is usually talked about in terms of two or three places (depending on whether you count the beginning of the next cycle), which are between the inbreath and the outbreath. That's also zero-point technology if you focus it on human breathing.

This new zero-point understanding has a geometry behind it, and that geometry is around the human body. The human body is always the measuring stick of creation.

### Male- and Female-Originating Spirals

To begin with we must understand that there are two kinds of spirals, depending on whether they are straight lines (male) or curved lines (female). We talked about this before. However, now we are going to introduce a new concept. The *originating point* of the spiral in this geometric pattern will further determine if it is male or female in a different way. In a double square there are four corners where a spiral can originate: top left, top right, bottom left and bottom right [see Fig. 8-14]. The two top positions produce male spirals, the two bottom positions, female spirals. The male spiral lines never pass through the center four squares; the female lines always do.

Figure 8-15 shows the two kinds of male and female spirals and how they move through this geometric pattern.

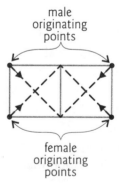

Fig. 8-14. The originating points.

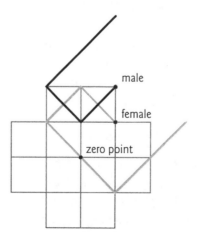

Fig. 8-15. The two kinds of spirals.

To make it clear, we will give an example. If the spiral begins at the top right point, it will be a male spiral relative to this geometrical pattern. In addition, the curved aspect of this male spiral would be female, and the straight-line aspect would be male. Every polarity always has another polarity within it, and within that new polarity there is always still another polarity. This division process will continue theoretically forever.

Fig. 8-16. The male-originating spirals with female curved lines

Figure 8-16 is an example of the male-originating spirals that begin at the top (meaning the greatest distance from center), but showing only their female (curved) aspect. This drawing shows all eight possible male-originating spirals that exist around the body, from a Fibonacci perspective, in their female (curved) form. They carry the Fibonacci sequence only as far as 5 (1-1-2-3-5). In this limited arrangement it's interesting to note how the curved spirals do a sort of loop-to-loop. The energy could actually become each other and recirculate. This Fibonacci movement is what I believe is really going on around the human body, not the Golden Mean that most books claim.

In Figure 8-17 we see male-originating spirals around the human body. Here we show the male (straight-line) aspect but only two with female curved lines.

Fig. 8-17. The male-originating spirals with male straight lines.

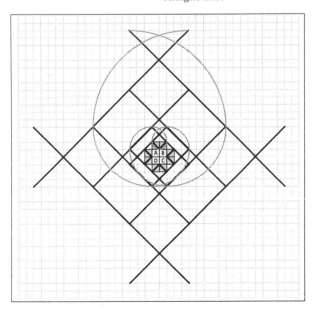

that never need charging. They showed how an ordinary gasoline motor can be converted to run on ordinary water with more power than gas. They showed panels that will produce boiling water forever as long as the outside temperature is above 40 degrees below zero Fahrenheit. They showed many other scientific inventions considered impossible by today's standards. When Lightworks was done, on a single day the video was released *and* the information put on a Web site ["Free Energy: The Race to Zero Point," 105-minute video by Lightworks (800) 795-8273, $40.45 ppd; www.lightworks.com]. This has forced the world to change direction. Two weeks later both Japan and England announced that they are very close to solving the cold-fusion problem. The world began to change.

On February 13, 1998, Germany issued a world patent on a free-energy machine based on carbon, a thin sheet of material that will produce 400 watts of electricity forever. This means that all small appliances such as computers, hair dryers, blenders, flashlights etc. will not need to be plugged into the system. It is the end of the old way and the birth of unlimited free energy.

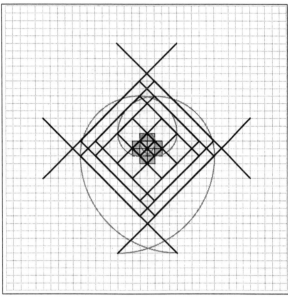

Fig. 8-18. The female-originating spirals with male straight lines.

Fig. 8-19. The binary sequence in mitotic cell division.

In Figure 8-18 we see the female spirals around the human body, which originate at the bottom, or closest points to center. Here we show primarily the male (straight-line) aspect of these female spirals. The female (curved) aspect of only two female spirals are shown (not all eight), which form a heart. Notice the pattern they create. One heart faces one way, and after it has been extended 180 degrees, a bigger heart faces the other way. Every one of these curved female lines passes through zero point at the exact center of the human body. This zero point is the creation point, or what we would call the womb. It is for this reason that females have the womb in their bodies and males do not. Males never pass through zero point. Later you'll see these heart-shaped relationships tied to many other natural phenomena such as light, eyes and emotions, to mention a few, so keep them in mind.

Now, with that understanding we're going to look at another sequence. There are thousands of mathematical sequences; I suppose on one level you could even say an infinite number. But in useful terms, there are many. A sequence can simply be 1, 2, 3, 4, 5, 6, 7, 8. In every one of the thousands and thousands of sequences known to man, three numbers are required to identify the pattern, the whole sequence—with the exception of the Golden Mean logarithmic sequence, in which case you need only two. This implies that it is probably the source of all other sequences.

According to my guidance, two sequences besides the Golden Mean are of major importance to nature and life. They are the Fibonacci sequence, which we just looked at, and the binary sequence we are about to look at. Here we will see the Fibonacci as female and the binary as male. They are really more than just female and male; they act more as mother and father. They are both primary, coming straight from the Golden Mean, just as the two primary colors that come from white light are red and blue.

### Binary Sequencing in Cell Division and Computers

The binary sequence [Fig. 8-19] is a mitosis that simply doubles each time, such as from 1 to 2 to 4 to 8 to 16 to 32. Instead of adding to the last number like we do in the Fibonacci sequence, we double it.

Let's look at the binary sequence for a moment. It goes 1, 2, 4, 8, 16, 32, doubling at each jump. In order to determine the characteristic of the sequence, all you need to do is take any three consecutive numbers in the sequence—like 2, 4 and 8. You double the 2 and get 4, and double the 4 to get 8. It takes three consecutive numbers to positively identify the doubling process.

In terms of a pronucleus's mitotic cell division, by the time the first cells form into the apple shape, there have been nine cell divisions, totaling 512 cells. Holding that in mind, look at these two facts:

Fact one (shown in Fig. 8-19): There are $10^{14}$ cells in the average human body. That's 100 trillion cells in the average person. That's a lot of zeroes. Fact two (in the same figure): An adult human body has to replace two and a half million red blood cells in every second of life. That definitely sounds like a lot. It would take you about two and a half months just to count to two and a half million if you were doing it day and night, 24 hours a day, seven days a week. Yet if we are to stay alive, our bodies have to create millions of new red blood cells every second to replace the dead ones. And the only way this can be achieved is through mitotic cell division.

You look at it and say, "Well, it's become 512 with only nine divisions, so it's going to have to really go for it to get up to this 100 trillion." But there's something almost magical that happens. Anyone who has studied mathematics knows this, but if you have never studied this before, it feels almost like magic. This is what happens [Fig. 8-20]: After the next ten divisions, cells have multiplied to over half a million. When it divides ten more times, there are 536 million.

According to Anna C. Pai and Helen Marcus Roberts in their book, *Genetics, Its Concepts and Implications*, it takes exactly 46 mitotic cell divisions to reach the $10^{14}$ cells of the human body. *It takes only 46 divisions!* It's magical to me that this number—46—happens to be the number of chromosomes we have in the average cell. Chance or coincidence?

These numbers are amazing. It's not amazing if you've studied it, because by then you're often immune to it. But it still amazes me.

I would like to talk about how computers work. I started to mention how we've got carbon and silicon arcing back and forth between each other. And who's making the silicon computers? *We* are—carbon-based beings. Out of all the various mathematical possibilities, we chose the binary sequence as the basis of how the computer works. It's the basis of the whole computer system, and it's also one of the primary bases of life itself. I feel sure it was not an accident that we chose the binary sequence, because we are life, and deep inside we know the importance of this sequence.

| Next 10 mitotic cell divisions | Next 10 mitotic cell divisions |
|---|---|
| 1024 | 1,048,576 |
| 2048 | 2,097,152 |
| 4096 | 4,194,304 |
| 8192 | 8,388,608 |
| 16,384 | 16,777,216 |
| 32,768 | 33,554,432 |
| 65,536 | 67,108,864 |
| 131,072 | 134,217,728 |
| 262,144 | 268,435,456 |
| 524,288 | 536,870,912 |
| (From 512 cells in the first 10 mitotic divisions to over a half-million in the second 10 divisions) | (From a half-million cells to a half-billion cells at the end of 30 mitotic divisions) |

Fig. 8-20. Next 20 mitotic cell divisions.

I know most of you probably know this, but nevertheless I want to show how a computer works. Imagine little light switches called computer chips, and when you turn on one of these lights, you see the number designated for that chip. If you turn on the 1 chip, you see 1. If you have five computer chips in your computer, they're designated 1, 2, 4, 8 and 16. You can turn these five chips on or off to get any number between 1 and 31. If you turn on just the 1 chip, you see the number 1. If you turn on the second chip, designated as 2, you see the number 2. The same for chip 4, chip 8 and chip 16.

By turning on *every combination* of those five chips and adding them up, you can come up with any number between 1 and 31. In other words, if you turn on the first chip, you get 1. Turn the second one on and get 2. And if you turn the first two on at the same time, you get 3. The next one you turn on is 4; 4 and 1 is 5; 4 and 2 is 6; 4 and 2 and 1 is 7. Then for 8, you turn on the 8 chip. Eight and 1 is 9; 8 and 2 is 10; 8 and 2 and 1 is 11; 8 and 4 is 12; 8 and 4 and 1 is 13; 8 and 4 and 2 is 14; and 8 and 4 and 2 and 1 is 15. Then for 16, you turn on the 16 chip. Adding the fifth chip gives you all numbers through 31 when they are combined in every possible way.

If you add just one more chip and call it 32, now you can get every number between 1 and 63. If you add another chip and call it 64, you can get every number between 1 and 127 and so on. If you have a computer that has 46 chips, *you can get every single number between 1 and 100 trillion*—just by turning 46 little chips on and off! This is what has enabled the unfoldment of knowledge that's happening so rapidly on the planet right now. And your body has been using this technology for millions of years!

## Searching for the Form behind Polarity

I studied the Fibonacci and binary sequences with the guidance of the angels, who were constantly leading me through it. The more I studied them, the more I personally believed that there must be geometry behind them, a secret form that created these number sequences. Since the angels said that the human body and geometry fields are the measuring stick of the universe, I suspected strongly that if these two sequences were like two mother/father, male/female components, then there must be a single geometric form hidden behind them, a form that generated both. I searched for a way to wed them.

I looked for this secret for years. For a long time I was very serious about it, then I gave up because I couldn't figure out what it was. But I always kept one eye open for an answer, always looking for a little clue that would maybe do it. And one day I got it.

# The Polar-Graph Solution

## A Sixth-Grade Math Book

A little boy I was taking care of was in the sixth grade, and he wanted to know about a particular mathematical problem. It was a relatively simple problem, but I didn't remember how to do it. I looked through his book to remember how it went so I could explain it. As I was going through his book, I saw the geometry I needed—in a sixth-grade math book! The author of the book didn't understand what *I* was seeing, because he was thinking along a totally different line. But I saw in the mathematics of it something I'd been looking for, and it was the key that tied these two primary sequences together.

I'm sorry that I don't remember the name of the book or the author—it was a long time ago—but it showed a polar graph and its relationship to a Golden Mean spiral. Figure 8-21 is a map of the South Pole on a polar graph. Notice the cross through the center, one line following the *x* axis and the other the *y*. Every circle does in fact have these lines crossing it. We demonstrated this by taking a flat disk about half an inch thick, randomly scattering sand all over it. We held it by a handle underneath and hit it with a wooden mallet. The sand would rearrange itself into a perfectly square cross like you see in this illustration. If we used a sound generator on the disk, the sand would change into many other geometrical patterns. But the very first pattern that emerges by striking a round disk at a low rate will be a perfectly square cross.

When you have a circle with a square cross over it, you take the radius of the circle as your measuring stick and call it 1

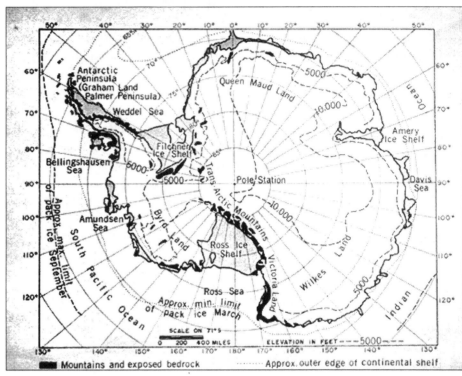

Fig. 8-21. Polar graph and map [from *World Atlas of Geomorphic Features* by Rodman E. Snead].

(that makes the calculations very easy). Drawing concentric circles the same distance outward from that first radius gives you a polar graph.

### Spirals on a Polar Graph

This is how a polar graph usually looks [Fig. 8-22], with 36 radial lines including the vertical and horizontal lines. These lines indicate 360 degrees in 10-degree increments. Then concentric circles are drawn, each one the same distance as the one before, creating eight equal demarcations along each radius, counting the inside circle as one. There's a great deal of reasoning behind a polar graph. Think first about what it represents. It is a two-dimensional drawing that attempts to show a three-dimensional sphere, one of the sacred forms, by projecting it onto a flat surface. It is the shadow form. Casting shadows is one of the sacred ways of obtaining information. Also, a polar graph has both straight lines (male) and circular lines (female) superimposed over each other—both male and female energies at once.

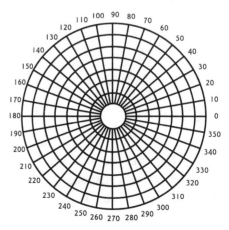

Fig. 8-22. Polar graph.

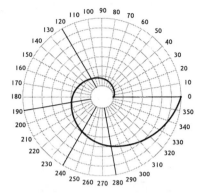

Fig. 8-23. Golden Mean spiral plotted
on a polar graph.

Think of the small central circle as a planet in space. From the surface of the planet, the author of the math book plotted a Golden Mean spiral— not Fibonacci, but Golden Mean. It starts at the zero radius on the circumference of the little "planet" in the center, and it is plotted one time around, from zero to 360°, or back to zero [Fig. 8-23].

Now, to figure out the value of any point, you would use the middle circle as a value of one (since it represents the distance from the center to the first circle, which we are calling the "planet"), then count outward to wherever the spiral crosses a radius. Thus on the radius at 260°(between the fourth and fifth rings) you would have counted outward to roughly 4.5. (Of course, on a computer you could be more accurate.) On the radial line at 210°, the spiral would have reached about 3.3. Does everybody understand that?

Now, look what happens to the actual data from zero to 360°. At zero degrees the spiral is exactly one circle (radial increment) away from center, because it's on the surface of that little sphere or planet. Then it goes around through different changes until it gets to 120°, where the spiral crosses the second circle. The spiral continues outward to the fourth circle, exactly where the 240° radial line sits. And it reaches the eighth (outer) circle precisely at the 360° (also 0°) radius. The radial increments have doubled (a binary sequence of 1, 2, 4, 8) at exactly 0°. 120°, 240° and 360°.

Notice Figure 8-24, which shows the crossing points of the spiral. The white stars to the left of the radial-increment column show where the binary sequence crosses a radius. The black stars show how the spiral advances, in a Fibonacci sequence (1, 2, 3, 5, 8), crossing radials at 120°, 190°, 280° and 360°. *Both sequences simultaneously reach full circle (360°), though in differing increments,* following this Golden Mean spiral. This spiral, shown on a polar graph, has integrated the binary and Fibonacci sequences!

I was so excited, I was doing cartwheels for a few days. I knew I had found something really extraordinary, even though I didn't fully know what it was. (This is another one of my weaknesses I have to admit to here. Once I saw it, I knew that if I decoded one of the patterns, it would be true for the other one, and I've never gone back even to look at the other pattern, which is probably equally as interesting.)

| Angle | Radial increment from center | Angle | Radial increment from center | Angle | Radial increment from center | Angle | Radial increment from center |
|---|---|---|---|---|---|---|---|
| 0° ✹ 1.0 ✹ | | | | | | | |
| 10° | 1.1 | 100° | 1.8 | 190° | 3.0 ✹ | 280° | 5.0 ✹ |
| 20° | 1.1 | 110° | 1.9 | 200° | 3.2 | 290° | 5.3 |
| 30° | 1.2 | 120° ✹ 2.0 ✹ | | 210° | 3.4 | 300° | 5.6 |
| 40° | 1.3 | 130° | 2.1 | 220° | 3.6 | 310° | 6.0 |
| 50° | 1.3 | 140° | 2.2 | 230° | 3.8 | 320° | 6.3 |
| 60° | 1.4 | 150° | 2.4 | 240° ✹ 4.0 | | 330° | 6.7 |
| 70° | 1.5 | 160° | 2.5 | 250° | 4.2 | 340° | 7.1 |
| 80° | 1.6 | 170° | 2.7 | 260° | 4.5 | 350° | 7.5 |
| 90° | 1.7 | 180° | 2.8 | 270° | 4.7 | 360° ✹ 8.0 ✹ | |

| Angle | 0° | 120° | 240° | 360° | *a binary sequence!* |
|---|---|---|---|---|---|
| Distance from pole | 1.0 | 2.0 | 4.0 | 8.0 | |

| Angle | 0° | 120° | 190° | 280° | 360° | *a Fibonacci sequence!* |
|---|---|---|---|---|---|---|
| Distance from pole | 1.0 | 2.0 | 3.0 | 5.0 | 8.0 | |

Fig. 8-24. Table showing distance of
spiral from pole, measured in radial
increments.

**Update: Other people have decoded the other pattern, and it is Fibonacci, as I suspected. What it really means to consciousness I have not researched.**

But I did analyze what a binary sequence does. The spiral crosses at 0, 120, 240 and 360 degrees. As you can see, that forms an equilateral triangle [Fig. 8-25]. If this binary spiral kept going outward, it would cross radii at further increments of 16, 32, 64 and so on, yet always hit those three 120-, 240-, and 360-degree radial lines as they too are extended.

You not only have a triangle, but you're actually looking at a three-dimensional tetrahedron, because the 120-, 240- and 360-degree radii extend to the center forming the top view of a tetrahedron as well as a side view.

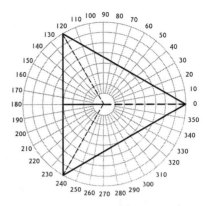

Fig. 8-25. Binary spiral forming a tetrahedron on polar graph.

### Keith Critchlow's Triangles and Their Musical Significance

Another image on this drawing is an equilateral triangle with the horizontal line running straight through the middle from 0 to 180 degrees. This is the side view of the tetrahedron. Now, you might not think that's important, and I probably would have never picked up on it, but another person did—Keith Critchlow. We don't know what he was thinking or how he arrived at this. He didn't know what you know right now when he did it. (He may know it now after he's seen this work, but he didn't when he wrote his book.)

Figure 8-26 is Critchlow's work. He drew an equilateral triangle with a line through the middle; then he measured to the middle of the center line (see black dot) and drew a line down to the corner and up to the top edge and then vertically down to the center line, as shown. Who knows why? Where that first diagonal line crossed the center line, he then drew a vertical line to the upper edge, then down to the same lower corner. Using the point where it crossed the center line, he repeated what he had done before, then did it once more to the left. You could keep going in both directions from your first line. By drawing this funny little form, he discovered something of great importance.

He says, "Continuing in this way" (in that pattern of construction), "each successive proportion will be the harmonic mean between the previous proportion and the total length, and all these proportions will be musically significant, ½ being the octave, ⅔ being the fifth, ⅘ being the major third, 8/9 being the major tone [step] and 16/17 being the half tone [half step]. In other words, he's comparing the measurement of these lines to musical tones.

He then tried measuring it in a different way, starting at a different point [Fig. 8-27] of the center line, at three-fourths (see black dot), and found that the measurements were 1/7, 1/4, 2/5, 4/7 , 8/11 and 16/19—and all these numbers are musically significant.

This is very, very interesting. It means that the harmonics of music are somehow related to the proportions of this central line moving through a tetrahedron. But he had to measure first to begin, and if you have to use a measuring stick, you're not at the core of sacred geometry; something's missing. If you're right in sacred geometry, you *never* have to use anything

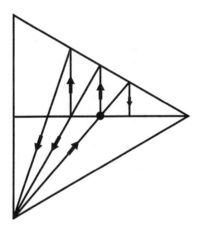

Fig. 8-26. Keith Critchlow's triangles.

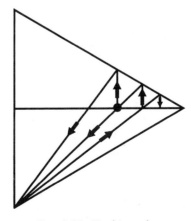

Fig. 8-27. Keith's work.

to measure. The measuring apparatus is built in so that you can calculate everything without having any kind of calculus or ruler or anything else. It's always built right into the system.

I experimented with his drawings and discovered that if I put the polar graph behind his pattern, I could reproduce his first pattern, which showed the octave—the halfway mark—without any measuring [Fig. 8-28].

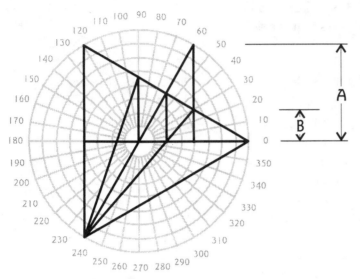

Fig. 8-28. Critchlow's triangles on the polar graph.

All I had to do was draw over a line that was already there from the lowest apex of the triangle through the center of the sphere to the opposite side of the triangle; when I dropped the line straight down, it divided the center line *exactly* in half, which was the octave point Critchlow had found. Then the other three lines could automatically be drawn.

I then discovered that the outermost circle of the polar graph, which circumscribes the equilateral triangle, was also harmonic to the central line: the vertical line at 60 degrees (line A) exactly overlies line B. There is a correspondence between the male (straight lines) and the female (curved lines) components inside and outside the triangle, and these proportions were all musically significant. *And I didn't have to measure anything!*

We have now taken this light-years beyond the above. A research team has found that you can draw these lines not only from the center, but from *any* of the nodal points inside the upper half of the triangle, and you will come up with all known harmonics in existence. In other words, if you draw a line from any of the points where the straight and curved lines cross from 0 to 120 degrees, then down to the corner of the primary triangle and start making your patterns, you'll come up with all the harmonic systems, not only the Western keyboard, but the Eastern systems as well—in fact, all known harmonic systems and many unknown ones that have never been used.

People who have done this research now believe that *all* the laws of physics can be derived from musical harmonics, now that the full system of harmonics has been revealed. I personally believe that the harmonics of music and the laws of physics are interrelated, and we now believe we've proven this mathematically and geometrically, though it is not fully shown here.

I was very excited at the time I was gathering this information, because the implications are incredible. It means that the harmonics of music are located inside a tetrahedron, and that these harmonics are now determinable. Since then we've discovered another geometric pattern behind the one shown in this illustration that reveals all the keys, and it has opened up all the inner meanings of what Egypt was about.

The Egyptians reduced their entire philosophy to the square roots of 2, 3, and 5 and the 3-4-5 triangle. Many people have given explanations for it, but there's another explanation hidden behind the geometry of the tetrahedron. That idea probably went over almost everybody's head, including mine, in a way. But it's there and we're working on it now.

### Black- and White-Light Spirals

While I was working on the harmonics of music, I got a postcard in the mail. The postcard was a polar graph with reflective surfaces [Fig. 8-29]. It had little reflectors in each component. I want you to see how light reflects off a polar graph. It reflects off what appears to be a Golden Mean or Fibonacci spiral.

There are two arms of the spiral, one opposite the other, exactly 180 degrees apart. Notice that between the reflecting arms the light goes very dark. The black-light spirals are rotating at 180 degrees to each other and 90 degrees to the white light. (We've seen that before in the swirling galaxy.) If you look right in the center, you can see that the two opposite arms are exactly 180 degrees to each other.

This is where we've seen it before [Fig. 8-30]. Here a white-light spiral comes out in one direction, and 180 degrees from it another white-light spiral goes out in the opposite direction. The dark arms—the feminine ones—come out between the light ones. That explains why the black light between the light arms of the spiral is different from the blackness in the rest of space [see Fig. 2-35], as scientists have discovered, because the black light within a spiral is the feminine energy, and the darkness out in space is Void, not the same. The scientists couldn't quite understand why it was different.

Fig. 8-29. Postcard with spiral.

Fig. 8-30. Swirling galaxy.

## Maps for the Left Brain and Their Emotional Component

There's one more simple teaching I would like to give here. Drawing the tetrahedron over the polar graph geometrically represents the harmonics of music. That drawing and the information I've given you on this subject comes into your understanding through your left brain. But do you remember how we went through those visualizations, where I was saying that every line on a page is not a line on a page, but a map of how spirit moves through the Void? So these drawings are maps—for the left brain.

But there's another component that's equally important to understand: Besides being a map of how Spirit moves in the Void, the lines on any sacred-geometry drawing also represent something else. *For every line in sacred geometry, there is always an associated emotional and experiential aspect.* There is not only a mental component, but an emotional component that can also be experienced. A sacred-geometry drawing can enter human consciousness through the left brain, but there is a way that it can also enter experientially through the right brain. Sometimes this emotional/experiential component is not obvious.

What does this mean? Let's use music as an example. Music can come into human experience as sound and be heard and felt inside us, or it can be understood by the left brain as proportion and mathematics. As you study sacred geometry, remember that both sides of the brain use the same information differently.

*[Here Drunvalo played a Sioux Lakota flute to give students a direct experience. He asked them to close their eyes and experience the music instead of mentally studying or thinking about it.]*

Form and the sacred geometry associated with it are the source, but the way this information enters the human experience is different. It's usually a lot easier to take in information experientially through the right brain than through the logical left brain, but they're equivalent. It's hard to see that they're equivalent, but they are. Throughout all this geometry, as you look at these triangles and squares around the body and the relating spheres and shapes, some kind of experience is associated with each geometry. Maybe you don't know what the particular experience is. It might take a whole lifetime to figure out what it relates to, but it's my belief that there is always an experiential aspect associated with every sacred geometrical form.

## Arriving Back at the Fruit of Life through the Second Informational System

Now I'm going to give a kind of bottom line for all this. Remember that we plotted this triangle, and its apexes hit at 0, 120 and 240 degrees, then we added these lines [see Fig. 8-28 on p. 224]? But in nature, like in the galaxy, there's not just one spiral, but two, going out from the center in opposite ways (see Figs. 8-29 and 8-30). So if you copy nature, you would have to plot two spirals, which will produce two opposing triangles on the polar graph [Fig. 8-31]. If you look carefully, it actually produces two tetrahedrons—more specifically, it's a star tetrahedron inscribed inside the sphere.

If you've seen Richard Hoagland's work, do you remember what the message on Mars at Cydonia was? It was a star tetrahedron inside a sphere. If you haven't seen Richard Hoagland's work, I suggest you look at what he showed the United Nations. Though science is just beginning to understand what this is about, what Mr. Hoagland showed them will probably make a lot of sense to you now.

Inside the star tetrahedron in the sphere, there's another star tetrahedron [Fig. 8-32]. And inside the smaller tetrahedron a sphere fits perfectly. If you take that size sphere and center it on each one of the points of the tetrahedrons, you end up with the Fruit of Life. If I rotate this drawing 30 degrees and get rid of some of the lines, you can see the result more clearly [Fig. 8-33].

What you just saw, only in reverse image, was the second informational system of the Fruit of Life. All the information above with the star tetrahedron, Golden Mean spirals, light, sound and the harmonics of music and so on came from this second information system.

I could have started with the Fruit of Life and gone back the other way, but it isn't how it happened to me. I wanted to show you that the second information system is accessed by connecting the concentric circles of the Fruit of Life with *radial* lines coming out *from the center*, rather than connecting all the centers together as we did to find the Platonic solids and the information on crystals. It is just a different way to superimpose male lines over the female lines of the Fruit of Life.

In the first system of information—Metatron's Cube—we came up with the structural patterns of the universe based on the five Platonic solids. These appear in lattice structures of metals and crystals and in many other patterns in nature that we didn't talk about. The diatoms that make up diatomaceous earth were one of the first life forms in the world, and diatoms are nothing but little geometric patterns, or functions of the patterns. What you have just been shown is how light, sound and the harmonics of music are interrelated through a star tetrahedral field inscribed inside a sphere that came directly out of the Fruit of Life, the third rotational pattern of Genesis [Fig. 8-34].

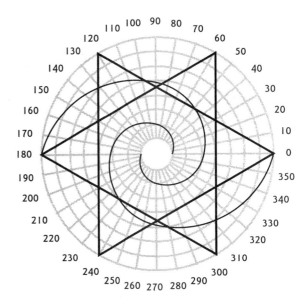

Fig. 8-31. Two spirals forming a star tetrahedron on a polar graph.

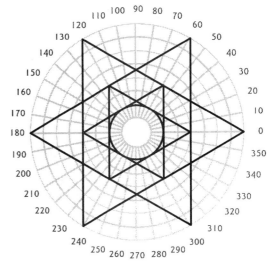

Fig. 8-32. A star in a star.

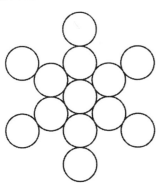

Fig. 8-34. Fruit of Life.

Fig. 8-33. Fruit over stars and sphere.

## AFTERWORD

It is now becoming clear that geometry—and thereby proportion—is the hidden law of nature. It is even more fundamental than mathematics, for all the laws of nature can be derived directly from sacred geometry.

In the second part of this work we will show you more of nature's secrets. We believe it will begin to change the way you see the world you live in. It will become clear that your body is the measuring stick or the holographic image of the universe, and that you, the spirit, play a more important role in life than society has taught us.

Finally (and this will be paramount in this work), you will begin to see how the geometries are located in the electromagnetic fields around your body that are about 55 feet in diameter. Remembering these fields is the beginning of human awakening, like a baby bird breaking into the light and out of the darkness inside its eggshell. The sacred and holy human lightbody, called the Mer-Ka-Ba by the ancients, becomes a reality. This Mer-Ka-Ba is the "wheels within wheels" of Ezekiel in the Bible. The pathway home through the stars becomes evident as the blueprint of creation emerges.

We are intimately connected to the Source of all life. In the remembering of this information will come an awakening that will dispel the myth of separation and bring you into the very presence of God. This is my prayer.

Until we meet again in volume two,
In love and service, Drunvalo

# REFERENCES

## Chapter 1

Liberman, Jacob, *Light, the Medicine of the Future*, Bear & Co., Santa Fe, NM, 1992.

Temple, Robert K.G., *The Sirius Mystery*, Destiny Books, Rochester, VT (www.gotoit.com).

Satinover, Jeffrey, M.D., *Cracking the Bible Code*, William Morrow, New York, 1997.

West, John Anthony, *Serpent in the Sky*, Julian Press, New York, 1979, 1987.

Cayce, Edgar: many books have been written about him; the Association for Research and Enlightenment in Virginia Beach, VA, is a source of an enormous amount of material. Perhaps the most well-known book is *The Sleeping Prophet* by Jess Stearn.

## Chapter 2

Lawlor, Robert, *Sacred Geometry: Philosophy and Practice*, Thames & Hudson, London, 1982.

Hoagland, Richard C.; see www.enterprisemission.com/ .

White, John, *Pole Shift*, 3rd ed., ARE Press, Virginia Beach, VA, 1988.

Hapgood, Charles, *Earth's Shifting Crust* and *The Path of the Pole* (out of print).

Braden, Gregg, *Awakening to Zero Point: The Collective Initiation*, Sacred Spaces/Ancient Wisdom Pub., Questa, NM; also on video tape (Lee Productions, Bellevue, WA).

## Chapter 3

Hamaker, John and Donald A. Weaver, *The Survival of Civilization*, Hamaker-Weaver Pub., 1982.

Sitchin, Zecharia, *The 12th Planet* (1978), *The Lost Realms* (1996), *Genesis Revisited* (1990), Avon Books.

Begich, Nick and Jeanne Manning, *Angels Don't Play This HAARP*, Earthpulse Press, Anchorage, AK, 1995.

## Chapter 4

Keyes, Ken, Jr., *The Hundredth Monkey*, out of print.

Watson, Lyall, *Lifetide*, Simon and Schuster, New York, 1979.

Strecker, Robert, M.D., "The Strecker Memorandum" (video), The Strecker Group, 1501 Colorado Blvd., Eagle Rock, CA 90041 (203) 344-8039.

*The Emerald Tablets of Thoth the Atlantean*, translated by Doreal, Brotherhood of the White Temple, Castle Rock, CO , 1939. Obtainable from Light Technology Publishing.

## Chapter 6

Anderson, Richard Feather (labyrinths); see www.gracecom.org/veriditas/ .

Penrose, Roger; see http://galaxy.cau.edu/tsmith/KW/goldenpenrose.html http://turing.mathcs.carleton.edu/penroseindex.html ; www.nr.infi.net/~drmatrix/progchal.htm .

Adair, David; see www.flyingsaucers.com/adair1.htm .

Winter, Dan, *Heartmath*; see www.danwinter.com .

Sorrell, Charles A., *Rocks and Minerals: A Guide to Field Identification*, Golden Press, 1973.

Vector Flexor toy, available from Source Books (see below).

Langham, Derald, *Circle Gardening: Producing Food by Genesa Principles*, Devin-Adair Pub., 1978.

## Chapter 7

Charkovsky, Igor; see www.earthportals.com ; www.vol.it/ ; www.well.com.

Doczi, György, *The Power of Limits: Proportional Harmonies in Nature, Art and Architecture*, Shambhala, Boston, MA, 1981, 1994.

## Chapter 8

"Free Energy: The Race to Zero Point" (video), available from Lightworks, (800) 795-8273, $40.45 ppd., www.lightworks.com .

Pai, Anna C. and Helen Marcus Roberts, *Genetics, Its Concepts and Implications*, Prentice Hall, 1981.

Critchlow, Keith, *Order in Space: A Design Source Book*, Viking Press, 1965, 1969 and other books are out of print; see www.wwnorton.com/thames/aut.ttl/at03940.htm .

Most of the books and sacred geometry tools, in addition to posters, kits, videos, tapes and CDs recommended in this workshop, are available from Source Books, P.O. Box 292231, Nashville, TN 37229-2231, (800) 637-5222 (in U.S.) or (615) 773-7652. Catalog available.

# Light Technology Publishing

## THE ANCIENT SECRET OF THE FLOWER OF LIFE

### VOLUME 1

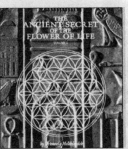

Once, all life in the universe knew the Flower of Life as the creation pattern — the geometrical design leading us into and out of physical existence. Then from a very high state of consciousness we fell into darkness and forgot who we were. For thousands of years the secret was held in ancient artifacts and carvings around the world, and encoded in the cells of all life.

Now we are rising up from that sleep, shaking old, stale beliefs from our minds and glimpsing the golden light of this new dawn streaming through the windows of perception. This book is one of those windows.

Here, Drunvalo Melchizedek presents in text and graphics the first half of the Flower of Life Workshop, illuminating the mysteries of how we came to be, why the world is the way it is and the subtle energies that allow our awareness to blossom into its true beauty.

Sacred Geometry is the form beneath our being and points to a divine order in our reality. We can follow that order from the invisible atom to the infinite stars, finding ourselves at each step. The information here is one path, but between the lines and drawings lie the feminine gems of intuitive understanding. You may see them sparkle around some of these provocative ideas:

- ✪ REMEMBERING OUR ANCIENT PAST
- ✪ THE SECRET OF THE FLOWER UNFOLDS
- ✪ THE DARKER SIDE OF OUR PRESENT AND PAST
- ✪ WHEN EVOLUTION CRASHED, AND THE CHRIST GRID AROSE
- ✪ EGYPT'S ROLE IN THE EVOLUTION OF CONSCIOUSNESS
- ✪ THE SIGNIFICANCE OF SHAPE AND STRUCTURE
- ✪ THE GEOMETRIES OF THE HUMAN BODY

ISBN-1-891824-17-1      228pp. $25.00

---

Not only is Drunvalo's mind exceptional, but his heart, his warm personality, his love for all life everywhere, is immediately understood and felt by anyone who meets him. For some time now he has been bringing his vast vision to the world through the Flower of Life program and the Mer-Ka-Ba meditation. This teaching encompasses every area of human understanding, explores the development of mankind from ancient civilizations to the present time and offers clarity regarding the world's state of consciousness and what is needed for a smooth and easy transition into the 21st century.

Drunvalo Melchizedek

---

*Embrace the expanded vision and understanding that Drunvalo offers to the world. Coincidences abound, miracles flourish and amazing stories of mysteries unveiled arise as the author probes the Ancient Secrets of the Flower of Life.*

### VOLUME 2

The sacred Flower of Life pattern, the primary geometric generator of all physical form, is explored in even more depth in this second volume. The proportions of the human body, the nuances of human consciousness, the sizes and distances of the stars, planets and moons, even the creations of humankind, are all shown to reflect their origins in this beautiful and divine image. Through an intricate and detailed geometrical mapping, Drunvalo Melchizedek shows how the seemingly simple design of the Flower of Life contains the genesis of our entire third-dimensional existence.

From the pyramids and mysteries of Egypt to the new race of Indigo children, Drunvalo presents the sacred geometries of the Reality and the subtle energies that shape our world. Finally, for the first time in print, he shares the instructions for the Mer-Ka-Ba meditation, step-by-step techniques for the re-creation of the energy field of the evolved human, which is the key to ascension and the next dimensional world. If done from love, this ancient process of breathing prana opens up for us a world of tantalizing possibility in this dimension, from protective powers to the healing of oneself, of others and even of the planet.

- ✪ THE UNFOLDING OF THE THIRD INFORMATIONAL SYSTEM
- ✪ WHISPER FROM OUR ANCIENT HERITAGE
- ✪ UNVEILING THE MER-KA-BA MEDITATION
- ✪ USING YOUR MER-KA-BA
- ✪ CONNECTING TO THE LEVELS OF SELF
- ✪ TWO COSMIC EXPERIMENTS
- ✪ WHAT WE MAY EXPECT IN THE FORTHCOMING DIMENSIONAL SHIFT

ISBN-1-891824-21-X      252pp. $25.00

---

No. copies  Total

**AIELLO**
This World and the Next One ......... $9.95 __ $ __

**ARGÜELLAS, JOSÉ**
AUTHOR OF **THE MAYAN FACTOR**
The Arcturus Probe ..................... 14.95 __ $ ___

**AVERY, FRANKIE Z**
Handbook for Healers ..................... 25.00 __ $ ___

**BACON, SUMMER**
This School Called Planet Earth ...... 16.95 __ $ ___

**BAIN, GABRIEL**
Auras 101 ..................................... 6.95 __ $ ___
Living Rainbows ............................ 14.95 __ $ ___

**BALL, LINDA**
Dimensional Journey ...................... 19.95 __ $ ___

**BATEMAN, WESLEY H.**
Through Alien Eyes ........................ 19.95 __ $ ___
Dragons & Chariots ........................ 9.95 __ $ ___
Knowledge from the Stars ............... 11.95 __ $ ___

**BEACONSFIELD, HANNAH**
Welcome to Planet Earth ................. 14.95 __ $ ___

**BRUCE, EDITH**
Keys to the Kingdom ....................... 14.95 __ $ ___

**BUESS, LYNN**
Children of Light, Children .............. 8.95 __ $ ___
Forever Numerology ........................ 17.95 __ $ ___
Numerology: Nuances . . ................. 13.75 __ $ ___
Numerology for the New Age ........... 11.00 __ $ ___

**CHAPMAN, CATHY**
Change Your DNA, Your Life! ......... 16.95 __ $ ___

**CLARK, GLADYS IRIS**
Forever Young ................................ 9.95 __ $ ___

**COHEN, MARK**
Ratho Shenzi (book) ....................... 19.95 __ $ ___
Ratho Shenzi (CD) .......................... 15 .95 __ $ ___

**COOPER, WILLIAM**
Behold a Pale Horse ....................... 25.00 __ $ ___

**deANGELIS, ANGELA/CONTINUITY OF LIFE SERIES**
Embracing Eternity ........................ 16.95 __ $ ___
Endings Are Beginnings .................. 16.95 __ $ ___
Transition and Survival Technologies 16.95 __ $ ___
Healing Earth in All Her Dimensions 16.95 __ $ ___

**DEERING, HALLIE**
Light from the Angels ..................... 15.00 __ $ ___
Do-It-Yourself Power Tools ............. 25.00 __ $ ___

**DONGO, TOM**
Mysterious Sedona .......................... 9.95 __ $ ___
Mysteries of Sedona—Book I ........... 6.95 __ $ ___
Alien Tide—Book II ........................ 7.95 __ $ ___
Quest—Book III .............................. 9.95 __ $ ___
Merging Dimensions ....................... $14.95 __ $ ___
Sedona in a Nutshell ....................... 4.95 __ $ ___
Unseen Beings, Unseen Worlds ........ 9.95 __ $ ___

**FALLON, NANCY**
Acupressure for the Soul ................. 11.95 __ $ ___

**FANNING, ARTHUR**
Soul Evolution Father ..................... 12.95 __ $ ___
Simon .......................................... 9.95 __ $ ___

**FANNING, ARTHUR/MEDITATION TAPES**
Black Hole Meditation .................... 10.00 __ $ ___
On Becoming ................................. 10.00 __ $ ___
The Art of Shutting Up ................... 10.00 __ $ ___

**GAUDETTE, RÉNÉ & McGUFFIN, MAGGIE**
The Wonders ................................. 14.95 __ $ ___

**GEORGE, TAMAR**
Guardians of the Flame ................... 14.95 __ $ ___

**GOLDEN STAR ALLIANCE**
I'm OK, I'm Just Mutating .............. 6.00 __ $ ___

**GOLDMAN, JONATHAN**
Shifting Frequencies ....................... 14.95 __ $ ___

**GRATTAN, BRIAN**
Mahatma I & II ............................. 19.95 __ $ ___

**JASMUHEEN**
Ambassador of Light ...................... 16.95 __ $ ___
In Resonance ................................. 24.95 __ $ ___
Harmonious Healing ....................... 16.95 __ $ ___

**JASMUHEEN/MEDITATION & HEALING TAPES**
Living on Light & Meditation .......... 10.00 __ $ ___

Prana Breathing & Meditation ......... 10.00 __ $ ___
Angel Meditation & Self Healing .... 10.00 __ $ ___

**KELLER, MARY LOU**
Echoes of Sedona Past ..................... $14.95 __ $ ___

**KINGDON, KATHLYN**
The Matter of Mind ........................ 16.95 __ $ ___

**KLARER, ELIZABETH**
Beyond the Light Barrier ................. 15.95 __ $ ___

**KLOTSCHE, CHARLES**
Color Medicine .............................. 11.95 __ $ ___

**LAMB, BARBARA/MOORE, JUDITH**
Crop Circles Revealed ..................... 25.00 __ $ ___

**LEWIS, PEPPER: GAIA SPEAKS**
1. Sacred Earth Wisdom ................. 19.95 __ $ ___
2. Awakening Humanity .................. 19.95 __ $ ___

**MANN, NICHOLAS R.**
SEDONA: Sacred Earth .................. 14.95 __ $ ___

**McCLURE, JANET**
AHA! The Realization Book .............. 11.95 __ $ ___
Light Techniques ............................ 11.95 __ $ ___
Sanat Kumara ................................ 11.95 __ $ ___
Scopes of Dimensions ..................... 11.95 __ $ ___
The Source Adventure ..................... 11.95 __ $ ___
Prelude to Ascension ...................... 29.95 __ $ ___

**McINTOSH, JOHN**
Millennium Tablets ......................... 14.95 __ $ ___

**MELCHIZEDEK, DRUNVALO**
Anc. Secret of the Flower of Life  I .. 25.00 __ $ ___
Anc. Secret of the Flower of Life II .. 25.00 __ $ ___
Living in the Heart, w/CD ............... 25.00 __ $ ___
Serpent of Light: Beyond 2012 ......... 19.95 __ $ ___

**MILLER, DAVID K.**
New Spiritual Technology/5D Earth 19.95 __ $ ___
Connecting with the Arcturians ...... 17.00 __ $ ___
Teachings from the Sacred Triangle . 22.00 __ $ ___

**MOORE, JUDITH**
Song of Freedom ............................ 19.95 __ $ ___
New Formula for Creation ............... 16.95 __ $ ___

**MOORE, TOM**
The Gentle Way .............................. 14.95 __ $ ___
The Gentle Way #2 ......................... 16.95 __ $ ___

**NAUMAN, EILEEN/LIGHT TECHNOLOGY PUBLISHING**
Homeopathy for Epidemics .............. 25.00 __ $ ___
Path of the Mystic ......................... 11.95 __ $ ___

**PHILLIPS, GLENN**
New Age Primer ............................. 11.95 __ $ ___

**PUTNAM, WILLIAM,**
Tale of Two Passes .......................... 29.95 __ $ ___

**ROEDER, DOROTHY**
Crystal Co-Creators ........................ 14.95 __ $ ___
Next Dimension Is Love ................. 11.95 __ $ ___
Reach for Us .................................. 14.95 __ $ ___

**ROTA, EILEEN MIRIANDRA**
Story of the People ......................... 11.95 __ $ ___
Pathways & Parables ....................... 19.95 __ $ ___

**RYDEN, RUTH**
The Golden Path ............................ 11.95 __ $ ___
Living the Golden Path ................... 11.95 __ $ ___

**SHAPIRO, ROBERT/SHINING THE LIGHT SERIES**
I: The Battle Begins ........................ 12.95 __ $ ___
II: The Battle Continues .................. 14.95 __ $ ___
III: Humanity Gets a Second Chance 14.95 __ $ ___
IV: Humanity's Greatest Challenge .. 14.95 __ $ ___
V: Humanity Is Going to Make It! ... 14.95 __ $ ___
VI: The End of What Was ................ 14.95 __ $ ___
VII: The First Alignment ................. 24.95 __ $ ___

**SHAPIRO, ROBERT/EXPLORER RACE SERIES**
1. The Explorer Race ...................... 25.00 __ $ ___
2. ETs and the Explorer Race ........... 14.95 __ $ ___
3. Origins and the Next 50 Years ...... 14.95 __ $ ___
4. Creators and Friends ................... 19.95 __ $ ___
5. Particle Personalities .................. 14.95 __ $ ___
6. Explorer Race and Beyond ........... 14.95 __ $ ___
7. Council of Creators .................... 14.95 __ $ ___
8. Explorer Race and Isis ................ 14.95 __ $ ___
9. Explorer Race and Jesus .............. 16.95 __ $ ___
10. Earth History & Lost Civilizations 14.95 __ $ ___

11. ET Visitors Speak ..................... 14.95 __ $ ___
12. Techniques for Generating Safety.... 9.95 __ $ ___
13. Animal Souls Speak .................. 29.95 __ $ ___
14. Astrology: Planet Personalities ... 29.95 __ $ ___
15. ET Visitors Speak #2 ................. 19.95 __ $ ___

**SHAPIRO, ROBERT/MATERIAL MASTERY SERIES**
A. Shamanic Secrets/Material .......... 19.95 __ $ ___
B. Shamanic Secrets/Physical ........... 25.00 __ $ ___
C. Shamanic Secrets/Spiritual .......... 29.95 __ $ ___

**SHAPIRO, ROBERT/SHIRT POCKET BOOKS**
Feeling Sedona's ET Energies ........... 9.95 __ $ ___
Touching Sedona ............................ 9.95 __ $ ___

**SHAPIRO, ROBERT/SECRETS OF FEMININE SCIENCE**
Benevolent Magic & Living Prayer .... 9.95 __ $ ___

**SHAPIRO, ROBERT/ULTIMATE UFO SERIES**
Andromeda .................................... 16.95 __ $ ___
The Zetas: History, Hybrids & .......... 24.95 __ $ ___

**STARRE, VIOLET**
The Diamond Light ......................... 14.95 __ $ ___
The Amethyst Light ........................ 14.95 __ $ ___

**STARR, ALOA**
I Want To Know ............................. 7.00 __ $ ___
Prisoners of Earth ........................... 11.95 __ $ ___

**STONE, JOSHUA DAVID, PH.D./ASCENSION SERIES**
1. Complete Ascension Manual ....... 14.95 __ $ ___
2. Soul Psychology ......................... 14.95 __ $ ___
3. Beyond Ascension ....................... 14.95 __ $ ___
4. Hidden Mysteries ....................... 14.95 __ $ ___
5. Ascended Masters ....................... 14.95 __ $ ___
6. Cosmic Ascension ....................... 14.95 __ $ ___
7. A Beginner's Guide to Ascension. 14.95 __ $ ___
8. Golden Keys to Ascension ............ 14.95 __ $ ___
9. Manual for Planetary Leadership.. 14.95 __ $ ___
10. Your Ascension Mission ............. 14.95 __ $ ___
11. Revelations of a Melchizedek ..... 14.95 __ $ ___
12. How to Teach Ascension Classes.... 14.95 __ $ ___
13. Ascension and Romantic ............ 14.95 __ $ ___
14. Ascension Index ....................... 14.95 __ $ ___
15. Be Financially Successful ........... 14.95 __ $ ___
**Special Offer—All 15 Stone Books ...179.00** __ $ ___

**SALTER, DAN AS TOLD TO NANCY RED STAR**
Life with a Cosmos Clearance .......... 19.95 __ $ ___

**VAN ETTEN, JAAP**
Crystal Skulls ................................ 19.95 __ $ ___

**VARIOUS**
Sedona Vortex Guide Book .............. 14.95 __ $ ___

**VYWAMUS**
Channelling: Evolutionary Exercises ..... 9.95 __ $ ___

**WARTER, CARLOS, M.D.**
The Soul Remembers ....................... 14.95 __ $ ___

**WELK, ANGELA**
Silent Self .................................... 9.95 __ $ ___

**Starchild Press**

**GOLD, BRIAN**
The Legend of Cactus Eddie full color 11.95 __ $ ___

**BADER, LOU**
Shadow of San Francisco Peaks ........ 9.95 __ $ ___
Great Kachina full color .................. 11.95 __ $ ___

**STINNETT, LEIA—ANGEL BOOKS**
A Circle of Angels .......................... 18.95 __ $ ___
The Twelve Universal Laws .............. 18.95 __ $ ___
All My Angel Friends ...................... 10.95 __ $ ___
Animal Tales .................................. 7.95 __ $ ___
Where Is God? ............................... 6.95 __ $ ___
Just Lighten Up! ............................ 9.95 __ $ ___
Happy Feet .................................... 6.95 __ $ ___
When the Earth Was New ................ 6.95 __ $ ___
The Angel Told Me . . . ................... 6.95 __ $ ___
One Red Rose ................................ 6.95 __ $ ___
Exploring the Chakras ..................... 6.95 __ $ ___
Crystals R for kids .......................... 6.95 __ $ ___
Who's Afraid of the Dark ................. 6.95 __ $ ___
Bridge Between Two Worlds ............. 6.95 __ $ ___
Color Me One ................................ 6.95 __ $ ___
**Special Offer—All 15 Angel Books.. 99.00** __ $ ___

# BOOK MARKET ORDER FORM
## BOOKS PUBLISHED BY LIGHT TECHNOLOGY PUBLISHING

NO. COPIES TOTAL

**ARGÜELLAS, JOSÉ**
The Mayan Factor .............................. $16.00 __$ ____

**ARMSTRONG, VIRGIL**
The Armstrong Report ........................ 11.95 __$ ____

**BABBITT, ELWOOD**
The God Within .................................. 12.95 __$ ____
Voices of Spirit .................................. 13.00 __$ ____

**BENTOV, ITZHAK**
Brief Tour of Higher Conciousness ....... 12.95 __$ ____
Stalking the Wild Pendulum ................ 12.95 __$ ____

**BREESE, CHRISTINE**
Reclaiming the Shadow Self ................. 15.95 __$ ____

**CARROLL, LEE**
An Indigo Celebration .......................... 13.95 __$ ____
The Indigo Children ........................... 13.95 __$ ____
Indigo Children: Ten Years Later ......... 15.95 __$ ____
Kryon–Book I, The End Times .............. 12.00 __$ ____
Kryon–Book II, Don't Think Like ......... 12.00 __$ ____
Kryon–Book III, Alchemy ................... 14.00 __$ ____
Kryon–Book IV The Parables of Kryon .. 17.00 __$ ____
Kryon–Book V The Journey Home ......... 14.95 __$ ____
Kryon–Book VI, Partnering with God .. 14.00 __$ ____
Kryon–Book VII, Letters From Home ... 14.00 __$ ____
Kryon–Book VIII, Passing The Marker .. 14.00 __$ ____
Kryon–Book IX, The New Beginning ... 14.98 __$ ____
Kryon–Book X, A New Dispensation ... 14.98 __$ ____
Kryon–Book XI, Lifting the Veil .......... 14.98 __$ ____

**CARROLL, LEE (DVDs)**
Kryon and Kirael in Austria ................ 18.00 __$ ____
Kryon in Argentina ............................. 20.00 __$ ____
Kryon in Austria ................................. 18.00 __$ ____
Kryon in Chile .................................... 20.00 __$ ____
Kryon in Mexico ................................. 18.00 __$ ____
Kryon in Moscow ................................ 18.00 __$ ____
Kryon Summer Light Conference I ....... 18.00 __$ ____
Kryon: The Whole Story ...................... 18.00 __$ ____
Prayer for Earth Meditation ................. 18.00 __$ ____

**CHATELAIN, MAURICE**
Our Cosmic Ancestors ......................... 14.95 __$ ____

**CHRISTINE, NICOLE**
Temple of the Living Earth ................... 16.00 __$ ____

**DANNELLEY, RICHARD**
Sedona: Beyond the Vortex .................. 14.95 __$ ____
Sedona Vortex 2K ............................... 12.00 __$ ____

**DAVENPORT, ANINA**
Reflections on Ascension ..................... 12.95 __$ ____

**DOREAL**
The Emerald Tablets of Thoth ............. 15.95 __$ ____

**FALZON, ALBERT/HORNBAKER, JEFF (DVD)**
Globus: The Meaning of Light ............. 30.00 __$ ____

**EMOTO, DR. MASARU**
Messages from Water ........................... 39.95 __$ ____
Messages from Water Vol.2 ................... 39.95 __$ ____
The Messages from Water III ................ 39.95 __$ ____
The Hidden Messages in Water ............ 16.95 __$ ____

**FISCHER, CHERI JAMIESON**
Love, Forgiveness & Hope ................... 14.95 __$ ____

**FORD, LANA J.**
Miracles & Other Ordinary .................. 19.95 __$ ____

**FREE, SCOTT**
Look Within ........................................ 9.95 __$ ____

**FREE, WINN**
Reincarnation of Edgar Cayce ............ $18.95 __$ ____

---

**GLATTAUER, MARGARET**
Don't Worry Be Happy ......................... 4.95 __$ ____

**GREER, STEVEN M., M.D.**
Contact: Countdown to Transformation 24.95 __$ ____
Disclosure .......................................... 24.95 __$ ____
Extraterrestrial Contact ...................... 24.95 __$ ____
Hidden Truth Forbidden Knowledge ..... 24.95 __$ ____

**GUSTAFSON, ERIC**
The Ringing Sound .............................. 19.95 __$ ____

**KENYON, TOM**
Mind Thieves ...................................... 18.95 __$ ____

**KENYON, TOM (AUDIO CASSETTE/CD)**
Angel Codes (CD) ............................... 26.95 __$ ____
Ghandarva Experience (CD) ................ 16.95 __$ ____
Imaginarium (CD) ............................... 16.95 __$ ____
Immunity (CD) .................................... 16.95 __$ ____
Infinite Pool (CD) ............................... 16.95 __$ ____
Lightship (CD) .................................... 16.95 __$ ____
Nuns of Gyantse (CD) .......................... 26.95 __$ ____
Sacred Chants (cassette) ..................... 13.95 __$ ____
Sacred Chants (CD) ............................. 16.95 __$ ____
Songs of Magdalen (CD) ...................... 16.95 __$ ____
Sound Transformations (cassette) ......... 13.95 __$ ____
Sound Transformations (CD) ............... 16.95 __$ ____
Voices from Other Worlds (CD) ........... 16.95 __$ ____
City of Hymns (cassette) ..................... 13.95 __$ ____
City of Hymns (CD) ............................. 16.95 __$ ____
Forbidden Songs (cassette) .................. 13.95 __$ ____
Forbidden Songs (CD) ......................... 16.95 __$ ____

**KING, JANI**
P'taah–The Gift (hc) ........................... 23.95 __$ ____
P'taah–An Act of Faith ....................... 23.95 __$ ____
P'taah–Transformation ....................... 19.95 __$ ____

**KNIGHT, JZ**
A Beginner's Guide to Creating Reality 19.95 __$ ____
A State of Mind: My Story .................... 24.95 __$ ____
Crossing the River ............................... 8.95 __$ ____
Forgotten Gods Waking Up .................. 8.95 __$ ____
From Sexual Revolution to God Revolution . 8.95 __$ ____
Parellel Lifetimes ................................ 8.95 __$ ____
Prophets of Our Own Destine ............... 8.95 __$ ____
When Fairy Tales Do Come True ........... 8.95 __$ ____
The White Book (hc) ........................... 19.95 __$ ____
Who Are We Really? ............................ 8.95 __$ ____

**KNIGHT, JZ (VIDEO)**
Ramtha World Tour VHS ..................... 19.95 __$ ____

**KOPPA, MARY FRAN**
Mayan Calendar Coloring Book ........... 8.95 __$ ____
Mayan Calendar Birthday Book ........... 12.95 __$ ____

**LEWIS, PEPPER (DVDs)**
Spiritual Leadership ............................ 20.00 __$ ____
The 5th Dimension: Akash & Ether ..... 20.00 __$ ____

**LEWIS, PEPPER (CDs)**
2009 & Beyond (4 CDs) ....................... 40.00 __$ ____
A New You (8 CDs) .............................. 99.00 __$ ____
Global Warming (2 CDs) ...................... 20.00 __$ ____
Moving Toward Spiritual Economy ....... 40.00 __$ ____
Releasing Judgement (2 CDs) .............. 20.00 __$ ____
Science & Metaphysics (3 CDs) ........... 35.00 __$ ____

**MAILE**
Principles to Remember ....................... 11.95 __$ ____

**MARECEK, MARY**
A View From the Other Side ................. 14.95 __$ ____

---

**McMANUS, DOROTHY**
Song of Sirius .................................... 8.00 __$ ____
Touched by Love ................................ 9.95 __$ ____

**MSI**
Second Thunder .................................. 17.95 __$ ____

**NAUMAN, EILEEN/BLUE TURTLE PUBLISHING**
Medical Astrology ............................... 29.95 __$ ____
Soul Recovery and Extraction .............. 11.95 __$ ____

**NORQUIST, ELLWOOD**
We Are One ........................................ 14.95 __$ ____

**PETTIT, ROBERT**
You Can Avoid Physical Death ............ 23.95 __$ ____

**RACHELE, SAL**
Life on the Cutting Edge ..................... 14.95 __$ ____

**ROTHER, STEVE**
Greetings from Home .......................... 17.95 __$ ____
Living in the 5th Dimension (DVD) .... 45.00 __$ ____
Re-member ......................................... 14.95 __$ ____
So I'm God . . . Now What? ................. 17.95 __$ ____
Spiritual Psychology ........................... 14.95 __$ ____
Welcome Home ................................... 14.95 __$ ____

**ROYAL, LYSSA/PRIEST, KEITH**
Visitors from Within ........................... 14.95 __$ ____

**SANDERS JR, PETE A.**
Access Your Brain's Joy Center ........... 14.95 __$ ____
Scientific Vortex Information ............... 9.95 __$ ____
Access Your Brain's Joy Center (cassette) 10.00 __$ ____

**SETI, D. NATHAN**
Life is the Father Within ..................... 19.75 __$ ____

**STECKLING, FRED**
Alien Bases on the Moon II .................. 19.95 __$ ____

**STERLING, FRED**
Guide to the Unseen Self ..................... 14.95 __$ ____
Kirael: The 10 Principles
of Consciously Creating ...................... 19.95 __$ ____
Kirael: The Genesis Matrix ................. 14.95 __$ ____
Kirael: The Great Shift ....................... 14.95 __$ ____
Kirael: Lemurian Legacy ..................... 18.00 __$ ____

**TAKA (AUDIO CASSETTE)**
Magical Sedona through the Didgeridoo 12.00 __$ ____

**TOBER, JAN (MEDITATION CDs)**
Guided Meditations ............................. 15.00 __$ ____
Color & Sound .................................... 15.00 __$ ____

**TOTEN, ED AND STACY**
M.A.S.S. 101 ....................................... 9.95 __$ ____

**TYBERONN, JAMES**
Metatron Speaks ................................. 27.00 __$ ____
The Energy & Geometry of Sacred Sites . 39.99 __$ ____

**VOSACEK, MARIA**
Dedicated to the Soul/Sole ................... 9.95 __$ ____

**WORK, RICH**
Awaken to the Healer Within ............... 16.50 __$ ____
Veils of Illusion .................................. 25.00 __$ ____

**POSTERS**
"The Mother Ship" 20 x 24 poster ........ 12.50 __$ ____
"Blessings from Sanada" 8 x 10 poster ..... 7.50 __$ ____

**BUMPER STICKER (FREE WITH ALL ORDERS OVER $30)**
"Peace to All Beings" 11 1/2 x 3 ............ $2.50 __$ ____
Quantity of 3 .............. 6.00 __$ ____

---

## BOOKSTORE DISCOUNTS HONORED—PLUS SHIPPING

☐ CHECK #    ☐ M.O.
☐ VISA    ☐ MASTERCARD
☐ DISCOVER    ☐ AMEX

CARD NO. _____
EXPIRATION DATE _____
SIGNATURE _____
(U.S. FUNDS ONLY) PAYABLE TO:

Name/Company _____
Address _____
City _____ State_____ Zip _____
Phone _____ Fax_____ Email _____
Ship to (if different from above)_____
Address _____
City _____ State_____ Zip _____

SIDE 1:  $ _____
SIDE 2:  $ _____
SUBTOTAL:  $ _____
SALES TAX:  $ _____
(8.5% – AZ residents only)
SHIPPING/HANDLING:  $ _____
($5.50 for 1 book, $1 for each additional book)
CANADA S/H:  $ _____
(30% of order)
TOTAL AMOUNT
ENCLOSED:  $ _____

PO BOX 3540 • FLAGSTAFF • AZ 86003  PHONE: 928-526-1345  1-800-450-0985
FAX: 928-714-1132  www.sedonajournal.com